I·D·E·O·G·R·A·M

I·D·E·O·G·R·A·M

Chinese Characters and the Myth of Disembodied Meaning

J. MARSHALL UNGER

 UNIVERSITY OF HAWAI'I PRESS
HONOLULU

Library of Congress Cataloging-in-Publication Data
Unger, J. Marshall.
Ideogram : Chinese characters and the myth of disembodied meaning /
J. Marshall Unger.
p. cm.
Includes bibliographical references and index.
ISBN 0-8248-2656-6 (cloth: alk. paper)   ISBN 0-8248-2760-0 (pbk.: alk paper)
1. Chinese characters. I. Title: Chinese characters and the myth of disembodied
meaning. II. Title.
PL1171 .U39 2003
495.1'11 — dc21
2003009996

Reprinted figures from:

Dave Barry Does Japan, by Dave Barry, copyright © 1992 by Dave Barry, used by
permission of Crown Publishers, a division of Random House, Inc. (New York).

Essential Kanji, by P. G. O'Neil, copyright © 1973 by P. G. O'Neil, used by permission
of John Weatherhill, Inc. (New York).

Gregg Shorthand, by John Robert Gregg, copyright © 1929 by John Robert Gregg, used
by permission of Glencoe/McGraw-Hill (New York).

Understanding Comics, by Scott McCloud, copyright © 1993, 1994 by Scott McCloud,
used by permission of HarperCollins Publishers, Inc. (New York).

Visible Speech, by John DeFrancis, copyright © 1989 by John DeFrancis, used by
permission of University of Hawai'i Press (Honolulu).

Writing Systems, by Geoffrey Sampson, copyright © 1985 by Geoffrey Sampson, used by
permission of Hutchinson (London).

Designed by Josie Herr

Printed by The Maple-Vail Book Manufacturing Group

To the memory of

JAMES DAVID MCCAWLEY

linguist · teacher · musician · gourmet · friend

Contents

Foreword

There is probably no subject on earth concerning which more misinformation is purveyed and more misunderstandings circulated than Chinese characters (漢字 Chinese *hanzi,* Japanese *kanji,* Korean *hanja*), or sinograms. The pernicious lies and naive myths that swirl around the sinograms have serious consequences not just for linguistics but for all the sciences. Most people passively succumb to the ubiquitous and outrageous tall tales concerning the sinograms, a large number of others energetically perpetuate them, while a handful of embattled warriors do their best to combat them. These three categories (the passive recipient, the active perpetrator, and the skeptical combatant) exist in about equal proportions both inside and outside sinogram-using societies.

But the tide may be starting to turn. I am just returning to my home in the Philadelphia area from a major international conference on "Modernization of Language and Script and the Program for Sinitic Spelling" (Yuwen Xiandaihua yu Hanyu Pinyin Fang'an), which was held in Beijing on 1 and 2 December 2001. The sponsoring bodies of this conference were the Chinese Department of Beijing University (China's most prestigious comprehensive institution of higher learning) and the Education Ministry of the government of the People's Republic of China. Support was also provided by the Chinese Academy of Social Sciences, which houses China's most important institutes for research on language and script. No greater authority could have been lent to the proceedings of this conference.

And what were some of the topics discussed at this landmark Beijing conference? Without attempting to be at all exhaustive, let me simply note the subjects that received the most attention: orthography (for Chinese today, this basically boils down to determining where whole words begin and end), computer inputting, Internet applications, the use of roman letters in Chinese writing practice, the spelling of proper nouns (an especially urgent matter because of the upcoming Beijing Olympics), competing spelling schemes, language pedagogy, internationalization and globalization, Sinitic topolects, and non-Sinitic minority languages. More than fifty outstanding scholars from China, Taiwan, Hong Kong, Singapore, Japan, Korea, and the United States earnestly debated these and other subjects during the intensive two-day meeting.

While unanimity of opinion could not be attained on every detail, of course, a firm consensus did emerge—namely, that romanized spelling of Chinese languages will continue to expand the scope of its applications in China (as elsewhere in East Asia) and that a de facto digraphia (sinograms and the alphabet) already exists. This is nowhere more poignantly evident than in the fact that the vast majority of computer inputting in China is now carried out with the aid of the alphabet—despite the existence of literally hundreds of shape-based codes.

I have focused on this memorable Beijing conference because it starkly reveals that the nature and status of sinograms at the beginning of the third millennium are not simply an intellectual curiosity for onlookers but a question that perplexes the best minds in China itself. Indeed Chinese, Japanese, and Korean reformers have been struggling for well over a century with the problem of how to modernize their antiquated sinographic scripts. They have not been helped by the obfuscations of Western theorists who elevate the characters to the (un)holy status of Ideogram. The very idea! It is preposterous to think that a motley collection of 170,000 characters (the latest count, but it will surely go higher), each consisting of anywhere from one to sixty-four brush strokes (with an average of about twelve strokes each), could possibly capture all human cognition and emotion (as expressed in all languages, no less), and do so *visually*. Yet this is exactly what doddering European philosophers and pipe-dreamers have been saying about Chinese characters since they first encountered them in the sixteenth century. This is sheer nonsense, of course, but the assumption that Chinese characters are ideograms persists to this very day. Unfortunately, this assumption wreaks havoc on general theories about language and writing, so it is not merely a harmless fantasy.

In this informative and entertaining book, J. Marshall Unger thoroughly demolishes the notion that Chinese characters directly convey meaning without any reference to specific languages and cultural contexts. To do so, he unleashes an amazing array of weapons ranging from the perceptions of a famous humorist to the techniques of specialists in memorization, from the secrets of shorthand to the mysteries of probability, from computer science and artificial intelligence to the profundities of philosophy. With a razor-sharp mind and deft pen, he exposes the self-contradictory folly of those who would assert some sort of independent, transcendental status for Chinese characters. Anyone who reads this book from beginning to end—parts of it are easy and fun, others are challenging and demanding—will surely come to the same conclusion as the author: in reality, there is no such thing as an ideogram.

VICTOR H. MAIR
8 December 2001
Honolulu

Acknowledgments

Although much of the material in this book is new, other material is expanded from lectures I have given and articles I have previously published in academic journals or as parts of books over the past twenty-five years:

Chapter 1: some of my remarks on Coyaud first appeared in the review listed under Coyaud (1985) in the References. I first told the story of Andreas Müller in Unger (1992). A more detailed discussion of how the Ideographic Myth got from the West to China and Japan may be found in Unger (1990). The discussion of DeFrancis' six myths is an expanded version of a short summary in Unger (1989).

Chapter 2: the discussion of the so-called Yukaghir love letter, as explained in the text, is derived from Unger and DeFrancis (1995).

Chapter 4: I also quoted Dave Barry's insights in my foreword to Nara and Noda (2003).

Chapter 5: this chapter is an expanded version of Unger (1991), my contribution to a festschrift for John DeFrancis.

Chapter 8: I have drawn material from my review of Gottlieb (2000) and two journal articles (Unger 1996 and 2001).

Bibliographic references, provided so the reader can study topics of special interest in greater depth, are as up-to-date as I have been able to make them.

I am grateful to many people who have spoken or corresponded with me about the topics I discuss: William Bright, Peter Daniels, John DeFrancis, Gerd Gigerenzer, Roy Harris, Michel Paradis, Jed Rothwell, and Victor Mair, whom I also thank for the Foreword. I am especially grateful to my wife Mutsuyo Okumura, who delivers criticisms with the aplomb of Mr. Spock on *Star Trek,* for her keen insights into modern Japanese culture and human psychology. None of these people, of course, is responsible for any errors I have failed to catch in the text.

Introduction

Eine falsche Hypothese ist besser als gar keine; denn daß sie falsch ist, ist gar kein Schade, aber wenn sie sich befestigt, wenn sie allgemein angenommen, zu einer Art von Glaubensbekenntniß wird, woran niemand zweifeln, welches niemand untersuchen darf, dieß ist eigentlich das Unheil woran Jahrhunderte leiden.

A false hypothesis is better than none at all, for that it is false does little harm. But if it becomes entrenched, if it gets generally accepted as a kind of creed that no one dares doubt or dares to examine—that is just the kind of mischief on which centuries come to ruin.

—Goethe, *Analysis and Synthesis*

Not so very long ago, when psychiatrists expected patients to free-associate "mouse" with "trap" rather than "pad," the word "inscrutable" was often heard in colloquial English followed by "Oriental." The phrase "inscrutable Oriental" had yet to become an embarrassing cliché. Times have changed, but a dinner menu full of Chinese characters remains for most Americans and Europeans the very picture of inscrutability.[1]

I have taught the Japanese language since 1975 to students in New Zealand, Hawai'i, Maryland, and Ohio. Before that I was officially a student of Japanese myself for ten years—though with Japanese, a native speaker of English never really stops being a student. Over the years, I have come to know hundreds of aspiring learners from just about every part of the world. Wherever I go, I am sure to find a knot of bright-eyed enthusiasts fascinated by those inscrutable Chinese characters, some so intensely that they lose sight of virtually all other aspects of the Japanese language. I know I am not misinterpreting their behavior, for I was once bitten by the bug myself.

This attachment to Chinese characters is in part just practical. If you want to read and write Japanese, then *kanji*, as the Japanese call them, simply must be learned. With a solid foundation in the spoken language, this can be a rewarding and enjoyable task. But the lure of *kanji* also has an aesthetic aspect that often leads to an infatuation with the tastes of East Asian calligraphy. The kind of people who find formal gardens oppressive or museum galleries crammed with treasures too overwhelming to enjoy may discover a new world of understatement and elegance in the casual asymmetries and quiet palette of brush writing and ink drawing. In extreme cases, the attachment becomes an obsession: the enthusiast begins to perceive a grand pattern underlying all the characters, evidently unnoticed even by generations of East Asians themselves. Like a chess player memorizing openings, he commits each new character to memory as if taking a steroid for the brain or stashing away a newfound pearl of wisdom in some inner lockbox of intellectual wealth.

Sooner or later, almost every student of an East Asian language falls prey to such feelings or knows a fellow student who has done so. This book is for them—not to discourage their efforts or lessen their enjoyment of the great forest of *kanji*, but to enhance both by placing the forest in a larger, sunnier landscape. Each of its nine chapters is, to use the quaint antiquarian phrase, a curious tale about Chinese characters. Some are long, some short, but all have unexpected twists and turns. Although I have added some cross-references and tried to arrange the chapters roughly on a scale from "popular" to "academic," the reader is invited to dip in at whatever place seems most intriguing. Each chapter takes up a different aspect of the lore of the so-called ideogram and raises questions that will, I hope, transform mere enchantment into deeper understanding. Some chapters may be a little rough for those without some background in linguistics, but none is beyond the grasp of the general reader—especially those contemplating a few months, if not a lifetime, of monkish devotion to a rosary of Chinese-character flashcards.

1 Agony and bliss

When a Russian hears or reads something that's arcane or unintelligible, a nice idiom is on hand and ready for deployment: *éto kitájskaya grámota* (это китайская грамота, "it's a Chinese writ"). Perhaps because the Cyrillic alphabet is based on the Greek, the phrase "It was Greek to me" (Casca's remark in *Julius Caesar*) never crossed from England to Russia; perhaps the idiom has to do with the history of Mongol subjugation and the long border that Russia shares with China. The aptness of the expression is, at any rate, clear enough.

Even more telling is the standard Russian translation of our stock phrase "Chinese character," which is *ieróglif* (иероглиф, literally "hieroglyph"), a word created from Greek roots (roughly "priest's carvings") to denote the picturelike writing seen on Egyptian monuments. A major misunderstanding of early orientalist thought in Europe (Clarke 1997; Said 1979) was that Chinese writing had something to do with ancient Egyptian; by jumbling together both unrelated times and places, *ieróglif* preserves that mistake like amber encasing a fly. The term "Indian" for "Native American" preserves Columbus' famous mistake, but *"ieróglif"* for "Chinese character" does even more, for it still has the power to evoke the fabulous, the exotic, the dimly understood.

From the writings of Tacitus, the great Roman historian of the first century, we know that Egyptian hieroglyphic texts could still be read in his time. But two centuries later, that knowledge had been lost, replaced by rationalizing legends about the picturelike symbols. These legends, in which each hieroglyph was said to possess a meaning, lay like dormant seeds in the topsoil of European thought during the Middle Ages, when, watered by the shower of direct reports from China of the sixteenth century, they sprouted and took root (Eco 1998).

Today we call that period of intense European change, rather misleadingly, the Renaissance (rebirth), but it was informed not just by a re-

1

connection with the civilizations of Rome and Greece but, more important, by something completely novel—namely the knowledge gained by
the explorations of the fifteenth century. It was this unexpected, incon-
trovertible evidence that the world was far bigger and more diverse than
anyone had ever imagined that, more than the printing press or Refor-
mation, jolted the European mind loose from its moorings. We should
savor the immense difference between the humane open-mindedness of
Montaigne and Shakespeare at the dawn of the seventeenth century and
the arid rationalism of Descartes and Leibniz after the Thirty Years War
that followed (Toulmin 1990). The shame of religious conflict, the ab-
surdity and cruelty of which was made even more painful by the self-
righteousness with which it had been prosecuted, caused sensitive minds
to recoil in horror and flee into mathematics and what we now call science. But since these early scientists were largely working on their own,
they often hit dead ends—even the incomparable Newton wasted many
days dabbling in alchemy. But of all the dead ends, none was more hotly
pursued than the search for the so-called Adamic language (Eco 1995).
Without the tantalizing vision of Chinese characters just then rising over
Europe's horizon to inspire them, one wonders how long the best minds
of the day would have continued to search for this apocryphal, logically
impeccable language.

SIX MYTHS ABOUT CHINESE CHARACTERS

Passing for the moment over the history of how the hunt for the perfect
language unfolded, let us jump ahead to the result: the intellectual bag-
gage about Chinese characters that we have inherited from the Renaissance and Enlightenment. John DeFrancis, in his classic book *The Chinese
Language* (1984), sums up that weighty legacy under six headings, and a
better summary would be hard to find. The source of all the confusion is
what DeFrancis calls the *Ideographic* Myth, the notion that Chinese characters represent meaning directly, without reference to language (that is,
speech) in any way. Its logical extension is the *Universality* Myth, according to which Chinese script allows for communication between mutually unintelligible dialects and languages. This leads in turn to the *Emulatability* Myth, which holds that Chinese script can serve as a model for a
general system of signs that transcends natural language. These first three

myths have little to do with the actual structure or history of the Chinese language or its writing system, in contrast with the remaining three: the *Monosyllabic* Myth, *Indispensability* Myth, and *Successfulness* Myth. Each of these—the names are more or less self-explanatory—makes a strong claim about language and the writing system, claims that have had significant social and political consequences.

The Ideographic Myth

The heart of the matter is the Ideographic Myth. And at the core of this myth lies a way of thinking about thinking—a theory of cognition and intelligence in which meanings are atomic entities that would exist in the universe whether human beings with brains existed or not. Such an outlook seems reasonable in the context of the sort of mathematical objects that Plato and others periodically trot out for the sake of argument: the point and straight line of Euclidian geometry, the ideal isosceles right triangle, the perfect circle, and the like. The definitions of such things are seemingly beyond dispute; we feel that we *discover* their existence, yet they are not real objects of the sort we apprehend with our senses. But one can argue persuasively that even these abstract entities are nothing but creations of the human mind (Lakoff and Núñez 2000). When we venture beyond the realm of mathematical abstractions, so much the weaker then is the notion of ideal, disembodied meanings floating "out there" in the world around us.

In terms of natural history, human language is, after all, speech. And to use speech one must not only learn the "code" of a particular language in the narrow sense but also embrace an open-ended set of agreements with others who inhabit the speech community.[1] Whether speakers agree or disagree about some topic of conversation, they share deep agreements of a much more fundamental kind—namely all the presumptions and presuppositions that make language use possible in its cultural context. These agreements are, at bottom, arbitrary because they concern the relationships between symbols and people's beliefs about reality. As individual language learners, we don't know how our culture and language got to be the way they are unless we take the time to study language consciously from a linguistic perspective. But fortunately we don't need to know such things to be effective language users. Language does not work by virtue of some inner logic inherent in its parts; rather, we make logic out of what the speech community gives us as we interact with others and entertain our own thoughts. Now let's apply these insights to the Ideographic Myth.

Consider, for example, the Chinese character consisting of three horizontal line segments (strokes). It stands for the Mandarin word *"sān"* (three). If we wanted to, we could decide to replace every occurrence of the sequence of letters *t h r e e* in English with this character 三 and agree to say "three" aloud every time we see it. We could even get fancy and let 三 also stand for the *t r i* in words like "tripod" and "tricycle" (but not, say, "trip" or "pastries"), using our knowledge of the fact that Greek *"tri"* and English "three" are etymologically related. But neither in Chinese nor in English does the character itself have any meaning apart from what is conveyed by the word or fragment we agree to represent by means of the character. In fact, with respect to the Chinese language, most characters are not graphically simple entities like 三 but graphically complex and functionally *phonographic*. That is, the typical character has a discernible graphic structure that makes it easy for someone who has learned the writing system to divide it into two parts called a *phonetic* and a *signific*. The phonetic indicates more or less how to pronounce the syllable represented by the character. The signific identifies a broad semantic category of the sort we would find in the main headings of a thesaurus; this heading may hint at the meaning of the words containing the syllable in question, though the connection (often tenuous in the first place) is frequently obscured by changes of meaning that have arisen over the centuries. Characters that lack this two-part structure (like 三) account for only about 15 percent of the characters in current use, and many occur as phonetics in more graphically complex characters. The number of such characters is small when we consider that the most common hundred characters account for nearly half of all those that appear in a typical modern Chinese text and that the most common 1,100 account for about 90 percent. Thus "if a reader of Chinese knew only a hundred characters, almost every other character in a piece of writing would be familiar to him. With a knowledge of 1,100 characters, only every tenth character would be unfamiliar" (DeFrancis 1984, p. 108). Furthermore, an analysis of the 1,100 most frequent characters shows that "in two-thirds of [them] there would be a useful phonetic clue to help the reader recall the pronunciation of the character" (ibid.).

These facts are indisputable yet widely ignored. To understand why, imagine that a student comes to a teacher with a piece of paper on which the word *"fēijī"* (airplane) is written thus: 飛機 (or in PRC simplified form 飞机). The teacher is unlikely to say, "These are two Chinese characters which together stand for the Mandarin word *'fēijī,'* which is the word for airplane." She will probably conflate these two facts and say, "Oh, that's the Chinese word for airplane" or even "That's airplane in Chinese." And the confusion only gets worse if teacher and student are speaking in Chinese itself. For if the teacher says, *"Zhèige zì shí fēijī"* (literally, "these characters are airplane"), she might intend either that "these characters spell the word *'fēijī'*" or "these characters (taken together) mean airplane." This is analogous to a situation that frequently arises in computer science, where one must carefully distinguish between numbers and numerals: how often we forget to be precise about whether we mean a number, such as 0, or a string, "0" (ASCII character 48)! The problem in both the Chinese and computer cases is that we usually do not bother to say whether we are talking about the symbols themselves (reference) or what they represent (use) because it is usually not relevant to our pragmatic needs. When we talk about meaning and writing themselves, however, such precision cannot be sacrificed.

Notice, by the way, that this example also demonstrates that the fallacy inherent in the Ideographic Myth is not unique to Chinese culture. It's a logical trap into which anyone can fall when discussing any form of writing.

The Universality Myth

Now if Chinese characters do not express meaning directly, how is it possible for speakers of Mandarin and Cantonese to communicate through writing? How is it possible to write a modern newspaper article and transcribe a Tang-dynasty poem in the same script? How is it possible for Japanese, who speak a completely unrelated language, to make sense out of Chinese texts? The Universality Myth is the exaggerated claim that these three things can all be fully accomplished with ease and the false belief that none of them could be done if Chinese were written with an alphabetic script. Neither the claim nor the accompanying belief is correct.

The so-called dialects of Chinese are as different from one another linguistically as French and Spanish or Dutch and English. All these are written alphabetically. Yet written communication between monolinguals who are unable to communicate in speech is often surprisingly effective, though of course a far cry from using the same language. So the situation in Europe and China is really not much different: a common writing system is a necessary but far from sufficient condition for (crude) cross-linguistic communication to take place. The same can be said for related dialects and languages separated in time rather than in space: without special training in the grammar and vocabulary of the archaic language, a Chinese classic like the *Analects* of Confucius is as much of a puzzle to a modern speaker of Mandarin as the original text of *Beowulf* is to a speaker of modern English. The presence of familiar characters masks the differences between the language of the texts and the vernacular of the reader but in no way removes them. Likewise, the use of Chinese characters in the writing of Japanese, which has sometimes been compared with the use of Hindu-Arabic numerals by speakers of different languages, is really not the same thing at all. The Japanese have not merely imported characters from China; they have more importantly borrowed actual words of Chinese—and, along with these words, the entire apparatus of literary Chinese itself. As DeFrancis points out, to cite the instance of Japan as evidence for universality "would imply that speakers of English might pronounce the French loanword *chauffeur* as 'driver'" (DeFrancis 1984, p. 157). The fallacy is in thinking that the ability of some well-educated Japanese to make sense of Chinese texts is due to the writing system, whereas in fact it is due to the total impact of Chinese culture on Japanese education and society, of which the characters are merely the most conspicuous of many vestiges.

The Emulatability Myth

As the Ideographic and Universality Myths gained currency in the West during the Renaissance, the Emulatability Myth was born—and this is the story we will examine in this chapter after summarizing the rest of DeFrancis' myths. Actually, DeFrancis is most upset with modern educators and reading theorists who believe that Chinese writing may hold the answer to dyslexia and other reading disabilities:

> In their eagerness to invoke the aid of the ideographic concept, psycholinguistic proponents of the Emulatability Myth have be-

come gullible victims of an inadvertent con game in which they have been sold a bill of goods about the nonphonetic or insignificantly phonetic nature of Chinese writing. This mistake has led them at best into errors of judgment and distortion of fact and at worst into academic hucksterism. They thereby do a disservice to the very cause they are seeking to promote by raising a question whether all their assertions, including the potentially persuasive claim of the superiority of the word or syllable approach over the letter approach to reading, are as poorly thought out and supported as those based on the Ideographic Myth. [1984, p. 176]

In Chapters 8 and 9, we will see how this controversy spills over into other areas, such as philosophy and computer science.

The Monosyllabic Myth

If the Ideographic Myth and its children, the Myths of Universality and Emulatability, were the end of the matter, things would be bad enough. But there is a second line of argument available to those entranced by the mirage of ideograms. The simplest apologist argument is the claim that Chinese characters reflect the morphology of the Chinese language — that is, the part of the grammar that describes the structure of words and fixed phrases. George Kennedy (1964) was probably the first to call this the Monosyllabic Myth. The linguistic truth of the matter is that many morphemes (the smallest meaningful units) of Chinese speech contain more than one syllable. Kennedy uses the example of *"húdié"* (butterfly), which, though written with two characters (one for each syllable), is really no different from English words like "orange" or "button." The *hú* and *dié* that the character dictionary confidently tells us both mean "butterfly" are only lexicographic ghosts, fictions made up to rationalize the writing system, which must use two characters to transcribe the word *"húdié"* because it has two syllables. Examples of this kind, and more, can be produced ad infinitum (Packard 2000). As we've seen before, speech comes first; writing follows.

Chinese certainly has a considerable number of monosyllabic morphemes. But then so does English, as many ESL learners discover to their dismay. It is also true that the syllables of Chinese have rather tightly constrained phonological shapes. The use of characters no doubt reflects a similar high degree of regularity in syllable structure in ancient forms of the language. But this observation merely strengthens DeFrancis' claim that Chinese has, after all, always had a phonetically oriented writing system in which morphemic and semantic considerations play only a secondary role. To claim that word-based or meaning-based characters were invented to accommodate the uniquely monosyllabic nature of Chinese linguistic morphology is to put the cart far ahead of the horse.

The Indispensability Myth

Such claims are commonplace, however, and anyone taken in by them is easy prey for the child of the Monosyllabic Myth, the Indispensability Myth, which runs as follows: since there are just a few more than a thousand phonemically distinct syllables in Mandarin (even taking tone-contour differences into account), the number of homophonic words must be many times greater in Mandarin than in, say, English, because Chinese (allegedly) lacks polysyllabic words. Hence characters serve the indispensable function of distinguishing homophones.[2] The truth is, of course, that a large number of words in Mandarin and other languages of the great Chinese language family contain two or more syllables. Those who insist, as did the Swedish philologist Bernhard Karlgren, that Chinese characters are indispensable for the writing of Chinese are typically concerned with literary Chinese *(wényán)* rather than everyday speech. Literary Chinese occupied roughly the same position of prestige in Chinese culture as Latin did in medieval Europe: it was a language that the educated could read and write; but Latin was probably spoken by more scholars over a longer period than literary Chinese ever was. One of the great achievements of Chinese poets and authors during the twentieth century has been to replace this artificial literary vehicle with a straightforward transcription of ordinary speech, or *báihuà*. Few today would advocate that China return to *wényán* as a standard style of writing. Yet as DeFrancis notes (1984, pp. 199–200), the Indispensability Myth lingers on as the residue of the discredited defense of just such a *wényán* standard.

Interestingly, the Indispensability Myth often comes up in discussions of Japanese and Korean. This is strange since Korean has a native alphabet (now called *han'gŭl*), of which Koreans are rightfully proud, and Japanese has two syllabaries *(hiragana* and *katakana),* by means of which vast amounts of Japanese literature were written, often by women. In principle, anything that can be written in Korean and Japanese can be writ-

ten exclusively with these native scripts. In the case of Japanese, the indispensability claim is sometimes given an additional twist: (1) a large
part of the Japanese lexicon is borrowed from Chinese or made up using
borrowed Chinese roots; (2) many syllables that sound different in Chinese end up with the same pronunciation in Japanese, which has a simpler
sound system; (3) therefore, there are an inordinate number of homophonic words in Japanese. The idea is that, however bad the confusion in Chinese, in Japanese it must be worse. One writer, Maurice Coyaud (1985),
hunting for homophonic two-character Sino-Japanese words (easy to do
using Japanese dictionaries, which list words by pronunciation) found
no fewer than 212 homophone groups containing two or more words.
This may seem a large number, but another writer, James B. Hobbs
(1986), found 3,625 homophone groups in English (a harder task because
of English spelling rules). True, many Sino-Japanese homonym groups
have more members than their English counterparts: a dictionary or
word-processor input routine will show you at least two dozen character combinations for *kōsei* (not counting proper nouns), but only ten are
commonly encountered in ordinary writing, and they have meanings as
disparate as "makeup, making(s)" 構成, "proofreading" 校正, "public wel-
fare" 厚生, "fixed star" 恒星, "rehabilitation" 更生, and "fairness" 公正;
moreover, these words rarely occur together except in dictionaries and
have different frequencies of occurrence. Foreign students are titillated
by the sight of so many homonyms in one place. But it is more interesting
to compare how many homonym groups different languages have—for
it has been argued time and again that the relative paucity of distinctive
syllables in Japanese necessitates an extraordinary number of homonyms,
yet English has more groups! The large size of some of the Sino-Japanese
homonym groups is perhaps to some extent a consequence of the simplicity of Japanese phonology, but it is mostly testimony to the creativity
of a small educated elite with time on its hands for several centuries.

Indispensability is also frequently invoked, though sometimes tacitly,
in arguments against script reform. It is noteworthy that, in every nation
of East Asia where Chinese characters are used except Taiwan, some kind
of script reform was instituted during the twentieth century. (Taiwan refuses to adopt the simplified characters of the People's Republic of China
for obvious political reasons and because it has its hands full accommodating the local language, for which there is no standard character-based

orthography.) Romanization, long resisted by the ruling elite in Vietnam, became the basis for popular literacy "overnight" when the Communist Party decided that education of the peasantry was essential to the expulsion of the Japanese and the French. Both North and South Korea have at one time or another abandoned characters in favor of exclusive use of *han'gŭl*. (See Chapter 2 for details.) In Japan, the end of World War II created an opportunity to implement reforms that had been planned long in advance. All this can only make one wonder how indispensable Chinese characters, at least in their pristine unreformed state, actually are.

The Successfulness Myth

This brings us to the last myth—the ultimate fallback position taken by diehard opponents of script reform whenever someone exposes the foregoing five myths, as we have done here. They grant that Chinese characters aren't ideographic, that the Chinese language isn't monosyllabic, and everything that flows from these elementary facts. But, they argue, since Chinese characters are used today in large, highly literate societies, none of the shortcomings or inconveniences entailed by their continued use are of any importance. This view has the merit of honesty; it abandons bogus claims about how Chinese characters work, switching the focus to practical questions about how, when, and in combination with what other symbols they should be used. Still it is flawed in three significant ways.

First, and most fundamentally, the Successfulness Myth evades the question of what exactly counts as literacy. When DeFrancis concludes that "Chinese characters appear to have failed insofar as the Chinese masses are concerned," he does so on the premise that "literacy should be defined as the ability to accomplish such relatively elementary tasks as corresponding about family matters and reading newspapers and instructions in various matters" (1984, pp. 205–206). Proponents of the Successfulness Myth seldom offer such explicit definitions of literacy.

Second, the Successfulness Myth presumes that literacy in so-called developed nations is not vastly superior to literacy in China. Many people believe, for example, that China cannot be far behind the United States when it comes to literacy. They have heard about the famous 1993 report "Adult Literacy in America" (National Center for Education Statistics), which stated that "47 percent of American adults had scored in the two lowest levels of the 1992 National Adult Literacy Survey. Even worse, 21 percent scored at the very lowest of its five literacy levels" (Baron 2002). But "it now turns out that the government report was wrong. A new analysis of the 1992 survey quietly concludes that less than 5 percent of the adult population is seriously illiterate." The problem was not with the test used to assess literacy, which amply sampled practical, everyday tasks, but rather with faulty assumptions in the 1993 statistical analysis of the data. To qualify as sufficiently literate, subjects had to score 80 percent on the test, which penalized many people who performed poorly in test conditions compared with "real life" situations.[3] Furthermore, the 1993 analysis did not take physical or linguistic factors into account. "One-quarter of those scoring at the lowest proficiency level . . . were immigrants who may have had limited proficiency in English; two-thirds were school dropouts; one-third were older than 65; 26 percent had significant physical or mental impairments; and 19 percent had visual problems that made it difficult for them to read." The real scandal of literacy in the United States is not that it is outrageously low but that it continues to correlate strongly with social and economic status despite nearly half a century of legislation aimed at providing educational equality to all Americans. China still has catching up to do.

Third, the Successfulness Myth overestimates the extent and, even more important, the quality of literacy in East Asia. A look at Japan is particularly instructive in this connection. When Japanese literacy was measured through a massive survey in 1948, few adults were found to be completely illiterate. But those who experienced no difficulties in reading and writing were also few in number, comprising just over 6 percent of the sample—that is, roughly 94 percent of Japanese adults had slight to severe trouble reading and writing for everyday purposes. Considering the class and gender biases at work in the administration of Japanese public education prior to the Occupation, this finding should not be surprising, yet it is easy to forget now that Japan has become the world's second-largest economy. It is only since the 1950s that virtually all school-age Japanese children have had to bear the full burden of what is generally agreed to be the most onerous writing system in general use today. The surge in the popularity of Japanese comics, or *manga,* starting in the 1970s showed that this new load was becoming heavy for a rapidly growing segment of the population. In the 1990s, "total book sales in the country have fallen from 900 million copies to 700 million, while sales of 'pocket books,' the popular paperbacks that were the staple of the commuter, have shrunk from 300 million to 230 million" (French 2000). Moreover:

> "Serious literature, that is where the sharpest decline is taking place," Toshiharu Sasaki, an industry expert with the Research Institute for Publications, told me. "The publishing industry's health goes in line with the reading habits of the public, and people are reading 2 to 3 percent less every year." . . . "In Japan, literature is no longer mainstream culture," commented Yoshinori Shimizu, a professor of literature and a book critic for Asahi Shimbun, Tokyo's leading newspaper. "My students have done very little reading. For them, whether it is classics or mystery novels, they are equally unknown." [ibid.]

If this is the trend in the East Asian nation most revered in the West for its economic success and devotion to education, it goes without saying that reports of great leaps forward in mass education in the People's Republic of China need to be taken with a grain of salt.

Beyond all this, the Successfulness Myth assumes that script reform in any of the countries of East Asia would necessarily have to be an "all or nothing" proposition. The history of writing practice in Korea, China, and Japan briefly alluded to here shows on the contrary that all reform packages to date have been mixed bags. Even in Vietnam, where the most radical reforms have been implemented, the legacy of Chinese writing has not been entirely forgotten. A more likely development than a Vietnam-style change in other Asian countries is the rise of digraphia (a term coined by DeFrancis)—the simultaneous use of two different writing systems for the same language. Though not officially acknowledged, digraphia is a practical fact of life for Japanese and many other Asian computer users (see Chapter 8) even though they seldom read texts in their native language in romanized format. Inputting raw language data in alphanumerics to initiate a conversion process that ultimately produces the characters they desire, they frequently need to read or type English, embedded in which words of their language take on romanized forms. It seems rather doubtful that people who use languages like English or Spanish on the Internet will ever assimilate the customary scripts of East Asia to the extent that Chinese, Japanese, and Koreans have already assimilated alphanumerics.

TWENTIETH-CENTURY *CHINOISERIE*

DeFrancis' six myths provide one way to understand how Renaissance and Enlightenment thinkers have molded our ideas about Chinese characters, but we can approach this topic from a different angle by looking at actual cases in which these ideas have played out. A prime example, of roughly the same vintage and flavor as the science fiction of H. G. Wells, is found in the life of Charles K. Bliss (1897–1985). Though his life was not easy, his love affair with Chinese characters and their silent world of meaning makes his adopted English name peculiarly appropriate.

Born Karl Kasiel Blitz to a struggling Jewish family living near the Russian border of the Austro-Hungarian Empire, Bliss was exposed to both multilingualism and anti-Semitism at an early age. He graduated from the Technical University of Vienna in 1922 in chemical engineering, a field in which he encountered the arcane language of technology and patents. Imprisoned in Dachau following the Nazi Anschluss of 1938, he gained release with the help of his wife Claire, a German Catholic, and departed for England. From there he traveled by way of Canada and Japan to the home of his cousin Paula in Shanghai, where at the end of 1940 he was reunited with Claire, who had reached Shanghai via Romania, Greece, Turkey, the USSR, and Manchuria. They remained together when the Japanese forced all the Jews in Shanghai into the notorious Hongkew ghetto. It was during this period in Shanghai that Bliss fell under the spell of Chinese characters, which he regarded as purely ideographic. In 1942, he came across the books of Basil Hall Chamberlain, the first professor of Japanese at the Imperial University in Tokyo, which afforded him a basis for study.

After the war, another cousin sent the Blisses entry permits for Australia, to which they immigrated in July 1946. As a refugee, Bliss encountered discrimination in employment and had to take manual labor jobs, but at nights and on weekends he worked with his wife on his project of "One Writing for One World and Understanding Across All Languages." This, he believed, could be achieved through a system of ideograms that he would devise on a completely logical basis. Around this time, he came across the writings of Leibniz on the dream of a *characteristica universalis,* which confirmed his beliefs and led to the 1949 publication in Sydney of *International Semantography: A Non-Alphabetical Symbol Writing Readable in*

All Languages. In this three-volume mimeographed typescript, Bliss explained his ideas about symbolic logic and semantics. Some examples of his graphic elements are shown in Table 1.

These examples just scratch the surface of Bliss' system. Symbols called *pointers* (< > ∧ v) can be combined with *elementals* to create *compounds*.

Table 1 Some Bliss "Elementals" and "Compounds"

Some Bliss "Elementals"

ʔ	ear	h	chair	⚡	electric	�	room
◉	eye	⊓	table	⌐	stairs	⊓	door
∠	nose	⋈	bed	⋏	woman	‖	repeat, copy, print
↓	hand	⟨	fire	—	ground	⏐⏐	limits
⚥	plant	⌣	water	⊗	wheel	⊔	open, opening
＼	pen	⌣	vessel	⋏	man	☐	closed, enclosed space
▯	paper	⏚	ship	⌂	house	⏐	line
♡	emotion	P	flag	∧	roof	♩	music
⌒	reason	⌄	wings	○	sun	⊠	mail
⋒	conscience	∘	mouth	⊕	time	△	safety

Some Bliss "Compounds"

⊐‖	elevator	⌂◉	theater	⊙	day
⊐h	waiting room	▯◉	theater tickets	⊙₁	Sunday
⋏⊐	chambermaid	⌂₂	second balcony	⊙₂	Monday
⋏⊓	doorman	⌂◉⚡	cinema	⚭↑	holiday
⊢⌐	entrance	⌂ʔ♩	concert hall	⊙↑	Spring
⌐⊢	exit	⌂◉♩	opera	⌂	morning

There are also signs called *indicators:* □ above an elemental marks it as a thing (noun), whereas ∧ marks it as an action (verb). Other indicators specify past or future tense and so on. Not surprisingly, sentences follow the overall gross syntactic order of English: time, location, subject, verb, object. The compound symbol for "please" (!♡) comes in sentence-initial position; the compound symbol marking questions (?:) does too. Since many languages have fundamentally different kinds of syntax, one must wonder why Bliss thought these particular practices were universal. This lack of concern for cultural differences, however, goes beyond grammar. To cite just one example, the use of the elemental ♡ for "emotion," ♡! for the verb "love," and so forth assumes that it is somehow natural both to associate the heart with feelings and to denote the heart with the symbol ♡. In East Asia, however, the heart has traditionally been regarded as the seat of the intellect, not the organ of passion, and ♡ historically has had no particular iconic significance.

Bliss' *Semantography* attracted the attention of such (mostly British) intellectuals as Bertrand Russell and Lancelot Hogben. Russell hardly needs an introduction; Hogben, who was professor of medical statistics at the University of Birmingham and a popular writer on science, had sketched out an artificial language he called Interglossa, his idea of an improved Esperanto. It should be remembered that, in the 1940s and 1950s, such schemes were not uncommon. Esperanto had been around for more than half a century; calendar reforms of various kinds had been proposed (some adopted by various companies); H. G. Wells and G. B. Shaw both supported duodecimalization (base-twelve arithmetic); and Shaw famously left a large sum in his will for the creation of a rational, space-saving English alphabet. Nevertheless, Bliss' ideas didn't arouse much enthusiasm at the time.

Despite this neglect and the death of Claire in 1961, Bliss published a second edition of his magnum opus in 1965 under the shorter title *Semantography (Blissymbolics)*. He coined the term Blissymbolics to strengthen his copyright claims. Interestingly, the first real recognition for Blissymbolics occurred in Canada in 1971, where it was used for work with children afflicted with cerebral palsy and other disabilities. In 1975, Bliss granted an exclusive license for the use of his symbols with handicapped children to the Blissymbolics Communication Foundation of Canada. But by 1977 he was at odds with the foundation, which he believed had ruined the logical purity of his work, not to mention his health and finances. A reconciliation was effected in 1982; since then, an organization called Blissymbolic Communication International (BCI) has claimed a perpetual, worldwide, exclusive license for the use and publication of Blissymbols for persons with language and learning difficulties.

The BCI website contains a lengthy bibliography describing how Blissymbolics is used to help those with mental retardation, aphasia, cerebral palsy, brain injuries, and other (sometimes multiple) disabilities. There are no doubt dozens of reasons why interventions and therapies using Blissymbolics work (to the extent they do work) in such contexts. But for BCI, the single underlying reason is that Bliss-characters are genuinely ideographic: "Blissymbolics is a *language* currently composed of over 2,000 graphic symbols [emphasis added]. Bliss-characters can be combined and recombined in endless ways to create new symbols. Bliss-words can be sequenced to form many types of sentences, and express many grammatical capabilities."

Considering the following Bliss left behind him when he died in 1982, one can say that he succeeded where Enlightenment scholars failed. Their attempts to create "real characters" are now seldom mentioned outside of specialist histories (Rasula and McCaffrey 1998; Porter 2001). Blissymbolics lives on, yet it is no more self-evidently logical or culture-free than the systems of sixteenth-century scholars. In this sense—the sense that Bliss himself thought most important—his work proves absolutely nothing about ideography except that certain utopian ideas periodically resurface throughout the course of history. Today's heavyweight contenders for the Cartesian mantle are not the enthusiasts of Blissymbolics but the computer scientists who believe in artificial intelligence (AI) and their allies in the field now called cognitive science. But let's backtrack and fill in the painful story we skipped over to learn DeFrancis' myths and find Bliss.

ANDREAS MÜLLER: FRAUD OR GENIUS?

In Descartes' day, a "computer" was a person who computed, not a machine, though Descartes himself was inclined to think of living things as nothing but machines, for he thought the soul was made of an essentially different kind of substance.[4] (Body and soul interacted, according to Descartes, in the pineal gland!) From this dualist perspective, reducing the body to the status of a mechanical system posed no obvious philosophical problems since all other features of individual selves could be ascribed to something else. But Descartes, Leibniz, and other rationalists realized that demonstrating how the brain and nerves caused thinking was going to take more than the kind of simple, elegant experiments that had enabled William Harvey to demonstrate the circulation of blood. This is why they found Chinese writing so fascinating: descriptions of it seemed to imply that if one could discover just the right inventory of basic semantic elements (surely a large number) and the proper syntactic rules for assembling them into logical propositions, then one could represent every thought that a human mind could entertain.

These tantalizing descriptions of Chinese writing can be traced back to the Portuguese missionary Gaspar da Cruz (sixteenth century), but his Italian colleague Matteo Ricci did perhaps more than anyone else to spread the idea. Like da Cruz, Ricci went to China carrying the idea of the ideogram with him. We know he didn't pick it up from the Chinese themselves because Chinese and Japanese sources do not explicitly claim that characters stand for meanings except when they ridicule naive pictographic theories of character etymology. Educated Chinese and Japanese were well aware that the overwhelming majority of characters consisted of a phonetic embellished with a signific and that the phonetics had once indicated similar-sounding syllables. For them the task of learning characters and how to use them properly was just the beginning of study: reading, memorizing, and emulating classic texts was the heart of the matter. And for this purpose, a careful distinction between words and characters was hardly an urgent consideration.[5]

To use a character as if it stood for a free-standing word of literary Chinese even though it was not actually so used in the classics was to commit an error both difficult to detect and easily excused. Recall George Kennedy's example of *"húdié"* (butterfly): to use just *"hú"* or *"dié"* to represent a free-standing noun meaning "butterfly" was seen not as a failure to know that *"húdié"* is a dissyllabic word but rather a failure to remember the missing character. This kind of thinking was encouraged by the practice of listing both characters in dictionaries as if each stood for a distinct word, which they did not. But the weak logographic theory of characters implicit in such scholarly practices never played a decisive role in shaping East Asian ideas about language and writing systems.

In Europe, things went differently. As already remarked, the standard

Russian word for "Chinese character" still belies the old mistake of thinking that ancient Egyptian writing was a universal ideographic code. In the 1760s, the French philosophes thought it perfectly reasonable to ask resident Chinese Jesuits whether they could read the Egyptian hieroglyphs. It all started with the Neoplatonists and the myth of Hermes Trismegistus. As the reports of sixteenth-century missionaries about Chinese writing made their way back into Europe, this tradition played a crucial role. While Francis Bacon and other early Renaissance writers regarded the shapes of Chinese characters as merely conventional and were relatively unconcerned with the details of how they functioned representationally, the obsessive Athanasius Kircher drew an analogy between them and the Egyptian symbols. From this point on, the idea that each Chinese character represented some essential idea, which was somehow encoded in its shape, became the dominant European view. How else could one explain the seemingly endless number of characters used in China? What easier way was there to explain the ability of Japanese and Vietnamese to "understand" the very same characters, even though their languages were different from Chinese? What's more, since Chinese characters were obviously ideograms, anyone who could discover the key to their decipherment would possess very valuable knowledge indeed. He would not only know how the Chinese literati managed to learn the myriad characters but would also possess a graphic key to all human knowledge.

One such scholar, Andreas Müller (1630–1694), believed he had found the key. He proceeded to devote the rest of his life, without success, to finding someone to purchase it from him. He tried to sell it to Leibniz' patron, the Duke of Brunswick (Braunschweig). Leibniz believed it was possible to construct a *characteristica universalis* for the representation and computational resolution of all logical problems—hence Voltaire's parody of Leibniz as Pangloss ("all tongues") in *Candide.* He was inclined to recommend that his patron invest in Müller's key, but he needed some evidence that Müller really had the goods promised. But Müller, explaining that the key was so simple that even describing it in outline would give it away, insisted on being paid in advance. Leibniz eventually lost patience, and Müller lost his chance. Bitter and impoverished, he took his precious secret with him to the grave.

Today Müller is almost entirely forgotten and the suspicion that he was just a charlatan clouds what little reputation remains to him. But it is quite possible that he had indeed discovered what his contemporaries had missed. The overwhelming majority of the characters, as previously remarked, contain a phonetic component that indicates with fair accuracy the syllable of Chinese for which the character stands. It is this heuristic value that allows those who know Chinese to learn the vast number of characters needed for everyday literacy. Linguists have known this for at least 170 years or so. Yet even today educated people who should know better — even some Chinese — still think that each and every Chinese character stands for a silent idea utterly unrelated to speech.

Müller's story has caught the attention of historians such as David Mungello and Jonathan Spence, but none, so far as I know, has suggested an explanation for Müller's behavior. David Porter, citing Mungello, mentions "Müller's successor in Berlin, Christian Mentzel (1622–1701), whose *Clavis Sinica, ad Chinensium Scripturam et Pronunciationem Mandarinicam* (Key to Chinese, to Chinese writing and Mandarin pronunciation) drew upon the Chinese lexicographic convention of classifying characters according to their radical elements and these latter according to the number of strokes they contained" (Porter 2001, p. 59). But Porter continues: "Mentzel believed that this system of lexical categories [the radicals] contained not only clues regarding the evolution of the characters, their pronunciation and meaning, but also the secret to the logical structure he presumed to underlie the language as a whole." Thus Mentzel missed what was right under his nose: Müller's secret may have been simply that many characters with similar pronunciation had the same residues left over when their dictionary radicals are removed. If this is true, then Mentzel, lost in details and obsessed with the ideal of an all-encompassing logic, missed the significance of this simplest but most telling observation. Porter, for his part, simply passes on to more self-indulgent European constructions of China.

Poor Müller! I fancy he may have been the only man of his generation in Europe to realize that Chinese characters were not ideograms. The agony he must have suffered! As every new page of the Chinese glossaries brought him ever more confirming evidence, he became increasingly aware that nothing but the utter simplicity of his discovery kept it concealed. He was trapped in a world without patents, only trade secrets. He had to rely on aristocrats. Peer review was in its infancy.

2 Cryptograms vs. pictograms

Voyages to previously unexplored regions brought Europeans into contact with new peoples who, though not so awe-inspiring as the Chinese, seemed to write in ideographic ways. As little as a hundred years ago, these new encounters led to scholarly misunderstandings that have been uncritically perpetuated ever since.

One example of such writing is the script of the Maya of Central America. Until the 1960s, it was generally believed to be ideographic and little of it was understood with any certainty. Even as late as 1981, despite the accumulating evidence that Mayan writing was a syllable-based script, some scholars held it up as a prime example of a genuinely logographic writing system (Baron 1981, pp. 170–175).[1]

We've all heard stories about Native American picture writing. Longfellow describes how his hero Hiawatha

> On the smooth bark of a birch-tree
> Painted many shapes and figures,
> Wonderful and mystic figures,
> And each figure had a meaning,
> Each some word or thought suggested.

He proceeds to give examples:

> Life and Death he drew as circles,
> Life was white, but Death was darkened;
> Sun and moon and stars he painted,
> Man and beast, and fish and reptile,
> Forests, mountains, lakes, and rivers.
> For the earth he drew a straight line,
> For the sky a bow above it;

White the space between for daytime,

. . . .

  Footprints pointing towards a wigwam
Were a sign of invitation,
Were a sign of guests assembling;
Bloody hands with palms uplifted
Were a symbol of destruction,
Were a hostile sign and symbol.

"Thus it was," concludes Longfellow, "that Hiawatha . . . taught the people
. . . all the art of Picture-Writing." Vigorous trochaic poetry, but how
does it fare as anthropology? Who says that Life and Death are white and
black and not the other way around? Why circles and not squares? What
makes footprints a better sign of invitation than, say, uplifted palms? The
answer must be that Longfellow was relying on some old account he'd
read, or perhaps he was just guessing.

In his 1989 book *Visible Speech*, John DeFrancis discusses accounts of
picture writing of the sort that probably inspired Longfellow. He demonstrates that no example of such so-called writing is part of a coherent
writing system capable of accommodating all the utterances of a spoken
language—as can all the ordinary writing systems familiar to us in everyday life. On this basis, he draws an important distinction between partial
and full writing systems. Any group of two or more people can concoct
an ad hoc signaling system to serve one or more special purposes, and such
improvisations have happened countless times throughout history wherever human beings dwell. But as far as we can tell, a full writing system,
coextensive with the generative capacity of an entire spoken language, is
an invention that has occurred precisely three times and in three locales
in all of history: once in ancient Mesopotamia; a little later in China; and
later still among the Maya of Central America. In all three instances, the
same innovation—the use of signs to form rebuses—enabled the passage
from partial to full writing.[2] Nevertheless, stories of picture writing en-
dure and have become part of the mythology that forms the background
for our uncritical thoughts about language. With brilliant scholarly de-
tective work, DeFrancis exposed what is perhaps the most egregious instance of sheer laziness and gullibility contributing to this mythology. It
is story that deserves to be retold.

THE NOTORIOUS YUKAGHIR "LOVE LETTER"

Figure 1 shows what was long alleged to be the best example of ideographic picture writing ever found. British linguist Geoffrey Sampson, in his widely cited book *Writing Systems* (1985), calls it "a copy of a letter sent by a girl of the Yukaghir tribe of northeastern Siberia to a young man." Here is how Sampson describes it:

> The conifer-shaped objects . . . are people. The second from the right is the writer (the row of dots represents plaited hair and thus shows that she is a woman); the next one leftwards, the recipient of the letter, was previously her lover, but has now gone off to live with a Russian woman (plaited hair, together with a skirt with panniers distinguishing Russian from Yukaghir costume). The Russian woman, naturally, has broken up the relationship between writer and addressee (line from head of the Russian woman cutting through the lines joining the two Yukaghir). . . . [Sampson 1985, pp. 28–29]

This is less than half of Sampson's description, but there is no point in belaboring the obvious: Sampson's interpretation is far too detailed for

Figure 1. Sampson's picture of the Yukaghir "love letter."

him to have figured it all out by himself. Just look at the picture and see if you could deduce everything in the foregoing paragraph, assuming that you had been given no background information about how the picture originated. And assuming for the sake of argument that you could in fact come up with Sampson's interpretation, how could you verify that it is the correct or only possible interpretation?

Without so much as a footnote of help from Sampson, John DeFrancis reconstructed the lineage of this Yukaghir "love letter," tracing it back to an original sketch by a political exile languishing in Siberia named Shargorodskii. By comparing sketches and interpretations in nearly a century of books and scholarly articles, DeFrancis worked out who copied what from whom. I drew a tree diagram (Figure 2) summarizing his findings for his 1989 book. As you can see, Sampson got his information from Diringer, who got his from Weule, who got his from Krahmer, who seems to have been one of only three people, prior to DeFrancis, who actually read Shargorodskii's report before writing about it. It appears that the German Weule was the person primarily responsible for creating the belief that the artifact in question was a "love letter."

Figure 3 shows Shargorodskii's original drawing. Compare it with Sampson's. Sampson has omitted a whole structure smack dab in the middle of the picture—a part that plays a key role in his explanation— yet gives the same hand-me-down report of its meaning he got, with the miscopied picture, from Diringer. The truth is, as Shargorodskii explained, that the original picture was something he picked up after observing a Yukaghir game something like Twenty Questions. Yukaghir girls carve pictures on birchbark about their love lives, challenging friends who look over their shoulders to guess what they're carving. The artifacts they make in this way are not letters at all. They're just by-products of semiritualized play. The whole idea that Shargorodskii reproduced an ideographic message is a scholarly fiction.

But it is hardly an innocuous fiction. James Elkins, oblivious of DeFrancis' findings, grounds his discussion of the Yukaghir pictures on the work of the Russian "I. P. Al'kora, who published the *only* account of these drawings in 1934" (Elkins 1999, p. 167; emphasis added). According to Elkins, Al'kora went so far as to offer an interpretation of certain groups of lines in the pictures: "He transcribes their collective meaning as 'I love you with all the strength of my soul' " (p. 168). Elkins' goal is to demonstrate the existence of a continuum leading from writing to picture through types of visual artifacts that he calls allography, semasiography, pseudowriting, subgraphemics, hypographemics, emblemata, and schemata. Gradations along this continuum are facilitated by introducing the concept of a *notation,* "an image employing organizational principles other than the formats associated with pictures or writing systems, especially reference lines and other geometric configurations" (p. 257).[3] As Elkins' "pseudo," "sub," and "hypo" prefixes make clear,

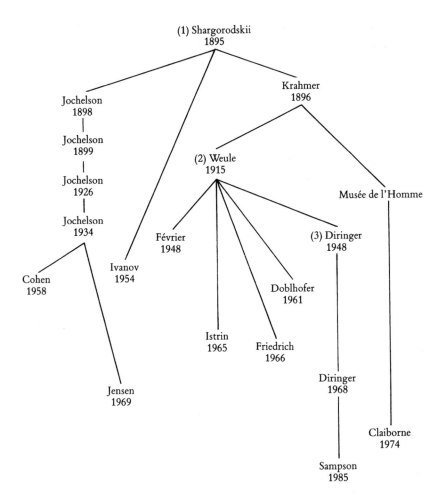

Figure 2. DeFrancis' tree of descent.
(Numbers in parentheses indicate distinct graphic versions.)

scripts beyond semasiography "are not 'full'—that is, they cannot express the entirety of a language" (p. 90). And since he includes the Yukaghir material under subgraphemics, he tacitly parts company with Sampson and concedes DeFrancis' point. Yet, Elkins insists, the Yukaghir images "are diagrams of emotional attachments, and *they are texts,* because they tell stories that can be read in a circuitous format. This is as close as any example I know of a fusion of notation and writing" (pp. 168–169; emphasis added).

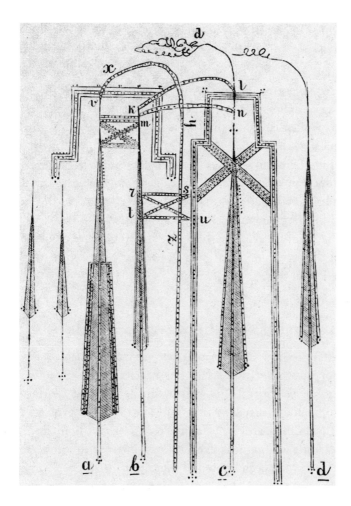

Figure 3. Shargorodskii's original picture.

The fiction of the "love letter" is harmful in a second way. Think for a moment about the fact that Sampson cited the Yukaghir love letter instead of Blissymbolics (see Chapter 1) to illustrate a semasiographic writing system. (Elkins uses other examples, but he too omits mention of Bliss.) Promoters of Blissymbolics, from Bliss himself onward, have not shied away from claiming that theirs is an authentic semasiographic writing system—that is, a full, coherent system independent of yet expressively coextensive with a natural language. But Bliss-characters are obviously artificial; their history is well known and to say that they are based on a universal language of symbols is about as appropriate as saying that McDonald's restaurants reflect the tastes and practices of all cultures because you can find one practically anywhere. The Yukaghir example, by contrast, has the look of the primitive; it seems to be a naive, spontaneous creation, an invention spawned by necessity. Did not these features influence Sampson's choice? Was he not attracted to the Yukaghir "love letter" because it looked like something that had arisen spontaneously in what Rousseau called the "state of Nature"?

Perhaps realizing how far out on a speculative limb he had gone, Sampson published an article in the journal *Linguistics* five years after DeFrancis had uncovered the true story of the "love letter." In this article he admitted his mistake but reasserted all his claims about picture writing (minus the Yukaghir evidence, of course) and the nature of Chinese characters. In essence, Sampson argued that it really doesn't matter whether the "love letter" was a message or not.

THE CLASSIFICATION OF WRITING SYSTEMS

In Sampson's terminology, writing systems can be *semasiographic* (ideographic) or *glottographic* (transcriptive of speech). DeFrancis, however, contends that all systems of signs worthy of being called writing systems are glottographic. (Partial writing, without the rebus principle, doesn't count.) In his 1994 article, Sampson concedes this point to a limited extent. Acknowledging that every alleged instance of a semasiographic writing system "has been limited to expressing messages relating to some narrow, limited domain," he then continues dismissively:

> Whether this makes semasiography so different from glottography that the word "writing" is inapplicable to the former, or whether

rather one should call existing semasiographic systems "writing" of an unusual, limited type, is purely a question of how one chooses to use the word "writing" and as such, surely, is not worth many moments' discussion. [p. 119]

But what about the observable differences between full and partial writing that underlie DeFrancis' distinction? In our rejoinder, we reminded readers that

> any physical act (e.g. touching your nose) or manipulation of matter (e.g. waving a red flag) can serve as an ad hoc signal provided its users make suitable prearrangements. There is nothing special about writing in this regard: there is no essential difference between agreeing that a wink means "I'm looking at a six-card major, partner" and agreeing that five triangles inscribed on a piece of clay will mean "The man who brings you this should also give you five sheep." Partial writing is different from full writing because it consists of nothing but a limited number of such ad hoc prearranged signals.[4] [p. 550]

This difference can be explained by means of a concept that Sampson himself introduced in his 1985 book. I alluded to it previously with the phrase "generative capacity," but perhaps Sampson's "expressive potential" is clearer. The basic idea is usually attributed to Noam Chomsky: it is possible to generate an *infinite* number of symbol strings using a finite number of symbols and a finite number of rules for arranging them; computer programs are examples of sets of rules that can act on sets of symbols to do so. For Chomsky this means that a program is the right model for the grammar of a language: the symbols are the entries in the language's lexicon; the commands in the program are the rules of its grammar. The beauty of such a model is that it offers an intuitively appealing explanation for how brains of finite capacity, working within finite time limits, can nevertheless produce and comprehend any grammatical sentence in a given language, even those neither uttered nor heard before. Sampson claims that groups of people are capable of constructing systems of this kind with symbols and rules completely unrelated to those of their community's speech. In his book, in fact, he goes so far as to say there is no reason in principle why a tribe of human beings could not have "expanded a semasiographic system, by adding further graphic conventions, until it was fully as complex and rich in expressive potential as their spoken language" (1985, p. 30). He thus asks us to believe it is just a quirk of history that we don't have any examples of such full-blown semasiographic systems.

The difficulty with this argument is that, in the natural world, there is no way to measure "expressive potential" except by the yardstick of naturally occurring languages. Whereas writing systems are clearly human inventions, language is a product of evolution. The languages a person picks up in early childhood are acquired; second languages and literacy, however, must be learned, like riding a bicycle or playing baseball.[5] Learning, unlike acquisition, requires conscious effort. Therefore, an indefinite increase in the "expressive potential" of partial writing must eventually outstrip one's capacity to learn. Since partial writing is by its very nature ad hoc, there is a limit beyond which it simply becomes unlearnable and impractical. In other words: Sampson is wrong to suggest that his hypothetical tribe could proceed continuously to a point at which it would "possess two fully-fledged 'languages' having no relationship with one another" (1985, p. 30). Long before they reached that point, their emerging "system" would hit a plateau of usefulness beyond which it would never rise.

What makes a writing system learnable and practical? In his 1989 book, DeFrancis points out that extremely detailed visual representations of speech—such as sound spectrograms (graphs of acoustical signals) and the highly technical notations used by linguists—are, despite their high degree of phonetic precision, completely unsuitable for the ordinary purposes to which we put writing every day. The reason is obvious: too much detail creates an unbearable burden. We don't need to know a writer's general tone of voice exactly, or her preference for pronouncing a word like "either," or any of the other minutiae that a truly extreme phonographic writing system captures—in fact, unless we are spared such minutiae, we cannot learn or use the system with any facility. People often say that the Spanish or Finnish writing systems are highly "phonetic," by which they simply mean that they have very few irregular spelling rules compared with, say, the awful writing systems of English or French. But from a wider perspective, no ordinary writing system comes close to the extreme cases of phonography we use for fieldwork or in the laboratory.

In our Toronto paper of 1988 and our 1994 rejoinder to Sampson, DeFrancis and I brought out the complementary point. All writing systems incorporate techniques that are logographic—that is, make use of linguistic structures beyond the merely phonological. In practice, these higher-level structures coincide with words, though written signs can stand for part of a word or for entire phrases. Signs that function entirely or partially as logograms are not at all like Sampson's semasiograms (ideograms) and are certainly not confined to writing systems that use Chinese characters. English spellings are full of logographic hints. There is a historical explanation for why the verb "know" is written differently from the negative "no." But for the reader the important thing is that the difference in spelling adds clues that facilitate recall which would not be present if these two words were notated in a strictly phonographic manner. (Indeed, even "no" isn't completely phonographic: think of how you pronounce "now.") Sampson and others seem to have overlooked extreme cases of logographic writing systems that are as unlearnable and impractical as the extreme cases of phonographic writing systems. These systems, we pointed out, are what are known in the field of cryptography as *codes*. Codes in this sense need to be carefully distinguished from *ciphers,* although both are used for military and commercial security.

> Ciphers are reversible algorithms for changing or transposing the characters that make up a message. If you know the rules of a cipher, you can encipher and decipher any message whatsoever. Codes, on the other hand, are prearranged ad hoc substitutions of symbols or words for other words, like "demon" for "general" and "party" for "attack." This simple method of concealing the phonetic identity of the words—their syntactic order can be left untouched—is all it takes to produce text that even a native speaker finds impenetrable.[6] When it comes to logography, it is such codes that represent the true limiting case, not Chinese characters. [1994, p. 550]

Once we are sensitive to the difference between codelike and cipher-like writing systems, we gain an important insight into so-called logographic writing systems like Chinese. Except for small, special-purpose codes that can be committed to memory with good reliability, codes are unlearnable and impractical. This is why military, commercial, and espionage organizations use codes for security. The possible disaster of having a copy of your codebook stolen without your knowledge is decisively outweighed by the certainty that no intercepted message can be decoded without a copy of the codebook. Therefore, as a general matter, it is considered good practice in cryptography to incorporate elements of code into systems of secret writing even when strong ciphers are being used. Yet one can in fact learn to read and write Chinese and Japanese. Though these writing systems may press the limits of human endurance, they do fulfill practical functions in the daily lives of millions of people; therefore, they cannot be as logographic as true codes even though they are reputed to be different in essence from all other kinds of writing.

Sampson seems to have been aware of this problem when he wrote the following passage in his 1994 article:

> Whether one regards such a system as essentially logographic with elements of a phonographic principle, essentially phonographic with elements of a logographic principle, or as too mixed to assign to either category, must depend on *a subjective judgment* as to how close and regular the relationship between pronunciations and written forms needs to be before one treats that relationship as the central organizing principle of a script. [p. 127; emphasis added]

In effect, this statement concedes that the graphic units of a writing system may not always serve the same representational functions, yet Sampson's own classification of writing systems (1985) pigeonholes each one on the basis of a "principle" upon which the system is allegedly based. Thus by 1994 Sampson had come to see that his categories were really just regions on a continuum. But then, we must ask, if writing system A is relatively more phonographic or logographic than writing system B, are the differences between them ever so great as to compromise the learnability and practicality of one system or the other? This crucial question is one that Sampson neglects. Unless one can produce hard data (not just classificatory theories) showing that the processing of, say, English texts and Chinese texts in the brain proceeds along different pathways, the hypothesis of a single pathway must be preferred.

To put it another way, Sampson's continuum looks like Figure 4. Writing systems like Finnish and Spanish are considered nearly ideal phonographies. English and French, which have numerous "irregular spellings," are less perfectly phonographic. Arabic and Hebrew, which usually omit vowel signs, have fewer such irregularities but require you to fill in a lot of phonological information on the basis of your knowledge of the structure of the language; hence, they are even less phonographic. But all systems that use Chinese characters are ipso facto logographic to an extent that alphabetic or syllabic writing systems can never approach. In fact, Sampson holds that Japanese is the most logographic writing system of all, because Chinese characters take different readings in Japanese writing depending on context. No ordinary writing systems occupy the middle terrain between phonography and logography, reflecting Sampson's insistence that, in each system, a certain "principle" of representation dominates. A more realistic view of the continuum looks like Figure 5.

According to this view, all ordinary writing systems are concentrated near the center of the continuum, reflecting the basic need to balance the ease afforded by phonographic techniques with the brevity that only logographic techniques permit. Too much of either results in a system that is impossible to learn or use freely in everyday situations. No ordinary writing system approaches the true extremes of phonography or logography—and these are not just theoretical extremes. Narrow phonetic transcriptions on the one hand and cryptographic codes on the other are flesh-and-blood examples of such extreme writing systems; they are suited to the special purposes to which they are put precisely because they lack the properties that all ordinary writing systems must possess.

Notice, incidentally, that Korean has been moved closer to the phonographic end of the central region in Figure 5. Although Chinese characters, called *hanja* in Korean, are still used in certain kinds of writing in both North and South Korea, most everyday writing is done in pure

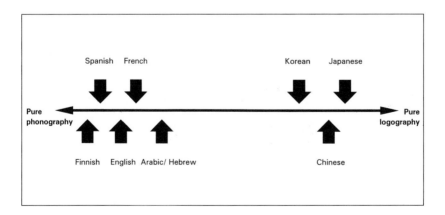

Figure 4. Wrong typology of writing systems.

han'gŭl orthography. In South Korea, a law against using *hanja* was promulgated in 1948; but in 1949, *hanja* were allowed when necessary if accompanied by *han'gŭl;* and in 1950, it was decided to use a mixture of *hanja* and *han'gŭl.* *Hanja* were abolished again in 1955; but in 1964, permission was given to include 1,300 of them in elementary and secondary school textbooks. This measure was followed by a 1968 presidential decree to use *han'gŭl* exclusively, which was applied to school texts in 1970; but in 1972, some 1,800 *hanja* were reintroduced in the schools. In North Korea, *hanja* were banned until 1964, when characters were reintroduced; 2,000 are taught to precollegiate students, 1,000 more to postsecondary students.[7]

I've rated Japanese as slightly more logographic than Chinese because of the many *kanji* that take multiple readings; some might feel that Chinese and Japanese should be reversed because Japanese writing also uses *kana,* which are highly phonographic. But in either case, the difference between both Chinese and Japanese writing and authentic logography is much more significant than the relative difference between them.[8]

In short, DeFrancis' distinction between partial and full writing remains fundamental. So long as we are talking about symbolic systems with the "generative capacity" or "expressive potential" of a naturally occurring (spoken) language, there appears to be no way to craft a system based strictly on two-dimensional, more or less permanent, visible patterns or marks other than by reference to a preexisting language. Of

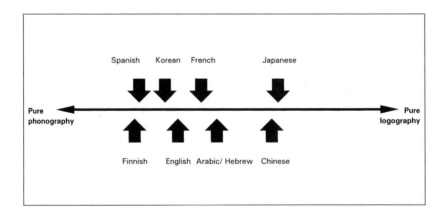

Figure 5. Right typology of writing systems.

course, there are well-known examples of visual and tactile languages—American Sign Language (ASL), and for example, the hand-manipulating language famously used by Helen Keller—but they neither qualify as writing nor enjoy the same position in natural history that speech does. The gestural symbols of such systems are as ephemeral as sound waves in the air, and they all owe much of their "expressive potential" to features they share with the lexicons and grammars of the speech communities in which they have developed. Though they have some structural features that lack simple analogues in speech, their robustness as evolving languages depends on other features, like finger spelling in ASL, that make it easy for them to borrow from ambient languages.

BUT ISN'T A PICTURE WORTH A THOUSAND WORDS?

Many people find all this hard to swallow because they live in a world saturated with print, whether formed by ink on paper or glowing phosphors on a screen. Linguists like DeFrancis seem to speak from an anthropological tradition in which peoples who possess the most primitive technologies are held up as most representative of the universal aspects of the human condition. But surely, the thought goes, my intuitions about how writing and pictures work can't all be mistaken: granted that speech is fundamental, there are lots of times when it seems that written words and pictures clobber me with meaning; I am just a silent observer. Meaning seems to just jump off the page at me. (Such considerations prompted Elkins' theory.)

Of all the artifacts of modern life, there is perhaps no better example of things that give rise to this intuitive feeling than the comic book. More than just a book in a specific language, comics seem to transcend language and culture because of their heavy reliance on pictures. Many American fans who think they understand Japanese *manga* are probably missing big chunks of meaning, but no matter. Misunderstandings happen all the time even when you're talking to people you know in your native language. So let's put it as a challenge: how come comics work if speech is primary?

The comics artist Scott McCloud (1993) has proposed a cogent theory that takes us a long way not only toward answering the challenge but also toward clarifying the connection between pictures and language—

which, of course, is exactly the connection that caused Sampson so much trouble when he came across the so-called Yukaghir love letter. McCloud develops a theoretical model of what he calls "the picture plane." He begins by arranging a variety of images along a single dimension as shown in Figure 6.

McCloud calls all these images *icons* because each can serve as an emblem for a face.[9] The photograph on the far left is, in fact, a photograph of a particular face. As we move to the right, the drawings become progressively more sketchy: detail is stripped away so that the face becomes less and less identifiable as the face of a particular person. (For this reason, McCloud suggests, it comes to resemble the sketchy self-awareness of the viewer's own face.) Eventually we hit the limit: the minimal cartoon. The vertical dashed line to its right marks the "language border." To its right, the graphic images are no longer icons of faces but rather emblems of chunks of language by means of which we think about faces. The most basic of these is the naked word FACE, a posterlike linguistic equivalent of the minimal cartoon. Then come progressively more elaborate pieces of language until, at the rightmost extreme, we run into language so freighted with metaphor that it takes a while to realize that it describes a face ("Thy youth's proud livery, so gaz'd on now . . .").

All these pictures and texts have one thing in common: they are all two-dimensional graphic images that can be taken as emblematic of a face

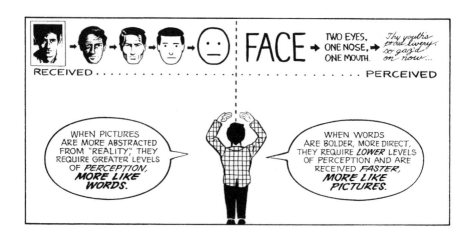

Figure 6. McCloud's continuum of images.

or faces in general. They vary in their degree of realism; as we move from left to right, the icon makes greater and greater demands on the viewer or reader. At the very least, we must acknowledge that the photograph on the left is a picture of something; as we move to the right, we must tolerate missing details or perhaps subconsciously fill them in. The cartoon is almost riddle-like in its simplicity. Then we cross over to FACE, which requires us to be minimally literate in English. Beyond that, we must participate even more; Shakespeare's words in Sonnet II won't conjure up "face" unless we are willing and able to play the "poetry game."

McCloud now adds a second dimension to his picture plane that cross-cuts the first (Figure 7). Along this new axis, the images grow graphically (rather than iconically) more abstract. The photograph is still a photograph, but it gets progressively grainier; the text is still a text, but it makes use of unconventional typography and unexpected layouts. Consequently, as Figure 7 shows, picture and text start to converge as we move higher along the dimension of graphic abstraction. (We can disregard McCloud's accompanying commentary about comics for the moment.)

The photograph, the sketch, the cartoon, the word, the phrase, the

Figure 7. McCloud's triangle.

metaphor—the differences become smaller and smaller as we move in the direction of ever greater graphic abstraction. This fact is embodied in McCloud's use of the triangle: graphic abstraction causes images of differing degrees of realism to converge. Near the apex of the triangle, pictorial and linguistic images become virtually indistinguishable. When people speak of Chinese characters being ideograms, it seems that it is this realm of convergent forms, where picture and text take on similar appearances, that they have in mind.

But as McCloud's model also shows, there is no special iconic or representational property of Chinese characters that makes them picturelike. To an educated native speaker of Chinese, a word, phrase, or passage in conventional Chinese script is just as plain and matter-of-fact as a word, phrase, or passage of an ordinary English text is to the average American. It is mostly the unfamiliarity of Chinese characters to the untrained eye and curious mind—their sphinxlike aspect—that compels the uninitiated to place them higher up in the triangle than they really belong.

Of course, McCloud's goal in laying out his "picture plane" was not to explicate writing. It was simply to create a map that could be used to analyze comics. Different artists, with different styles and priorities, will occupy certain regions on this triangular surface. For example, one distinctive feature of the famous Belgian artist Hergé's *Tintin* is his placement of moderately cartoony characters against "unusually realistic backgrounds" (McCloud 1993, p. 42). Hergé "ventures very little into the upper world of non-iconic abstraction" in either text or picture, and his texts cluster near to the dotted line in the foregoing rectangular figure, or Language Border (p. 54). Figure 8 shows three more examples of how McCloud uses his map.

Despite his focus on comics, McCloud intends his model to embrace all graphic art. He does not shy away from saying where he would place typical works of Monet, Mondrian, Rembrandt, and Matisse on his map of the graphic universe. (They go on the "left face," "top," "lower left," and just above the center of the base, respectively.) And while he does not explore the implications of his model as a unifying theory of picture and text, we are free to do so.

Let's strip down the "picture plane" to its essentials by removing the illustrative figures as in Figure 9. (The descriptive labels are the ones suggested by McCloud.) The space defined by the triangle contains all black-

Figure 8. How McCloud uses his map.

and-white, two-dimensional graphic images, so it is certainly adequate for virtually all ordinary writing, including fancy typography and arty layouts. Below the Representational Edge (line *AB*), additional formal elements come into play, most notably color. As with black-and-white, different ways of using color can be plotted along the axis of graphic abstraction. At the left extreme would be realistic coloring. A more middle-of-the-road approach is found in the work of Hergé, who "captured the magic of . . . flat colors with unprecedented subtlety" despite the fact that "comics printing was superior in Europe and for Hergé, flat colors were a preference, not a necessity" (p. 190). In the United States, the four-color process was until the 1970s pretty much the most artists could hope for, so

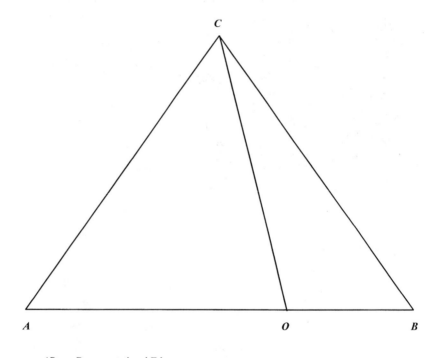

AB	Representational Edge
CA	Retinal Edge
CB	Conceptual Edge
CO	Language Border

Figure 9. McCloud's picture plane.

they perfected the use of more iconic, cartoonier, bright primaries. Ordinary texts can also be printed using color, so the area to the right of the Language Border (line CO) can be extended downward as well.

Likewise, one could extend the model across the Retinal Edge (line CA) by introducing the third dimension of space we get with sculpture or holographic images. A similar extension beyond the Conceptual Edge (line CB) is easy to imagine: from texts we move on to whole books, libraries, and electronic networks. From this viewpoint, the significance of the triangle is that it demarcates the domain within which human beings have found a robust balance between practicality and flexibility. The need for ordinary writing systems to maintain a balance between phonography and logography, explained earlier, can thus be taken as a special case of this general theory. In this sense, McCloud's model offers us a way to define writing of all kinds without having to refer to the transcriptive nature of ordinary writing. We will return to this idea in Chapter 9. For now, it is enough to note that this is about as far as anyone can go in accommodating the long line of scholars who (in more ways than one) have stumbled on the Yukaghir "love letter."[10]

3 The Great Wall of China and other exotic fables

As I mentioned in Chapter 1, Gaspar da Cruz was probably the first European to come up with the contagious idea that Chinese characters are hieroglyphic-like ideograms. Many others more famous, like Matteo Ricci, abetted him, but it is fitting that John DeFrancis zeroed in on da Cruz—for it was also he who initiated the Western legend of the Great Wall of China. The Great Wall, so the story goes, was built in ancient times by a corvée labor force of unimaginable size. It stretched from the sea to the interior deserts of western Gansu, blocking the northern entry into the fabled land of silk. No architectural project in antiquity, we are assured, equaled the size or cost of the Great Wall. The pyramids of Egypt, the Roman roads and aqueducts, were stupendous achievements, yet only the Great Wall, among all human buildings, is so vast that an astronaut standing on the Moon can see it with the naked eye (weather on Earth permitting, of course). After all, it's right there in one of the *Believe It or Not* cartoons of Robert Ripley (a famous lover of Chinese women if not China itself). But why cavil? Has not the Great Wall fueled the imaginations of writers down to Kafka? Is it not, thanks to the propaganda apparatus of the Chinese Communist Party, the very symbol of the Chinese nation?

THE HANDWRITING'S ON THE WALL

Despite the ubiquity of the Great Wall idea throughout the literate world, it is almost impossible to find a reference to it in Chinese literature prior to the Ming dynasty. It was during that isolationist period of late imperial Chinese history that most of the structure now called the Great Wall was constructed. Though some of that construction was new, much of it simply linked together preexisting fortifications and towers scattered here and there across Inner Mongolia, an area that had for centuries wit-

THE GREAT WALL OF CHINA

nessed wars, migrations, and the rise and fall of many Chinese dynasties. The original legend probably began with Arab traders, the same traders who collected the material now associated with the fictional Scheherazade. Da Cruz was just a gullible bystander in a faraway marketplace. Thus the story of the Great Wall that "everyone knows" is no less a construction than the snake of masonry upon which tourists walk today.

So, too, Chinese characters exist but the stories about them are exaggerated. Judging from the gorgeous profusion of shapes one finds in even the simplest Chinese document, it certainly seems impossible that they could have anything in common with the alphabetic writing systems of Europe or other parts of Asia. From this seed of misunderstanding have sprouted entire theories of knowledge and history. Merlin Donald, in his otherwise persuasive attempt to situate the rise of human culture in an evolutionary context, stumbles over ideograms, much as Sampson and Elkins stumbled over the Yukaghir "picture writing" examined in Chapter 2. But the most egregious recent example of mistaken theorizing is undoubtedly to be found in *The Alphabet Versus the Goddess: The Conflict Between Word and Image* by Leonard Shlain (1998).

It is Shlain's contention that, in some primordial era, there was harmonious equality among men and women. In the case of China, known to be one of the world's cradles of literacy, the rise of patriarchal misogyny was, according to Shlain, a consequence of the invention of writing. Shlain relies so heavily on the six myths about Chinese writing enumerated by John DeFrancis (see Chapter 1) that, lifted out of the context of his book, his chapter on China could easily be mistaken for an academic parody. Shlain begins by identifying the well-known Chinese yin-yang symbol as the emblem of the alleged time of innocence before patriarchy took hold:

> The Chinese yin/yang symbol portrays the equality and complementarity of the two sexes. Consisting of two fluid teardrops nestled head to heel, each half extends deep into the hemispheric territory of the other. In the head of each half is a small circle composed of the essence of its opposite; each side contains within it the seed of its reciprocal. [p. 179]

This harmonious intertwining of the sexes did not last long, however:

> Paradoxically, Chinese culture has been one of the world's most rigid patriarchies. For the better part of Chinese history, and espe-

cially in the last thousand years, the status of Chinese women has been abysmal. During this period, polygamy has been the norm, and many men have treated secondary wives as little better than slaves. Often, the primary function of the chief wife was to head a reproductive enterprise whose most coveted products were sons. Indoctrinated from birth to kowtow to their husband's demands, wives often had to adapt to their lowly station by effacing their own personalities. [p. 179]

Passing over the sweeping generalizations and mishmash of historical periods in these few lines, let us simply ask: what precipitated this horrible fall from marital harmony?

Mounting archaeological evidence points to an egalitarian culture in pre-literate China and has raised the following question: does the historical condition of women represent the way things always were or was there an earlier time when Chinese women enjoyed higher status? . . . Chinese written language also contains several suggestive incongruities. For example, family names are ubiquitous in all cultures acquainted with writing. Ancient Chinese family names were built up from the symbol representing "woman." If patriarchy had been in existence long before the recording of Chinese history, why would men choose to construct their patronymics upon the spine of a maternal symbol? [p. 180]

Quite apart from the unexplained "archaeological evidence," Shlain's comments on Chinese are simply wrong. Someone evidently told him about Mandarin *"xíng"* (surname 姓), which includes the signific 女, now used to write *"nǚ"* (woman). Perhaps he was told that *"bǎixíng"* (peasant 百姓) is etymologically "hundred surnames," legendarily because there were only a hundred surnames in ancient times. At any rate, the element 女 most certainly does not occur in the characters used to write all family names, which are, incidentally, not "patronymics" (like the Russian Ivanich, Hebrew ben-Gershon, or Swedish Johansen). But this does not stop Shlain:

Other clues abound. An ancient written Chinese character for "wife" also meant "equal." [I have no idea what characters he's thinking of.] The character for "roof" over the character for "woman" denotes "peace." [That is, 安 is a feminist ideogram.] In ancient times, a wife kept her own name after marriage. [This is standard practice in China even in these late and evil days of patriarchy.] These tantalizing nuggets suggest that at the outset of writing, women still enjoyed considerable equality. And then things began to change. [Sheer speculation.]

Shlain's account of how the introduction of writing led to antifemale discrimination comes in two parts. First he repeats what DeFrancis calls the Monosyllabic Myth:

> Spoken Chinese . . . has *no* distinct parts [of speech]. Depending on the dialect, Chinese contains 400 to 800 monosyllabic sounds or, as linguists call them, "vocables," none of which signifies a specific word. Instead, the meaning of each syllable depends *entirely* on the place (syntax) it occupies in relation to the preceding and following vocables. . . . Each Chinese vocable has four to nine "tones." The meaning of each vocable can vary according to the singsong manner in which it is spoken. . . . For example, the vocable *[y]i* can have sixty-nine different meanings, *shi* fifty-nine, and so on. Thus, monosyllables, although limited in number, allow a speaker to express many diverse ideas and meanings. [p. 181]

(I regret having to use so many ellipses to bring coherence to Shlain's text, but his digressions are simply excessive.) The alleged monosyllabicity of Chinese is supposed to justify the ideographic nature of the Chinese writing system, which Shlain contrasts with alphabetic writing as follows:

> While the Indo-Aryans and Semites found economical ways to translate the *sounds* of the voice into abstract *letters,* the Chinese transformed mental *ideas* into concrete *images.* Their use of a pictographic written language instead of an alphabetic one strongly affected their historical development. Along with ancient Hebrew, Chinese is the oldest continuously used written language. A Chinese scholar can read the most ancient script, because it does not fundamentally vary from the present writing style. Chinese dialects may so differ from region to region that neighbors might not understand each other. Yet, throughout Chinese culture, all can read the written language. It is a testament to how well formed the written language was at its inception that it has undergone so few modifications over thousands of years.

Alphabets are specific to their cultures and not easily translatable even though the *principle* behind alphabets has also remained virtually unchanged after thirty-five hundred years of usage. Alphabets attempt to correlate one letter, or letter combination, with each of the forty-three distinctive sounds, or phonemes, that the human voice can easily articulate. While this feature facilitates learning an alphabet, it impedes communication between different language groups, even within the same alphabet, as any Portuguese letter writer paired with a German reader can attest. [pp. 181–182]

(Notice the casual invocation of the Universality Myth en passant.) I trust the reader understands that human phonation is not in fact limited to forty-three sounds; that phonemes are language-relative, not universal; that Hebrew is not the oldest continuously written language of ancient West Asia; and that a smart German can dope out a lot in a Portuguese letter *because* the roman alphabet, and the culture that goes with it, is the common inheritance of most Europeans.

Shlain believes that "written Chinese has . . . no parts of speech, and none of the complex rules of grammar typical of Western languages" (his second statement to this effect), ignoring the fact that morphology and syntax are not the same—and Chinese has plenty of both (see Packard 2000). But this is the first of many mix-ups. Instead of "common nouns and verbs," for instance, Shlain says that Chinese has "symbols called 'radicals,'" of which there are "only 216 basic" types. He thus confuses not only speech with writing but also significs (see Chapter 1) with radicals, which are just graphic parts of characters used as headings in Chinese character dictionaries. The great Kāngxī dictionary has 214 (not 216) such headings; the characters assigned to a radical (heading) are listed under it in ascending order by number of residual strokes. These headings hardly exhaust the number of graphic components in complex characters; some have variant forms; others look like (but are never analyzed as) combinations of simpler radicals. While the sets of radicals and significs overlap, therefore, they are not the same. In short, the 214 traditional radicals do not constitute a set of mutually exclusive elementary shapes, let alone shapes with fixed linguistic connotations. Hence it is wrong in multiple ways to say, as Shlain does, that "a complex Chinese ideogram [is] built up from as many as eight different radicals."

Not content with his crude justification of the Ideographic Myth, Shlain moves on to the overall layout of Chinese texts: "Unlike horizontally beaded alphabetic words, traditionally [Chinese characters] have been arranged in vertical columns. This difference affects the way the information they convey is perceived." He continues:

Consider for a moment the most common use of vertical information in alphabet writing-lists. Lists make clear the holistic intercon-
nections of separate items. Verticality calls upon the right brain's *all-
at-once* perception and allows us to organize the list's components in
relation to one another. A menu in a restaurant presents the courses
in a vertical layout so that the patron can perceive the concept of a
dinner in its entirety. For the same reason, a theatrical performance's
playbill lists its segments vertically. [p. 182]

One wonders where Shlain found evidence to support this extravagant
claim. How could there be any? It is patently self-contradictory: in traditional Chinese format, menus, playbills, and other lists are written horizontally from right to left just as English lists are written vertically from
top to bottom. The direction of lists is perpendicular to the ductus (flow)
of the text in English or Chinese — or, I might add just to slip in a writing
system with right-to-left lines, Hebrew. It's just ethnocentric to say that
"rearranging a vertical list of items horizontally makes the relationships
of the parts to the whole more difficult to perceive." American "telephone
directories would be nearly impossible to use if the names were arranged
across the page," of course, but that's exactly how you'll find entries in a
Chinese dictionary or encyclopedia with traditional top-to-bottom lines
of text.

Having thus explained the characters themselves and their traditional
format, Shlain claims that they all entail "feminine" psychological features — namely "synthesis, holism, simultaneity, and concreteness." (Why
these elements are especially feminine is something of a mystery.) Here
are the features of the Chinese language that allegedly prove this femi-
ninity:

The Chinese written language does not contain tenses to indicate
past, present, and future; the Western grammatical quagmire called
"verb conjugation" does not exist. There is no conditional pluper-
fect future declension in Chinese. And accordingly, in their culture
the Chinese did not conceptualize the time frame of a week, or the
notion of Sunday. [p. 183]

Although Shlain may once have had a bad experience with German or
French irregular verbs, anyone who has actually interacted with Chinese-
speakers knows that they are quite capable of expressing themselves on
matters present, past, future, and contrary-to-fact, just like any other

human being over the age of four. Either Shlain thinks that "written Chinese" has nothing whatever to do with Chinese as it is spoken or else he must think that Chinese-speakers inhabit a bleak world devoid of history, hope, and holidays. Of course there is no traditional character for "Sunday," but this is merely a fact of Chinese cultural history and has nothing whatever to do with the structure of the Chinese language or Chinese ideas about time.

These are the main points in Shlain's argument, but his chapter on Chinese brims over with additional errors. A brief sampling in the style of a term paper (left-hand side) with marginal corrections (on the right) may prove helpful:

Calligraphy is a highly developed art in the East. In contrast, Western readers care little about the font displayed when they are reading. [p. 183]

What about Islamic calligraphy? Is the whole world just East versus West? Why don't we still use black-letter gothic?

The ideogram for "autumn" is the superimposition of the radical for "crops" upon the one for "fire." [p. 183]

They burn off the rice-fields <u>after</u> the harvest—the "fire" radical is just phonetic.

The left-brained alphabet cultures have been more aggressive in war, conquest, and exploration. The writers of ideographic characters built a wall around their country to keep foreigners out and discouraged exploration. [p. 184]

Mongolian, Korean, Japanese—all traditionally written top to bottom like Chinese. Not warriors?

On Great Wall, see Waldron (1989). What about early Ming voyages as far as Africa?

Alphabet cultures, due to their extremely dualistic form of writing, are more inclined to impose their systems of belief on others and, therefore, religious persecution is commonplace, whereas religious tolerance has been the way of the gestalt-based ideographic cultures. [p. 184]

Dalai Lama? Falun Gong?? Taiping Rebellion??!

The alphabet users' sophisticated abstract science combined with their bellicosity led them to colonize the people of the patterns. [p. 185]

Better see Needham, Science and Civilisation in China (currently 7 vols.). Imperialism in the Americas, India, Africa?

If I have been harsh with Shlain, it is because his book got the royal treatment from a distinguished New York publishing house. The webpage trumpeting the book's insights is as slick and colorful as any to catch the eye of the gullible net surfer. (See the URLs listed in my References.) But perhaps I shouldn't complain. For the sheer volume of ignorance contained in Shlain's discussion of Chinese proves beyond a shadow of a doubt that the pseudoscientific mythology of Chinese characters which forms the focus for this book is very much alive. Perhaps it is not as potent an academic theory as it once was, but as an inferior substitute for honest science fiction, it apparently sells well.

HOW WE REALLY READ

If Shlain and others like him are so mistaken about Chinese characters, the alphabet, and all that, then how does reading actually happen? What's the real story? Let's take a look at Japanese, the more complex of the two cases. By way of a preface, let me quote the famous Japanese diplomat and educator Nitobe Inazō, today pictured on the ¥5,000 bill. Nitobe (1972, 4:274–275) once wrote: "The blind man can be better educated than his more fortunate brethren who are endowed with good sight; for the former, by acquiring the forty-seven letters of the *I-ro-ha* syllabary, through the Braille system, can read history, geography or anything written in that system; whereas he who has eyesight cannot read the daily papers unless he has mastered at least 2000 characters." More eloquent testimony to the fact that language remains the same no matter how it is written would be hard to imagine. And this fact is the starting point for any serious investigation of how Japanese (or any other kind of) reading works.

There is a widespread belief that the use of Chinese characters *(kanji)* in Japanese texts adds a layer of indefinable meaning to those texts not present in their spoken or phonographically transcribed form. But there is now empirical evidence proving that this alleged superlinguistic stratum of meaning is an illusion. Though there is a certain subjective correlate to this illusion, which we will examine later on, it lacks a physical correlate that plays a role in the cognitive processes of reading or writing. (Think of movies or television: subjectively we see pictures move due to the persistence of vision; in fact, we are seeing a very rapid succession of slightly differing still images.)

The truth is that *kanji* work the same way all ordinary systems of writing work. They combine phonographic cues to speech sounds with logographic information that identifies word-level chunks of speech (Chapter 2). The logographic information saves space and keeps texts from getting too detailed for everyday purposes; the phonographic information assures that texts do not get so dense that learning the writing system becomes like memorizing a codebook. A balance must be struck between both kinds of information, but there are multiple ways to do so. In the case of Chinese characters, mnemonic phonetic information is embedded in the graphic structure of most characters.

But even when used in Japanese writing, in which supporting phonetic context is provided by syllabic script, *kanji* are recalled principally by sound. This can be demonstrated experimentally. Table 2 shows the stimuli used. The "target" lines in Table 2 show actual words of Japanese. In each numbered line, the second *kanji* is a mistake; the result is a nonword. If we assume that *kanji* are ideograms or logograms, then the words on the far right give the core meanings in Japanese of the second *kanji* in each line. The pronunciation of each *kanji* compound is shown in the center in italics; the meaning of each compound is given if it is a real word.

Now compare examples 1 and 2 in Table 2. The false and true *kanji* do not resemble each other. In example 1, they do not share a core meaning but do take the same pronunciation. In example 2, it's the other way around: the false and true *kanji* share a core meaning but cannot be pronounced the same way. By analyzing hundreds of pages of text written by educated Japanese, Richard Alan Horodeck showed that they produced mistakes of type 1 ten times more often than any other kind, including type 2. This shows that so-called core meanings seldom play a role in *kanji* recall. Shared pronunciations often cause the writing of false *kanji,* however, even when the false and true *kanji* don't look anything like one another.

Next compare examples 3 and 4. Here the false and true *kanji* do look very much alike. Their core meanings are unrelated. The difference is this: in example 3, the false and true *kanji* can take the same pronunciation; in example 4, they cannot. Suppose we plant mistakes like these in texts and ask educated Japanese to read them for comprehension. If *kanji* are recalled by meaning, we would expect our readers to notice mistakes of both kinds often and at about the same rate. But as Horodeck discovered, readers don't do this: they are particularly bad at catching errors of type 3. These went unnoticed about five times more often than all other kinds of errors, including those of type 4. If a *kanji* causes the pronunciation demanded by context to be subvocalized, the reader tends to move on even when the *kanji* is wrong. Core meanings just don't matter much. (Ironically, when using Japanese script on computers, type 3 errors are the kind

Table 2. The Horodeck Model

		Writing Errors		
Error Type	*Kanji*	Pronunciation (reading of 2nd *kanji* italicized)	Word Meaning	"Core meaning" of 2nd *kanji*
1. S+ F− M−	不恐	fu*kyō*	*nonword*	FEAR
Target	不況	fu*kyō*	"business slump"	STATE
2. S− F− M+	迅早	jin*sō*	*nonword*	EARLY, FAST
Target	迅速	jin*soku*	"rapid"	FAST

		Reading Errors		
Error Type	*Kanji*	Pronunciation (reading of 2nd *kanji* italicized)	Word Meaning	"Core meaning" of 2nd *kanji*
3. S+ F+ M−	予側	yo*soku*	*nonword*	SIDE
Target	予測	yo*soku*	"forecast"	MEASURE
4. S− F+ M−	埋投	mai*tō*	*nonword*	THROW
Target	埋没	mai*botsu*	"bury"	SINK

Error type key: S = sound, F = form, M = meaning.

S+ false *kanji* can be pronounced like target
S− false *kanji* cannot be pronounced like target

F+ false *kanji* looks like target
F− false *kanji* looks different from target

M+ false *kanji* has "core meaning" similar to target's
M− false *kanji* has "core meaning" different from target's

typically produced by popular Japanese word-processors. The same can be said in the case of Chinese. In other words: these pieces of software generate the kind of *kanji* error most difficult to detect while proofreading. We'll return to this point in Chapter 8.)

The foregoing discussion is brief but gets to the heart of the matter in regard to the reading and writing of Chinese characters. The interested reader can find copious bibliographic references and a thorough discussion of experimental techniques and clinical studies of patients with brain injuries in such technical surveys as Paradis, Hagiwara, and Hildebrandt (1985) and Kess and Miyamoto (1999). But as we can see from Shlain's pronouncements, discourse on the psycholinguistics of Chinese characters in the general literature seldom rises above the level of popular "left-brain/right-brain" theories. The basic idea behind such theories is that the left side of the brain is analytic, verbal, and coldly rational whereas the right side is devoted to the visual, tactile, and imaginative aspects of human cognition. Not surprisingly, a lot of experiments designed to demonstrate "hemispheric laterality" in users of Chinese characters are poorly structured, improperly carried out, or interpreted with circular, self-confirming logic.

In fairness, it should be pointed out that junk science of the left-brain/right-brain variety is by no means limited to the study of reading and writing. A Japanese weekly magazine recently ran a short article by Senzaki Manabu (2001) in which he describes his experience as a test subject at "a certain university" that he graciously does not name. Senzaki is a high-ranking professional *shōgi* player. (*Shōgi* is Japanese chess, a game if anything even more complicated than Western chess, since its board contains eighty-one rather than sixty-four squares and its rules allow you to introduce a piece captured from your opponent on your own side in lieu of making a move.) When Senzaki was about twenty, he was invited to participate in a psychology experiment and gamely showed up though suffering from a severe hangover. As anyone who has been wired up for an electroencephalogram knows, the adhesive used to glue the electrodes to the scalp can make even a sober person feel queasy. After asking Senzaki a few easy questions to get him to relax, the experimenter instructed him to count mentally by sevens (7, 14, 21, 35, 49, . . .). Soon he was feeling nauseous. Just then he was asked to say the next number out loud. He had more urgent things to think about, so he blurted out "161," adding 140 and 21 in his head, maintaining the appearance of complete cooperation. Then, refocusing on keeping his stomach under control, he prepared himself to say "301" (7 × 43) and closed his eyes as if in deep concentration. So it went. He merely called out larger and larger multiples of seven whenever asked for a number.

After several such tests, the experimenter asked Senzaki to play some *shōgi*. His opponent was an indescribably cute female lab assistant, dressed in a revealing miniskirt, who barely knew the rules of the game. Naturally, a pro can make a strong move after just glancing at a position for a few seconds. Senzaki's attention was focused entirely on the lab assistant and how he might be able to wangle her phone number. He didn't need to think about the game at all. Nevertheless, the next day the professor in charge remarked: "It's just as we thought. Pro *shōgi* players are really sharp!" Senzaki wondered whether ogling the girl's legs had distorted his alpha waves, but the professor has since passed away—which is why Senzaki was willing to lay bare this youthful indiscretion to promote his books on *shōgi* in a popular magazine.[1]

When it comes to reading and writing with Chinese characters, the typical pop-psych move is to associate an alleged left-hemisphere preference for linguistic, analytical thinking with alphabets and syllabaries and to associate a complementary right-hemisphere preference for spatial, holistic thinking with Chinese characters. In reality, this is no more warranted by the experimental evidence than the conclusions of the unidentified professor about the brains of *shōgi* players. It is true that Broca's and Wernicke's areas of the brain, active in the production and processing of linguistic signals, are located in the left hemisphere. It is also true that, just as most subjects in a randomly selected group will exhibit right-handedness, one can design experiments in which most subjects will show a kind of "left-brainedness" when doing verbal production and perception tasks.[2] In fact, Michel Paradis (1998) goes so far as to argue that the accumulated neurolinguistic clinical and experimental evidence justifies "treating sentence grammar independently of pragmatics" in the way postulated by Chomsky. But Paradis also points out that the corresponding areas of the right hemisphere are predominantly involved in the handling of metaphorical senses, context, and the relevance of linguistic acts.

Right-brain injuries may not result in a breakdown of the more obvious features of linguistic production or comprehension, but they often compromise the ability to rise above literal meaning and deal with metaphorical or figurative expressions. This is why Paradis urges us to "distinguish between the linguistic 'sentence' and the pragmatic construct 'utterance.'" He continues:

> The former is independent of context and its semantic interpretation can be derived from the meaning of its words and its underlying grammatical structure; the meaning of the latter requires, in addition, inferences from its various contexts (situational, discourse, general knowledge). . . . It has been amply demonstrated that (context-independent) sentence grammar . . . is subserved by areas of the L[eft] H[emisphere], and that consequently damage to specific areas of the LH results in language structure deficits (. . . in phonology, morphology, syntax, and the lexicon, in both comprehension and production). There is increasing evidence that the pragmatic aspects of language are subserved by the RH, and that consequently damage to specific areas of the RH results in content-dependent language deficits (. . . in the use of presupposition, inference, anaphora, cataphora, sarcasm, indirect speech acts, idioms, metaphors, and any aspect of the non-literal interpretation of sentences, in both comprehension and production, including the recognition and production of affective prosody, as well as disruption of discourse structure and conversational conventions). [Paradis 1998, pp. 4–5]

This is a very different view of hemispheric laterality than the one typically invoked by those who say there is something transcendentally unique about Chinese characters among all other varieties of writing. It reminds us that a text written in Chinese or Japanese cannot be successfully created or read without the participation of both hemispheres of the brain—that is, the participation of both linguistic and pragmatic competence—and is therefore no different psycholinguistically from a text in any other of the world's languages.

In our computer-oriented age, we tend to zero in on the code-like aspects of language and to think of meaning as mere information, measurable in bits. But from a less biased perspective, we see that many parts of the brain contribute to the pragmatic success of linguistic and, more generally, semiotic (sign-based) behavior. Whether we use audible words or visual signs that symbolize words, the task of making and finding meaning in the words involves much more than merely creating or apprehending a linear pattern. When it comes to language in the brain, there is no Great Wall dividing the hemispheres any more than there was a Great Wall dividing all of China in the Han dynasty.

4 Dave Barry vs. the intellectuals

Humorist Dave Barry is not your average modern American—and not just because he's outrageously funny. He understands the Ideographic Myth perfectly, though I wonder whether he's aware of the depth of his understanding. A few years ago, he published a book called *Dave Barry Does Japan* that presents a classic statement of the popular view of Chinese characters. Although it is rather long, I cannot improve on it, so I'm going to quote it in full, complete with illustrations:

> Learning to speak Japanese isn't so bad, but learning to read it is insanely difficult. Start with the fact that, for some malevolent reason, the Japanese use four different systems, which are often intermixed, in addition to characters sometimes arranged vertically, in which case you read right to left, but sometimes arranged horizontally, in which case you read left to right. (I might have gotten some of this wrong, but, trust me, there's no way you'd be able to tell.) Also sometimes there's a mixture of horizontal and vertical writing, using several different character systems.
>
> That's not the hard part. The hard part is that the major Japanese writing system consists of—why not?—Chinese characters, which represent words, not sounds. So for each word, you need a different character, which means to be even moderately literate you have to memorize thousands and thousands of characters. This wouldn't be so bad if the characters looked like what they're supposed to represent. For example, if the character for "dog" looked like this:

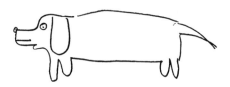

And "bird" looked like this:

And "politician" looked like this:

Then you could form a simple sentence like this:

And even a child would easily understand the meaning ("The bird smiled when the dog ate the politician"). But the Japanese/ Chinese characters don't look anything like the concepts they're supposed to represent. They all look approximately like this:

And every one of those marks is important. If you put one teensy little line in there wrong, you could change the entire meaning of the character, from something like "man holding broom" to "sex with ostriches."

Sometimes it seems as though the whole point of the Japanese writing system is to keep non-Japanese people from understanding what the hell is going on. The only Westerner I met in Japan who had actually learned to read Chinese/Japanese characters was Tom Reid, who works for The Washington Post. He was always trying to explain it to me. He'd write down something that looked like this:

Then he'd say, "OK, this character means 'library infested with vermin.' See, this line here"—here he points to a line that appears identical to all the other lines—"looks like a tree root, right? And books are the root of knowledge, right? Get it? And this line—he points to another random line—looks like the whisker of a rat, right? You see it, right? RIGHT?"

I'd always say that yes, I thought I saw it, although what I really thought was that Tom had spent too many hours studying rats' whiskers. [Barry 1992, pp. 21–24]

OBVIOUSLY A JOKE . . . OR IS IT?

Dave Barry's name rarely makes it into *The New York Review of Books,* but writers whose names do show up there frequently say more or less the same thing. Consider, for instance, the collection *The Empire of Signs: Semiotic Essays on Japanese Culture* (Ikegami 1991). Its title alludes to a famous French book on Japan, *L'Empire des Signes* by Roland Barthes (which I prefer to call *Roland Barthes Does Japan*). At any rate, in one of the essays in this anthology, under the imposing title "Characters That Represent, Reflect, and Translate Culture in the Context of the Revolution in Modern Art," a Japanese scholar named Mukai Shūtarō writes as follows:

> Unlike the alphabet, which has developed a linear form of representation, the writing systems of Chinese and Japanese . . . represent a situation of equilibrium unique in the history of mankind in which the signs function not simply as signs with which one builds sentences, but as signs which by virtue of their pictorial representation and sequencing retain their potential for creating groups of images which are visually meaningful. [Ikegami 1991, p. 72]

At this point Mukai inserts a footnote referring to *Le geste et la parole* by the French archaeologist André Leroi-Gourhan. Leroi-Gourhan is the world's leading authority on the famous animal paintings on the walls of the Lascaux Caves. Here is what he says about *kanji*:

> The manner in which Chinese writing fits Japanese spoken language is something like trying to write French by selecting from among postage stamps the picture that approximately corresponds to the meaning of the words to be transcribed, and assembling them in rows: Both grammar and the phonetic content are completely lost. The characters were borrowed at a strictly ideographic level. [Leroi-Gourhan 1993, p. 207]

This is about Japanese, but perhaps this is where Shlain (Chapter 3) got the idea that Chinese has no grammar. After all, if written Japanese lacks grammar, how much more so must Chinese, with its uninterrupted lines of characters?

Similar ideas were voiced by the celebrated Soviet film director Sergei Eisenstein. Writing of *kanji* in 1929, he proclaimed:

> [The combination] of two hieroglyphs of the simplest series is to be regarded not as their sum, but as their product, i.e., as a value of another dimension, another degree; each, separately, corresponds to an object, to a fact, but their combination corresponds to a concept. From separate hieroglyphs has been fused—the ideogram. By the combination of two "depictables" is achieved the representation of something that is graphically undepictable.
>
> For example, the picture for water and the picture of an eye signifies "to weep"; the picture of an ear near the drawing of a door = "to listen";
>
>> a dog + a mouth = "to bark";
>> a mouth + a child = "to scream";
>> a mouth + a bird = "to sing";
>> a knife + a heart = "sorrow," and so on.
>> But this is—montage!
>
> Yes. It is exactly what we do in the cinema, combining shots that are depictive, single in meaning, neutral in content—into intellectual contexts and series. [Eisenstein 1949, pp. 29–30]

Notice the telltale "hieroglyphs," which the translator has naively transferred from Russian to English (see Chapter 1). Perhaps Russian cultural
beliefs about Chinese explain some of Eisenstein's confusion.

And this brings us back to France. For it was the philosophes of the
Enlightenment who thought that Chinese characters were a way-station
on the road of human progress from Egyptian hieroglyphs to civilized
writing. In his famous essay "Signature Event Context," the deconstructionist Jacques Derrida quotes Condillac on this notion of progress with
enthusiastic approval. As previously remarked, the roots of the idea that
hieroglyphs and *kanji* have something to do with one another goes back
to Western antiquity and is not seen in East Asian writings until long after
the arrival of the Catholic missionaries. The earliest text I have found
in which a Japanese says that *kanji* are ideograms was published in 1894
by Inoue Tetsujirō, who was initiated into philosophy in Tokyo by the
American Ernest Fenollosa (about whom more presently) and culminated
his education in Germany.

The delicious irony of this piece of history is especially piquant when
one reads the pronouncements of postmodernists like Derrida. Mary
Erbaugh (2002, pp. 206–209) has conveniently collected a representative
assortment: Derrida deplores the alphabet as a tool of Western hegemony
because it has no relation to "natural representation," no resemblance or
participation, no symbolic [or] "iconographic" relationship. Michel Fou-
cault regrets that in Western culture "writing refers not to the thing but
to speech." Julia Kristeva insists that, in Chinese script, "meaning/sound/
thing [are] fused into a single traced mark—into an ideogram . . . *la langue*
and 'the real' are one and the same thing." Erbaugh (2002) comments:
"Postmodernist claims that alphabets breed bureaucracy while characters
nurture poets should seem hilarious to anyone who has strangled on red
tape in Tokyo or Beijing" (p. 207). More important, but only slightly less
hilarious, is the contrast between the sweet tones in which the postmodernists extol the alleged uniqueness of Chinese characters and the sour
opinion of the famous Chinese dictionary writer of the first century, Xŭ
Shēn, who wrote that those who etymologize characters pictorially are
"mediocre scholars and crude people."

But let us cross the Atlantic to the United States. Figure 10 shows the
analysis of a poem in classical Chinese cobbled together by the turn-of-
the-century art critic and collector Ernest Fenollosa (Inoue's mentor at

the Imperial University in Tokyo) and Fenollosa's literary executor, the American poet Ezra Pound. Pound thought that he and Fenollosa knew more than anyone else about Chinese poetry: "If our universities had been worth half a peck of horse-dung," he wrote, "something would have been done during the last quarter of a century to carry on Fenollosa's work. . . . The state of Chinese studies in the Occident is revolting, squalid . . . English and American professors are moles" (Fenollosa 1968, p. 37). In reality, the level of Pound's ignorance was as colossal as his ego (Kennedy 1964). As a result, his analysis of the poem can best be described as an exercise in literary narcissism. Just as the mythical Narcissus fell in love with his own reflection, Fenollosa and Pound fell in love with their own aesthetic preconceptions, which they projected onto Chinese poetry by means of naive pictorial etymologies of characters.

As can be surmised from just the single page in Figure 10, Fenollosa's approach is to examine all the teensy little lines in each character and fabricate plausible etymological stories about them. String these stories together in linear order and you divine the meaning of the poem. Dave Barry would be proud. Spoken language has nothing to do with it. This particular analysis appears in an essay by Fenollosa edited and published by Pound in 1920 together with the following so-called translation:

> The moon's snow falls on the plum tree;
> Its boughs are full of bright stars.
> We can admire the bright turning disc;
> The garden high above there, casts its pearls to our weeds.

Whatever one thinks of this as English verse, the question for us is: does it have anything to do with the Chinese text?

In the Chinese, read as Chinese, no snow descends from the moon. Nothing is falling; the ground is, in fact, implicitly free of snow. There is no simile comparing flowers with stars, for no "stars" are mentioned anywhere in the text. The "disc" is actually a mirror. (Traditional Chinese mirrors are round, like a bright full moon.) In English, a "turning disc" conjures up a phonograph record, but the Chinese verb in the poem refers to a different kind of rotation, namely the gradual passage of the moon across the nighttime sky. The characters in the third line labeled "CAN" and "ADMIRE" do not form a single verb phrase; they stand

月 MOON	輝 RAYS	如 LIKE	晴 PURE	雪 SNOW
sun disc with the moon's horns	bright + feathers flying. Bright . . . . Upper right abbreviated picture of wings; lower, bird = to fly . . . short-tailed bird	woman mouth	sun + azure sky. Sky possibly containing tent idea. Author has dodged a "pure" containing sun + broom	rain + broom. cloud roof or cloth over falling drops. Sweeping motion of snow; broom-like appearance of snow
梅 PLUM	花 FLOWERS	似 RESEMBLE	照 BRIGHT	晃 STARS
tree + crooked female breast	man + spoon under plants abbreviation, probably actual representation of blossoms. Flowers at height of man's head	man + try = does what it can toward	sun + knife mouth fire	sun bright. Bright here going to origin: fire over moving legs of a man
可 CAN	憐 ADMIRE (*be in love with*)	金 GOLD	鏡 DISC	轉 TURN
mouth hook . . . fish-pole or sheltered corner	fire heart + girl + descending through two	Present form resembles king and gem; but archaic might be balance and melting-pots	gold + to erect sun legs (running)	carriage + carriage tenth of a cubit (?) Bent knuckle or bent object revolving around pivot
庭 GARDEN	上 HIGH ABOVE	玉 JEWEL	芳 WEEDS	馨 FRAGRANT
to blend + pace, in midst of court		king and dot. *Note:* Plain man + dot = dog	plants cover knife. I.e. growing things that must be destroyed	. . . fragrance from a distance . . . sun under growing tree (cause of fragrance)

Figure 10. Fenollosa's analysis of a poem in classical Chinese.

for a two-syllable adjective meaning "pitiful" or "precious." No "pearls" are "cast" from "high above there" because (passing over the forced allusion to St. Matthew and proceeding directly to Gertrude Stein) there is no "there" there, let alone any casting, throwing, or strewing of anything. The characters in line 4 identified as "JEWEL" and "WEEDS" are not two separate words; they represent a compound noun that poetically refers to the plum blossoms mentioned in line 2. And if we really want to delve into etymology, the original sense of the noun represented by the character labeled "JEWEL" is "jade." One good thing—actually the only good thing—we can say about Pound's translation is that he wisely chose "bright" for the character glossed by Fenollosa rather overliterally as "GOLD."

Let me stress that none of these faults is a matter of poetic license. They are simply mistakes in translation that anyone who knows the language of the original can spot. Although I make no claims to being a poet, the following translation (my own) at least gives the reader a glimpse of what the Chinese text actually says:

> *Wherever the moonlight shines looks like pure snow;*
> *The plum blossoms seem to sparkle.*
> *How melancholy the mirror as it arcs through the sky!*
> *In the garden, the jade-white flowers are fragrant.*

In this version, the poem's forced parallelism between the first and second couplets becomes obvious. The words labeled "GOLD-DISC" in line 3 refer back to the "MOON-RAYS" in line 1 just as the words labeled "JEWEL-WEEDS" in line 4 refer back to the "PLUM-FLOWERS" in line 2. As my colleague Lao Yanshuan once forcefully reminded me, connoisseurs of Chinese poetry look upon such blatant echoing as hack technique, especially in a short quatrain. Moreover, classical Chinese poetry of the first millennium often had tonal prosody and it always rhymed. In this poem, the final syllables of the two couplets do not rhyme. In modern Mandarin, they are *huǎng* and *xīng,* respectively, and they sounded no more alike in Middle Chinese. These facts all strongly suggest late foreign authorship. Most likely, what Fenollosa left to Pound is a gentlemanly foray into Chinese poetry by a Japanese, perhaps one of Fenollosa's teachers. Such a cultivated Japanese would have read such a poem, not in Chinese, but in the stilted kind of classical Japanese called *yomi-kudashi,* in which a gloss is forced onto each *kanji,* which are read off in the scrambled order demanded by Japanese syntax, with Japanese inflectional endings adjusted and particles thrown in as needed. In this case, the first line requires moving Fenollosa's "LIKE" to the end; adding an ending to it, "RAYS" (a verb in Japanese), and "PURE"; and inserting a couple of particles, finally yielding *tsuki kagayaku wa kiyoki yuki no gotoshi,* which contains not a single word of Chinese and sounds to a modern speaker of Japanese rather like a line of Chaucer in the ears of an American college student.

The problem, in short, is not one of artistic sensitivity, delicate nuance, or interpretive shading. Quite literally every detail in Pound's rendition is wrong; yet it remains in print, on many a college reading list, perennially influential. Both fiction and poetry are fine with me, but I am forced to conclude there is really only one difference between what Dave Barry says about *kanji* and what Pound, Eisenstein, Leroi-Gourhan, and all the rest have to say about them.

Only Dave Barry knows that he's making it up!

THE REAL REASONS THAT JAPANESE
IS HARD TO READ

OK, you may say, so Dave Barry is as smart as some intellectual bigwigs. (You knew that already!) But if all those teensy little lines in *kanji* aren't the problem, what does make reading Japanese hard? The chief problem is that most *kanji* can stand for more than one string of sounds according to the rules of the Japanese writing system. To recover the words represented by *kanji* and to use the right ones when writing, you have to know which readings are correct in which contexts. In practice, this can be tricky even for educated native speakers.

In earlier books, I tried to convey the flavor of the difficulties involved by referring to the "spelling rules" in a newspaper handbook and by analyzing a single sentence of modern Japanese character by character. Here I offer a third approach. Going through a quiz book about *kanji* of the sort that Japanese might read for entertainment, I have culled the following list of "stumpers" and classified them for ease of explanation. Remember, it is words like these that Japanese themselves find hard to read correctly.

If you have never studied Japanese, don't worry about the details: just try to imagine that you are a native speaker of Japanese. You know all the words in italics and what they mean; long ago in school, you crammed "spelling facts" like the following into your head. But now, after years as a salaryman or housewife, you're getting a little rusty. When a seldom encountered phrase hits your eye in a magazine article or when, having taken pen to paper, you're trying to remember how to write some fixed expression, you suddenly stop and wonder whether you've got it right.

Let's start with Sino-Japanese morphemes (words or word parts) that were imported from China (in the earliest period by way of Korea) along with the *kanji* themselves. A Sino-Japanese morpheme may be followed by a native Japanese morpheme in a compound. These are called *jūbako-yomi* because *jūbako* (*jū* + *hako* 重箱 "stacking boxes") is such a word. Here are some other examples:

業腹   *gōhara (gō + hara) [ni omou]* "be much vexed at; resent"
      (**gyōfuku* or the like)
諸訳   *showake (sho + wake)* "intricacies; diverse circumstances"
      (**shoyaku*)
利幅   *rihaba (ri + haba)* "profit margin" (**ribuku* or the like)

Likewise a native morpheme may be followed by a Sino-Japanese morpheme in a compound. These are called *yutō-yomi* because *yutō* (*yu* + *tō* 湯桶 "teapot-shaped pitcher") is such a word. Some other examples:

更地   *sarachi (sara + chi)* "empty lot" (**kōchi*)
野天   *noten (no + ten)* "roofless; open to the sky" (**yaten*)
間尺   *mashaku (ma + shaku) [ni awanai]* "doesn't pay; isn't
      worthwhile" (**kenjaku* or the like)

(In linguistics, asterisks are used to mark nonexistent or hypothetical forms. Here "starred" forms are sometimes heard but are considered mistakes.)

Since you cannot depend on a compound containing only morphemes of one kind, errors are often made when readers encounter an uncommon phrase. Sometimes they associate a native morpheme with a character that correctly stands for a Sino-Japanese morpheme, as in the following:

天馬空を行く   *tenba kū o iku*, "sweeping all before you [like Pegasus crossing the sky]" (**tenba sora o iku*)

群を抜く   *gun o nuku*, "come out on top [of others]" (**mure o nuku*)

頭が高い   *zu ga takai*, "be arrogant" (**atama ga takai*)

Alternatively they may think a Sino-Japanese morpheme is meant when a native one is actually intended:

実のある話   *mi no aru hanashi*, "a substantial discussion" (*jitsu no aru hito* 実のある人 is also possible but means "a sincere person")

生きる証   *ikiru akashi*, "living proof" (**ikiru shō*)

真に受ける   *ma ni ukeru*, "take as true; take [a joke] seriously" (**shin ni ukeru*)

Traditionally a few native words were used whole in order to gloss strings of two or more characters (a practice called *jukujikun*). Thus a string of Sino-Japanese morphemes may be mistakenly associated with the string of characters:

玄人   *kurōto*, "expert" (**genjin*)

気質   *katagi*, "character, spirit" (**kishitsu;* not to be confused with *katagi [na]* 堅気 "honest, respectable")

昨日   *kinō*, "yesterday" (*sakujitsu* is possible but not colloquial)

Similar errors arise due to relics in modern Japanese writing from a writing style loosely called *kanbun.* Until recently, a technique for parsing literary Chinese *(kanbun)* and reading it off in a form of classical Japanese *(yomi-kudashi)* was a staple of elite Japanese education. Consequently, in certain situations, Japanese would write literary Chinese (often with some license) expecting the reader to know the rules for mechanically "translating" the text. Fossils from *kanbun*-style writing are often misread today:

所謂   *iwayuru*, "so-called" (**shoi* or the like)

為替   *kawase*, "[currency] exchange" (**itai*)

勿忘草   *wasurenagusa*, "forget-me-nots" (**mochibōsō* or the like)

Kanbun expressions can also give rise to ghost forms, that is, false readings or even false words. For example:

間髪に容れず   *kan-hatsu ni irezu,* "[so close] one cannot insert a
　　　　　　　　hair" (**kanpatu*)
屋上屋を重ねる *okujō, oku o kasaneru,* "[as wasteful as] putting a
　　　　　　　　roof over a roof" (**okujō-oku no shō-iinkai,*
　　　　　　　　"redundant subcommittee")
鬼面人を驚かす *kimen hito o odorokasu,* "[bluffs like] a demon mask
　　　　　　　　intimidating people" (**kimennin o odorokasu,*
　　　　　　　　*kimenjin o odorokasu)

So far, we've looked only at confusions between Sino-Japanese and native morphemes. Actually, there are different kinds of Sino-Japanese morphemes because the Japanese borrowed words from Chinese at different historical epochs. As a result, many *kanji* have multiple Sino-Japanese readings. Before the eighth century, so-called *go-on* morphemes entered the language probably by way of early states on the Korean peninsula. During the eighth century, a massive layer of borrowings directly from Tang China, called *kan-on,* was laid down. In the thirteenth century, the Japanese monks who brought Zen Buddhism from China also brought new ways of pronouncing Sino-Japanese morphemes, now called *tōsō-on.*

When a given *kanji* is associated with more than one Sino-Japanese morpheme, one morpheme is typically more frequent than the others, and different kinds may be mixed in the same compound. For example:

京都　Kyōto (**Keito,* all *kan-on; *Kyōtsu,* all *go-on*)

Consequently, it often happens that a rare *go-on* is misread as a common *kan-on,* as in:

殺生　　　 *sesshō [na],* "cruel"; *sesshō [suru],* "kill" (**sassei*)
杜撰　　　 *zusan [na],* "slipshod; defective" (**tosen*)
一期一会　 *ichigo-ichie,* "once-in-a-lifetime encounter" (**ikki-ikkai*)

Or perhaps a rare *tōsō-on* is misread as a more common *go-on* or *kan-on,* as in:

行燈 *andon*, "paper-covered night light" (**kōtō*)
胡乱 *uron [na]*, "suspicious"; *uron [ni omou]*, "suspect" (**koran*)
塔頭 *tatchū*, "minor temple [building]" (**tōtō*)

Sometimes a *kanji* is rare or takes rare Sino-Japanese readings. Compare the readings for the common *kanji* in the following sets:

容体 *yōdai[buru]*, "give oneself airs"; 風体 *fūtei*, "appearance, dress" (the second character in both words is usually *tai*)

蛇行 *dakō [suru]*, "meander"; 蛇口 *jaguchi*, "spigot" (the first character in both words is uncommon)

出納 *suitō*, "receipts and disbursements" (the first character is usually *shutsu*); 納戸 *nando*, "storage room; back room" (納 is usually read *nō*)

In extreme cases, there is only one word in modern standard Japanese in which a *kanji* takes a particular Sino-Japanese reading. Note how the second *kanji* in each of the following words is read:

風情 *fūzei*, "air, appearance; taste; elegance" (**fūjō*)
遊説 *yūzei*, "canvassing, barnstorming" (**yūsetsu*)
疾病 *shippei*, "sickness" (**shitsubyō*)

When confronted with a character that calls for a Sino-Japanese reading you are unsure of, you can always look for a phonetic element embedded in the character and guess its Sino-Japanese reading on that basis. Unfortunately, this approach doesn't always work:

弛緩 *shikan*, "relaxation," as in *dōtoku no shikan*, "moral laxity" (not **chikan* [compare *chikan* 痴漢 "masher, lecher"]. The 也 in the rare 弛 brings to mind the 地 in such common words as 地図 *chizu*, "map")

甦生 *sosei [suru]*, "regain consciousness" (also written 蘇生; not **kōsei* even though *kōsei*, "revival, rebirth," is written 更生)

進捗 *shinchoku*, "progress, advance" (not **shinshō*. The 歩 in the rare 捗 brings to mind the 渉 in the common word *kōshō* 交渉, "negotiation")

Recent Chinese and Korean loanwords are often pronounced to sound roughly like the way they are pronounced in Chinese and Korean today—which renders any attempt to apply traditional readings useless:

飲茶　　 *yamucha* (*incha, *nomicha), "[Cantonese] dimsum"
釜山　　 *Pusan* (*Huzan), "Pusan [Korea]"
麻婆豆腐 *mābo-dōfu* (*maba-tōfu), "Sichuan tofu"

Over the course of the centuries, sound changes have occasionally affected Sino-Japanese morphemes after entering Japanese. Some are unique to particular words:

所為　 *sei*, "reason, account" (< *soi* < *shoi)
反古　 *hogo*, "wastepaper, trash" (< *hōgo* ~ *hōgu* < *hanko)
億劫　 *okkū*, "an eternity" (< *okukō)

Other sound changes, though quite rare, occur in more than one word. The third example in the following list shows that such changes occasionally can affect native morphemes as well as Sino-Japanese morphemes:

反応　　 *hannō*, "response" (**han'ō*)
雪隠　　 *setchin*, "[Zen temple] toilet" (*setsuin)
生っ白い *namatchiroi*, "pale, wan" (*namasshiroi)

Sometimes there is an unexpected doubling (gemination) of *p, t, ts, ch, k, s,* or *sh:*

素気 *sokke, suge [nai]*, "curt, blunt" (*soki, *suke, or the like)
気風 *kippu*, "generosity" (*kippu no yoi yatsu*, "jolly good fellow"; *kifū*, "character, disposition," written with the same characters, is a different word)
初端 *shoppana*, "very first, beginning" (*happa, *shotan)

Sometimes a Sino-Japanese morpheme consisting of two short syllables drops the second syllable in a particular word:

読経　 *dokyō*, "chant sutras" (*dokkyō)

牡丹餅   *botamochi*, "rice dumpling with bean jam" (**botanmochi*)
音頭   *ondo [o toru]*, "lead the chorus" (**ondō*, **onto*)

A Sino-Japanese morpheme that begins with *b, d, g, j,* or *z* may show up with the corresponding voiceless sound in certain words like the following:

読本   *tokuhon*, "reader [textbook]" (**dokuhon*)
神道   *shintō*, "Shinto" (**jintō*)
時化   *shike*, "stormy weather" (**jike*)

Conversely, a Sino-Japanese morpheme that begins with *h, t, ts, ch, k, s,* or *sh* may show up with the corresponding voiced sound in certain words:

寸胴   *zundō [no]*, "tubular; sleeveless" (**sundō*)
上戸   *jōgo*, "a drinker" (**jōko*)
精進   *shōjin [ryōri]*, "vegetarian [fare]" (**shōshin*)

Native morphemes offer a few special problems of their own. Sometimes several different characters or strings of characters can stand for the same native word:

親子、父子、母娘   all *oyako*, "parent and child"
早い、速い   both *hayai*, "fast; early"
分かる、解る、判る   all *wakaru*, "be clear, be understood"

Names are notorious in this regard. For example: 和男、和夫、和雄、一男、一夫、一雄、一生、数雄、数夫 are all possible spellings of the man's personal name Kazuo, as is 一郎 (which can also be Ichirō) and several other strings.

In a few instances, one of the morphemes associated with a *kanji* is neither native Japanese nor Sino-Japanese. For example:

零   *zero*, "zero"
頁   *peiji*, "page"
弗   *doru*, "dollar"

Characters not used in China were occasionally invented in Japan and therefore lack a Sino-Japanese reading or else have a contrived one:

働く   *hataraku,* "work"; 労働 *rōdō,* "labor" (by analogy with 動 *dō*)
峠   *tōge,* "mountain pass"
匂い   *nioi,* "scent"

Such characters can be particularly puzzling to Chinese-speakers learning Japanese as a second language.

Finally, there are problems of homography. One character compound may be used for two distinct, independent words. For example:

物心   *monogokoro [ga tsuku],* "begin to take notice"; *busshin,* "matter and mind"
一見   *ikken,* "one look"; *ichigen [no kyaku],* "a chance/casual [customer]"
希有   *keu [na],* "rare"; *kiyū,* "[chemical] rare earth element"

Names such as 土井 (Doi or Tsuchii) offer many comparable examples of homography involving native words.

In other cases, the homographic words are embedded in longer compounds:

文書   *bunsho,* "documents"; 古文書 *komonjo,* "ancient documents" (saying *"kobunsho"* is a sure sign that one is not a true scholar of *komonjo!*)
眼鏡   *megane,* "spectacles, eyeglasses"; 天眼鏡 *tengankyō,* "magnifying glass"
人身   *jinshin,* "human body"; 人身御供 *hitomi-gokū,* "human sacrifice"

Cases of quasi-homography occur when putting two characters in reverse order results in a new word:

多数   *tasū,* "great number"; 数多 *amata,* "a lot, much"
食餌   *shokuji,* "diet"; 餌食 *ejiki,* "food; prey"
隙間   *sukima,* "crack, crevice"; 間隙 *kangeki,* "gap; opening; breach"

Even single characters may stand for more than one native word:

暇   *hima,* "leisure"; *itoma,* "leisure"
傍   *soba,* "side"; *hata,* "side"
被る *kōmuru,* "cover up"; 頬被り *hōkaburi/hokkamuri [suru],* "put in a
      kerchief on the head; ignore"

The point of this bestiary of troublesome *kanji* and their readings is
not to belittle Japanese writing for its quirks—how could anyone who has
had to learn the awful English spelling system be so cold-hearted!—but
rather to give a feeling for the hundreds of niggling little uncertainties
and hesitations the disciplined Japanese reader must learn to resist, overcome, or live with. No wonder the average Japanese finds the notion that
kanji are ideograms so congenial. When the goal is to finish reading or
writing something quickly, you learn to work around the thorns of doubt
and misunderstanding that prick you along the way. So long as you take
care to use the right characters when writing and avoid reading aloud too
often, literacy is your own private affair. Perhaps it is this incentive for
silence that gives rise to the notion that the Japanese approach to language
is uniquely visual.

5 How would a magician memorize Chinese characters?

Why don't more students of Japanese know about Harry Lorayne? His book *How to Develop a Super-Power Memory* (1957) brims over with sound advice on memorization that has stood the test of time. It's a minor classic among magicians, amateur and professional. To quote from the jacket of my first-edition copy:

Tie a string around your finger?
Carry a bulky memo pad?
Shove pieces of paper in your pocket?
Never again will you have to resort to makeshifts in order to remember an important fact.
Now, at last, with the LORAYNE "LINK-METHOD" OF MEMORY, you will be able to:

- *recall faces and names even years later*
- *memorize a speech or a script in minutes*
- *remember the lay or play of cards in bridge, gin, poker or pinochle or other card games*
- *memorize the Morse Code in 30 minutes*
- *remember the entire contents of a magazine*
- *have a photographic memory for a panel of numbers or objects*
- *In short, remember prices, details, codes, dates, calories, facts, routes, events, school work, lectures—anything of need or interest to you!*

Harry Lorayne, who has trained his own memory to the point where he is acclaimed as having *the most phenomenal memory in the world,* has written the most practical, lucid and definite memory-training book ever written, . . .

AN EXTRAORDINARY MAN

Now as most students of Japanese seem to know instinctively, the only thing better than being able to count cards undetectably at a blackjack table is being able to memorize all 1,945 *kanji* on the government's currently approved list before setting foot in Japan. To say that they are preoccupied with the memorization of *kanji* would hardly do justice to the burgeoning number of study guides, decks of flashcards, learners' dictionaries, workbooks, and, most recently, computer programs that cater to their seemingly insatiable demand for ever more potent means of making Chinese characters as instantly recognizable as the faces of their friends and relations. (I haven't read any claims of using hypnosis, but I wouldn't be surprised if I came across one someday.) Leaving aside the wisdom of approaching the task of learning how to read and write Japanese using these methods, you'd think that students would pay more attention to the mnemonic techniques explained by Mr. Lorayne, who regularly astounded audiences by memorizing the faces of dozens of total strangers—together with their names, phone numbers, occupations, addresses, and other particulars—and recalling them all, in any order desired, with breathtaking speed and flawless accuracy.

Harry Lorayne himself performed his feats as entertainment; he never pretended to be anything other than what we might call a mental strongman. Performers who specialize in what in the trade is called "mental" or "head" magic, playing the role of a mind reader, make use of the same techniques but less openly. By injecting a theatrical element of challenge and mystery into the proceedings, they make them more entertaining. Others who claim to be psychics (a name, like unicorns, for beings that don't exist) use the same mnemonic techniques to carry out premeditated deception for profit. But only a snob would turn up her nose at these ruses simply because of their popularity among actors and criminals. Although Lorayne does not describe them in sophisticated academic jargon, they are far from primitive; on the contrary, they represent the fruit of centuries of experimentation and practical experience. These tricks, simple once you know the secret, are good enough to fool even the shrewdest spectator when executed with appropriate misdirection and sangfroid. They are definitely worth examining in detail, for they have much to tell us about how—and how not—to tackle *kanji*.

THE THREE TECHNIQUES

Lorayne recommends three techniques for instant memorization, which he refers to as the "link system," the "peg system," and the method of "substitute words." I doubt Lorayne would claim them as his own inventions—magicians and charlatans have periodically reinvented and refined them for centuries—but they do work, and he has every right to be proud of his skill in using them.

Links

Linking refers to the imaginative association of a pair of tangible objects or meaningful words that have no apparent connection with one another. Suppose you need to link "carpet" with "paper." (Why you might want to do this will become clear later.) You imagine (literally try to see in your "mind's eye") a single visual scene in which "carpet" and "paper" are somehow associated. In Lorayne's words:

> The association must be as *ridiculous as possible*. For example, you might picture the carpet in your home made out of paper. See yourself walking on it, and actually hearing the paper crinkle under foot. You can picture yourself writing something on a carpet *instead* of paper. Either one of these is a ridiculous picture or association. A sheet of paper lying on a carpet would not make a good association. It is too logical! Your mental picture *must* be ridiculous or illogical. Take my word for the fact that if your association is a logical one, you will *not* remember it. [1957, p. 40; emphasis in the original]

To assure that familiar objects will be combined in utterly fantastic ways, Lorayne specifically recommends (1) imagining the items out of proportion, (2) picturing the items in violent action, (3) seeing exaggerated amounts or numbers of items, or (4) substituting one object for another (pp. 45–46). If you need to associate "car" with "hamburger," for example, you might think of your own car smashing into a gigantic hamburger (especially if you've been embarrassed by bumping your car into something and squirm every time you recall it). Or imagine yourself driving down the road behind the wheel of a giant hamburger. Or picture a busy street filled with hundreds of honking hamburgers instead of cars.

Pegs

Although links form the foundation of Lorayne's system, much of its real power comes from what he calls pegs. These are based on a simple enciphering procedure for numbers. In Lorayne's version (there are others), the ten digits are associated with consonant phonemes of English as shown in Table 3. You simply ignore vowels, the glides /y/ and /w/, and /h/. Only the *pronunciations* of words are considered, not their spellings.[1]

In accordance with these rules, every integer can be associated with a peg; Lorayne recommends the pegs shown in Table 4 for one- and two-digit numbers. You can choose whatever pegs are most congenial, but stick to one peg per number after settling on it. Pegs for three-digit and longer numbers are easily constructed as needed. For example, the twelve-digit string 633752741631 (the dates of the first Sundays in the twelve months of 1957, the year Lorayne published his book) can be remembered as "chum mug linger dishmat" (63 37 5274 1631) using the foregoing cipher.

Now suppose you have to remember an ordered list of twenty objects. By forging ridiculous links between the objects and the pegs for 1 through 20, you can, says Lorayne, easily recall an object given its number in the list or vice versa. What's more, the order in which you commit each item to memory doesn't matter. Linking objects to the peg words rather than directly to numbers is more reliable because numbers typically contain multiple morphemes whereas most pegs are monomorphemic. Numbers lack sufficient individuality to permit memorable associations with random words;[2] they are too much like one another. Short, semantically heterogeneous words are easier to keep separate and to link with other words.

Notice carefully that the regular phonetic cipher underlying the pegs facilitates their translation to and from numbers but does not participate in the linking process.[3] Linking, according to Lorayne, requires irregularity (lack of logic) and works only if you can easily visualize both items to be linked. Links and pegs are thus in a complementary relationship.

Table 3. Lorayne's Phonemic Cipher for the Decimal Digits

1. /t, d/	6. /ʃ/, /tʃ/, /ʒ/, /dʒ/
2. /n/	7. /k, g/
3. /m/	8. /f, v/
4. /r/	9. /p, b/
5. /l/	0. /s, z/

Note: /ʃ/ is the *sh* in "ship"; /tʃ/ is the *ch* in "chair"; /ʒ/ is the *s* in "measure"; /dʒ/ is the *j* in "journal."

Let's make this idea more definite—it will be important when we return to *kanji* later on.

Linking requires imagining two things in a familiar context, that is, a context you know a lot about and react to "automatically." The irrationality of the linkage arises precisely from the clash between the contrived relationship of the items you imagine and the normal relationships you expect in the imagined context. If either item is highly abstract or hard to visualize (equality, anger, sleep), a suitable context may not readily suggest itself or even exist. The peg system for the numbers shows how to cope with this sort of situation: first, treat each abstract item as part of a system (such as the numbers in order) rather than as an isolated entity; second, use ordinary words that refer to easily visualized things as tags for the elements of the system; third, associate tag words with elements of the system by means of a simple, compact set of rules, specifically a

Table 4. Harry's Personal Peg List

0. zoo	10. toes	20. nose	30. mice	40. rose
1. tie	11. tot	21. net	31. mat	41. rod
2. Noah	12. tin	22. nun	32. moon	42. rain
3. ma	13. tomb	23. name	33. mummy	43. ram
4. rye	14. tire	24. Nero	34. mower	44. rower
5. law	15. towel	25. nail	35. mule	45. roll
6. show	16. dish	26. notch	36. match	46. roach
7. cow	17. tack	27. neck	37. mug	47. rock
8. ivy	18. dove	28. knife	38. movie	48. roof
9. bee	19. tub	29. knob	39. mop	49. rope
50. lace	60. cheese	70. case	80. fez	90. bus
51. lot	61. sheet	71. cot	81. fit	91. bat
52. lion	62. chain	72. coin	82. phone	92. bone
53. loom	63. chum	73. comb	83. foam	93. bum
54. lure	64. cherry	74. car	84. fur	94. bear
55. lily	65. jail	75. coal	85. file	95. bell
56. leech	66. choo choo	76. cage	86. fish	96. beach
57. log	67. chalk	77. coke	87. fog	97. book
58. lava	68. chef	78. cave	88. fife	98. puff
59. lip	69. ship	79. cob	89. fob	99. pipe

phonetic cipher. In other words: Lorayne's links and pegs are mutually reinforcing methods of memorization that depend on different principles.
Linking is a visual strategy that depends on imagining *irrational* gestalts;
pegging is a linguistic (auditory) strategy that depends on constructing
rational rules for organizing speech forms in pairs. Each strategy is better
suited to situations in which the other is hard to apply.

Substitute words

This complementarity is found as well in Lorayne's third technique—
the method of substitute words—which he uses when he must remember information that has no intrinsic meaning for him. Lorayne explains
"meaning" in this context quite precisely by means of the well-known
example of the five lines of the musical staff marked with a treble clef:

> The letters, E, G, B, D, and F don't mean a thing. They are just letters,
> and difficult to remember. The sentence "Every Good Boy Does
> Fine" does have meaning, and is something you know and under-
> stand. The new thing, the thing you had to commit to memory, was
> associated with something you *already* knew. [1957, p. 16; emphasis
> in the original]

That is, meaning in this case just indicates that what you memorize is
linguistically well formed—for example, forms a grammatical sentence.
(After all, have you ever heard anyone say "every good boy does fine" except as a mnemonic?)

Now suppose the performer must associate faces with names. (One of
Harry's stunts involved greeting patrons as they entered a nightclub; during the act, he would ask people to stand up at random. He'd instantly
call out their names.) Names like Baker or Lincoln readily call up a visual
image, but many do not. Lorayne's description of how to deal with them
is clear even without the book's cartoon illustrations:

> No. 3 is Miss Standish. I would select her "bang" hairdo. You could
> "see" people *standing* on the bangs and scratching themselves vio-
> lently because they *itch.* Stand itch—Standish. Of course, a *dish*
> standing would serve the same purpose, but I like an association into
> which I can inject some sort of action. Now look at Miss Standish
> and *see* the picture you've decided on, in your mind's eye.
> No. 4 is Mr. Smolensky. Don't let the name scare you, it's easy

to find a substitute thought for it. I would see someone *skiing* on Mr. Smolensky's very broad nose, and taking pictures (while skiing) with a *small* camera (lens). Small lens ski—Smolensky. See how simple it is? I have chosen Mr. Smolensky's broad nose; you might think that the receding chin is more obvious. Choose whichever you think is most obvious, and *see* the picture of the skier taking pictures with a small lens. [1957, p. 144]

Notice how both the rational/phonetic and irrational/visual techniques play a role here. The "meaningless" proper noun (typically a single morpheme) is expanded via a phonetic cipher (punning) into a string of morphemes associated with visualizable things, which form a memorably absurd constellation linked to the features of the face in view. You gain mnemonic leverage, so to speak, by increasing the number of morphemes, just as you do when using pegs to remember numbers: you have more morphemes to remember, but they are easier to recall. You purposely describe a real sight to yourself as a ridiculous combination of things that aren't there, just as in linking. Instead of wasting effort on trying to fix something in your mind that has no prior "meaning" for you, you devote your energy to bringing into play loaded words you are likely to recall.

One application of substitute words that Lorayne recommends is memorizing foreign-language vocabulary items: find an English phrase that "sounds like" the foreign word and visually link the word's meaning to the (non)sense of the English phrase. A good example of this process would be so-called G.I. Japanese phrases like "a ring a toe" for *arigatō* (thank you) and "don't touch your mustache" for *dō itashimashite* (you're welcome)—accompanied in Lorayne's method by a heroic effort to imagine handing over a ringed toe as a gesture of gratitude or granting permission to leave the upper lip untouched as the epitome of modesty. Mnemonic techniques of this kind, of course, aren't good for anything but ad hoc memorization of isolated lexical items, the sort of thing frantic students do when they cram for a written vocabulary test in high school or college. True proficiency can never be acquired by imposing an alien phonology and irrelevant semantics (not to mention unwarranted cultural expectations) onto the structures of a language that must be used spontaneously and without self-consciousness. Substitute words may be great for doing an act in a nightclub, where the audience changes and the performer must deal with new information every evening, but they're far from ideal for other purposes.

APPLYING THE TECHNIQUES TO *KANJI*

This word of caution brings us back to the topic that prompted our long digression into Harry Lorayne's bag of tricks: the memorization of Chinese characters.

We have all seen books that attempt to teach *kanji* by rationalizing their shapes. They start with a picture that somehow illustrates the alleged core meaning of the *kanji* and then, by a process of gradual distortion and transformation, move from the picture to the visual shape of the *kanji* itself. Today computer programs use animation to enliven the metamorphosis. Apparently the underlying assumption behind all these materials is that the "meaningless," unfamiliar, and hard-to-distinguish shapes of the *kanji* befuddle the student. By seeing how an "inscrutable" shape like 馬 can be derived from a picture of a horse, for example, the student allegedly acquires a trusty mnemonic link. What do Lorayne's professional insights tell us about this?

To answer this question, we need to specify goals so that we can measure success or failure in memorization. Suppose the goal is to recall the "meanings" of a hundred *kanji* at sight as quickly as possible. (This is analogous to Harry's name-recall bit.) For the sake of argument, let's assume that the "meanings" are expressed as English tag words.[4] Each tag reflects the sense of the *kanji* when it is used to write, entirely or partially, a word of Japanese. The *kanji* 馬, for example, would get the tag "horse" when used to write *"uma"* 馬 (horse) or *"jōba"* 乗馬 (horseriding).[5] The graphic appearance of a *kanji* is to a person's face as its tag is to the person's name. So the student needs, according to Lorayne, to see in the image of the *kanji* a bizarre thing or event that somehow brings to mind the tag word. For example, I could imagine 馬 as the face of a man in profile, facing left, wincing in anguish, his right hand slapped over his brow and eyes (crossed lines at top depict fingers), screaming in despair at the top of his lungs (mouth wide open, four dots for teeth and tongue) in a *hoarse* voice. Hoarse—horse. No good seeing a horse itself in the *kanji*—too logical! If Lorayne is right, pictorial rationalization of *kanji* for the sake of memorization is wrong.

Interestingly, one of the most popular courses for memorizing *kanji*—the two-volume treatise of James Heisig (1977; 1987)—rejects the rationalization approach in favor of the very method that Lorayne recommends. To associate 滅 with the English gloss "destruction," for example, Heisig instructs the student to see 滅 as a graphic combination of 氵, 戌, and 火. Earlier in the book the student has been taught to link 氵 with "water," 戌 with "march," and 火 with "flame." So to link 滅 with "destruction," the student should envision "a *march* of *flames* demonstrating against the Fire Department, but being doused with *water* by the police riot squads" (1977, p. 128). This is Lorayne's irrational imagery in spades. Notice also that although 氵 and 火 are traditionally called the "water" and "fire" radicals, respectively, the character 戌 has nothing to do with "march." It is just the eleventh of the twelve zodiacal signs used in Chinese calendrical calculations—the Dog to be specific. The link between 戌 and "march" is Heisig's invention, the link he found most convenient given the occurrence of 戌 within more complex *kanji,* about which he needed to make up other mnemonic stories, and the most consistent given his links for graphically simpler shapes.

Here is a more advanced example. To forge a link between 墓 and "grave," Heisig tells the student to see 墓 as 莫 plus 土. Previously the student has been taught to link 莫 with "graveyard" by analyzing it graphically as a compound of ⁺⁺, 日, and 大, which are linked with "flower," "sun," and "St. Bernard," respectively. Thus:

> The element shown here [莫] should be taken to represent a modern **graveyard**. Gone are the cobwebs and gnarled trees, the tilted headstones and dark, moonless nights that used to scare the wits out of our childhood imaginations. Instead, we see brightly colored *flowers* placed before the tombstone, the *sun* shining gloriously overhead, and a cuddly great *St. Bernard* sitting at the gate keeping watch. [1977, p. 85]

Combining this derived link with the more primitive link of 土 with "soil" ("a mound of earth piled on the ground"; p. 61), Heisig treats 墓 as follows:

> The mound of *soil* with crude wooden crosses set at their head suggests those boot-hill graveyards we all know from cowboy lore. The only odd thing about this kanji is that the *soil* comes *under* the grave-

yard, rather than to its left, where we might expect [it]. Just think of the bodies as "lying under boot-hill" if you have any trouble. [1977, p. 86]

Once again, the similarity with Lorayne's linking technique is unmistakable. Note also that whereas ⁺⁺ and 日 are traditionally called the "grass" and "sun" (or "day") radicals, respectively, other parts of Heisig's account are less satisfactory. Most glaring is the fact that 莫 doesn't stand for any word of Japanese or Chinese meaning "graveyard"—that's just the English word Heisig found handiest for his purposes.[6] Likewise he links 大 with "St. Bernard" because it resembles 犬; more traditionally, 大 would be linked to "great" and 犬 to "dog," so linking both to "St. Bernard" does double duty but ignores East Asian traditions, languages, and cultures. The story for 土 is the traditional one, but Heisig says he uses it faute de mieux. As Lorayne would have said, it's too logical, not wild enough to be memorable.

Now let's consider a different goal: training students to link *kanji* with *Japanese* glosses. Consider, for instance, a Japanese dictation test. This is like Harry Lorayne running over to a member of the audience as soon as the person's name or phone number is called out: the Japanese word or word fragment represented by the *kanji* is the name; the *kanji* itself is the person's face. Now for persons fully literate in Japanese, the *kanji* and their readings have become so familiar that a character is often said to be (or to mean) a word it is used to write. Pointing to 書, for instance, one might say *"Kore wa kaku to iu ji desu"* (This is the character for "write") or *"Kono ji wa kaku desu"* (This character is [or means] "write") by way of identification. In reality, of course, it is the word *kaku,* not the character 書, that has the meaning "write" in Japanese. Meaning simply rubs off on the character by virtue of the role it plays in the orthography.[7] Nevertheless, almost everyone slips into the habit of talking sloppily about *kanji* as if they directly symbolized the sense of their readings. What connection could have greater logical power than that? So we have a paradox: the naive learner, following Lorayne's instructions, needs to forge an illogical link between a Japanese word and a character so that hearing the former will conjure up the image of the latter; yet improvement in reading occurs precisely as this linkage becomes less and less illogical. Indeed, the sign of total mastery is that the linkage is so "logical" that any other linkage becomes, literally, unthinkable.

One way out of this paradox is to resort to the "G.I. Japanese" mentioned earlier—that is, "hearing" Japanese words in terms of another, completely unrelated, language system. For the reasons stated earlier, this is a bad idea for anyone except those bent solely on passing puzzle-like quizzes and tests. A second solution would be to ask the student to dream up ridiculous linking thoughts in Japanese. This might work for native speakers, but it's inconceivable that a nonnative student who knew enough Japanese to play Lorayne's game in Japanese would need mnemonic devices to memorize *kanji* in the first place!

There is a third way out based on a judicious combination of links and pegs, and Heisig applies it in volume II of his course in teaching *kun* readings of *kanji* to students.[8] *Kun* readings originated as Japanese glosses, or rough translations, of the Chinese words for which the various *kanji* stood. As we've already seen, students are supposed to have linked 滅 with "destruction," 墓 with "a grave," and so on before launching into this part of their studies. They now memorize a list of *kanji* that can be read using exactly one syllable of Japanese. These are like Lorayne's pegs. Heisig suggests, for instance, using 歯 (teeth) for *ha,* (because *ha,* "tooth," is the traditional *kun* for 歯), using 蚊 (mosquito) for *ka* (because *ka* is the traditional *kun* for 蚊), and so on: 帆 (a sail) is *ho,* 呂 (backbone) is *ro.* This approach lacks the rationality of Lorayne's phonetic cipher. But since there are only about a hundred phonemically distinctive syllables in Japanese, and since the student must learn these links anyway, no harm is done making them the primitives from which other links are developed.

Now let's say you want to remember that 墓 stands for the Japanese word *"haka."* All you have to do is

> first picture a specific **grave** that you know. . . . Now exhume the contents of the **grave** in memory, turn back the lid on the coffin, and discover a smiling corpse, completely intact except for the fact that it has *mosquitoes* buzzing about in the hollow in its mouth where the *teeth* used to be. (Or, alternatively, you might picture the corpse of a giant *mosquito* smiling through its large, white *teeth.*) [Heisig 1987, p. 86]

The *kanji,* its *kun* reading, and an English equivalent for this *kun* reading are all linked because you have already learned the pegs 歯 (teeth) for *ha* and 蚊 (mosquito) for *ka.*

Here's an example that shows how to handle a *kanji* followed by one or more *kana* (Japanese syllabic letters). In 滅ぼす, we have a *kanji* followed by two *hiragana,* which phonographically represent *bo* and *su.* The whole combination stands for the verb *"horobosu"* (destroy [it]). Presumably the student knows the values of the elements in the *hiragana* and *katakana* syllabaries, so the problem boils down to remembering that 滅 in this word is to be read (pronounced) *"horo."* This is to be done by using the pegs 帆 (a sail) for *ho* and 呂 (backbone) for *ro:*

> Paint yourself a picture as vivid as the phantom ship in Coleridge's "Rhyme of the Ancient Mariner." See the ghosts and demons and goblins flying *kites* stretched with human skin and tailed with *backbones,* fluttering gently in the breeze—a portrait of **destruction.** [1987, p. 296]

The resemblance to Lorayne's technique is absolutely uncanny.

I once had a chance to talk with Heisig in person. I asked him whether he had ever been an amateur magician. He said no—reinforcing the observation that mnemonic techniques such as Lorayne's are periodically rediscovered. However it happened, Heisig chanced upon what the modern MBA would call the "best practices" of head-magic experts. But as a procedure for efficient learning, it obviously has little if anything to do with reading Japanese as Japanese. Heisig's method is a thoroughgoing technique for memorizing the equivalent of a dictionary, much as a magician might memorize the order of the cards in a stacked deck—a fine trick,[9] but not the secret to winning poker.[10] It can help students decode Japanese texts much as vocabulary coaching can help them pass standardized tests of verbal ability, but unless the students ultimately learn Japanese (the language itself), it can never rise above the level of mere decoding. (To his credit, Heisig freely acknowledges in his books that his mnemonics are merely temporary scaffoldings which fall away as the student learns more and more Japanese. Or as Harry might say, you have to be careful on Saturday night not to get confused by the links you made up on Friday night!)

The lesson to learn from Harry Lorayne and other mental magicians is that we can do seemingly miraculous things with short-term memory if we make systematic use of cleverly interlocking patterns of speech. Bizarre visualizations set up conjunctions we verbally describe using a regular phonetic cipher; there is little overlap in the useful domains of the two techniques, which must be artfully combined. This conclusion confirms the observations of generations of Japanese language teachers who have found that the students with the most thorough grasp of the spoken language are the ones who go on to become the most successful readers and writers. Beginning students seldom make use of the "logical" pictorial links between *kanji* and readings that so many guidebooks recommend. Instead they use their growing knowledge of Japanese speech, as limited as it may be, to forge idiosyncratic, illogical, and perhaps even embarrassing associations between *kanji* forms and various Japanese words or word fragments. Or as Harry might say: the secret to a mighty *kanji* memory does not reside in some grand, logical web of meanings.

6 Lord Chesterfield and the Mandarins

There was a time, not so long ago, when American comedy writers could expect audiences to know all about female secretaries who took dictation from their male bosses and typed their letters. Whether the gag was about an empty-headed Marilyn Monroe look-alike who couldn't take shorthand to save her life or a Plain Jane wearing glasses who made up for her looks with superhuman mental agility and a razor-sharp tongue, everyone in the audience could be counted on to relate to the situation. Nowadays, American television sitcoms like *Drew Carey* get laughs by doing the same shticks with an ironic reversal of gender roles. But on the long-running British series *Are You Being Served?* you can still see the old dictation sketches, filled with farcical double entendres, pretty much unchanged. Perhaps this is because it has taken longer for British businesses to go electronic—if Marshall McLuhan were still with us, he would probably make this a flat assertion. Before the electronic revolution, the conservative middle-American idea was that typing was women's work (newspaper reporters and professional writers excepted). If a guy typed, he did it "hunt and peck." Girls took home economics in high school to prepare themselves to become moms; they took shorthand and typing to get a respectable job while waiting for Mr. Wonderful.

Of course, this was already a false picture of the world even before personal computers came along. Plenty of men learned shorthand and touch typing. For anyone in the middle class, court reporting and similar skilled jobs were attractive: they paid well, they offered security, and there was no shortage of them in sight. Business, banking, industry, and government depended on skilled stenographers and typists. Before World War II, magazines were published for those in the profession, replete with tips from national stenography champions. According to *Dissertation Abstracts,* no fewer than seventy-seven doctoral dissertations and masters theses about Gregg shorthand, the dominant American system, were written between 1937 and 1986.

LONGHAND, SHORTHAND, AND CALLIGRAPHY

Shorthand was done in by a combination of technological advances. First came chord-keying dictation machines; while based on shorthand spelling techniques, they eliminated the need to work with a pen. The Dictaphone and other recording technologies of the 1960s diverted some of the demand for shorthand, but by no means did it in. The end followed IBM's introduction of the first commercial personal computer in 1980. Almost immediately it became not only acceptable for male bosses to learn to handle a keyboard but actually prestigious.[1] Today Gregg and other handwritten systems are joining the slide rule as relics of a bygone era. But for most of the twentieth century, government and industrial management without shorthand was simply inconceivable, and tens of thousands of Americans and Europeans (mostly women) studied Gregg assiduously.

We're talking about ordinary Americans who populated the world of Norman Rockwell and golden-age movies, not sophisticated, well-traveled yuppies and dinks of the 1990s. We are talking about a period when, in most places in the United States, pizza, let alone Chinese food, was considered foreign. Who would imagine that these steak-and-potatoes folks were experiencing the same kinds of psychological conditioning in their study of Gregg that most Japanese youngsters were going through in their efforts to become literate? Yet this is exactly what was happening.

This may sound overly dramatic, but a touch of drama is called for because a careful examination of Gregg shorthand exposes the fallacy of exoticism. As detailed in Chapters 1 through 4, Western writers have not hesitated to jump from the superficial difference in appearance between Chinese characters and the roman alphabet to baroque theories about prehistory, the mind, art, and cultural differences of every description. Leaving aside the many illogical steps and unsubstantiated claims to be found in such theories, a major reason why so many of them appear plausible is the widespread but baseless belief that there must be something utterly different about Chinese characters. Shorthand turns out to be a crushing counterexample that makes such a belief impossible.

To see how shorthand undercuts the fallacy of exoticism, we need to start with writing in longhand. When longhand was the *only* way to write final drafts, Western beliefs about handwriting were surprisingly similar to Chinese and Japanese beliefs about calligraphy and characters. As

Tamara Thornton (1996) explains, we have forgotten the great variety of "hands" that once coexisted in our own culture, each with its own occupational, class, and gender associations; the difficulty of preparing pens, ink, and paper for writing; the public tolerance of restricted literacy, in which not all who could read were expected or encouraged to write; the belief that a person's handwriting revealed his or her innermost character; the popularity of handwriting interpretation and its affinities with astrology, palmistry, and phrenology. Small wonder that Lord Chesterfield complained in the 1700s so bitterly of his son's graceless and illegible handwriting! (He wasn't much different from the typical Chinese literatus of his day.) In the 1800s, the fierce competition to find materials and new techniques for manufacturing pencils (Petroski 1989) testifies to their economic importance.

Technological changes that took hold about a century ago started driving a wedge between writing in the East and the West. When Commodore Perry "opened" Japan in the 1850s, Japanese methods of creating and handling commercial documents did not surprise their American counterparts greatly; after all, in America the principal means of organizing papers was the pigeonhole desk. Indeed the introduction of filing cabinets in the early twentieth century was a truly revolutionary innovation (Norman 1993, pp. 159–160). The Japanese have yet to take full advantage of such filing techniques (which now have computer analogues) because the procedure corresponding to alphabetization in the Japanese writing system is fraught with many special difficulties (Unger 1987, pp. 51–58). In the same way, the typewriter transformed the ways Americans did business; but Japan, which had no trouble assimilating the pencil, never made effective use of typewriter technology (Koestler 1961, pp. 180–181; Unger 1987). In America, the typewriter gave shorthand a new lease on life: dictation in the office became commonplace. In Japan, though Japanese shorthand (sokki) was developed in the Meiji period, it never spread far beyond the legislature and the courts because, without the typewriter, transcribing stenographic texts was a slow process.

Filing cabinets, typewriters, and shorthand can be found in Japan, of course, and the greatest changes in American attitudes toward handwriting have occurred, according to Thornton, in the decades since the end of World War II. Still, it is clear that the Japanese writing system has become more exotic in Western eyes primarily because of technological developments that have had different impacts in the West and East. We in the West are tantalized by theories that purport to have isolated some special principle underlying the use of Chinese characters because they offer an easy way to solve the riddle of why anybody who partakes in modern global technology should persist in using them.

As the foregoing analysis suggests, shorthand before the typewriter was a technology that East and West could share on a more or less equal footing. But it turns out that the similarities run much deeper than that. When we examine Gregg shorthand objectively from the perspective of linguistics, we see that it is structurally very similar to Chinese and Japanese writing. In fact, even the aesthetics and rhetoric associated with Gregg shorthand bear remarkable similarities to the aesthetics and rhetoric surrounding Chinese calligraphy.

A SAMPLE OF GREGG

Let us plunge right into an example of Gregg shorthand taken from a textbook published during its heyday, 1929. In the example shown in Figure 11, I've added an English transcription of the text above each line of writing. The dated content of the text may be amusing, but what's really noteworthy is how much linguistic information is conveyed by the sparse outlines (shapes) of which the text consists. This compression is achieved by means of several techniques—primarily writing the pronunciation of each word, rather than its English orthographic representation, and leaving out many sounds in high-frequency words and phrases. This compression is what makes it possible to write Gregg quickly enough to keep up with the normal flow of speech. Speed is also enhanced by limiting the number and kinds of shapes allowed, specifying precise rules for the order and direction of every pen stroke, allowing frequently occurring combinations to be run together, and not relying on graphic distinctions such as stroke thickness that are difficult to execute (a basic flaw of earlier shorthand systems such as Pitman).

Anyone who has studied *kanji* knows there are rules about how they are to be written. For the most part, you start writing a character from its top and/or left side. Horizontal strokes are made left to right, vertical strokes top to bottom; diagonal strokes that resemble/are written downward to the left. When horizontals and verticals cross, the horizontal is

Dear Sir, I have an opening immediately for a man with a thorough knowledge of French and Spanish, to go abroad with a committee representing the officials of this company. If present plans are completed the party will leave next week on the Île de France and remain overseas between six and eight months. The officials already have expressed the opinion that it will be necessary to employ a college man not over 35 of good family. It will be of especial value if he has some knowledge of finance ¶ You will readily agree that getting such a man is no easy task. I feel that since you know so many college men as well as your own fellow classmates you may be able to send one of them for this job that really has a future in it ¶ May I ask you to phone my office soon. Yours truly

Figure 11. Gregg letter transcribed.

usually drawn first. Boxlike enclosures are made with a vertical stroke on the left, a hook for the top and right side, then any material that goes inside, and finally the bottom horizontal. There are, however, many exceptions to these general rules. A complete description would take us far beyond the scope of the present discussion. And despite the best efforts of East Asian school systems to pound the rules into their charges, there is a certain amount of nonstandard practice. Ask a hundred Japanese to write the characters 左 (*hidari*, "left") and 右 (*migi*, "right") and you'll find that quite a few make the first two strokes of each (the part they seem to have in common) in the same order. Yet according to the official rule, the horizontal stroke is supposed to be written before the slanting curve in 左 and after it in 右. (Don't ask why!)

Figure 12 shows a page selected at random from a standard reference for English-speaking students studying *kanji,* with tiny numbers indicating the start of each stroke. This sample (O'Neill 1998, p. 164) also illustrates certain other features of *kanji* that will be important later on. In Chinese, most characters (though not all) stand for only one syllable. In Japanese, the corresponding ancient Chinese syllables were borrowed and changed to fit the phonology of Japanese. (Sometimes, because of borrowings at different times, a *kanji* will have two or three Sino-Japanese readings. It just so happens that the eight *kanji* in Figure 12 have only one apiece in the modern language.) Most Chinese characters are graphically composed of two components: a phonetic and a signific. For the purpose of categorizing characters in dictionaries, a certain number of significs (214 in the famous eighteenth-century dictionary of Emperor Kāngxī) were chosen as chapter headings; they were called radicals (that is, roots) by Western scholars for this reason. Nowadays, many people use the term "radical" loosely to refer to any identifiable graphic component of a *kanji,* but it is not true that every *kanji* is a pastiche of radicals selected from the set of 214. Nevertheless the overwhelming majority of characters, like the eight shown in the figure, can be analyzed into a signific (or radical) and a phonetic. The author has indicated this with the "R" and "P" designations following the Mandarin pronunciation (given in the old Wade-Giles system) of each character. (The asterisk after the P means that the phonetic element is a *kanji* all by itself; this is not always the case.)

Phonetic elements provide good heuristic clues to the sound of the syllable represented by the *kanji* in which they appear. John DeFrancis (1989)

沈	沈	1097; 85/4. CHIN, *shizu(meru/mu)* sink [SHEN², CH'EN² • R water & P*] 沈没 — *chinbotsu* — sinking 沈着 — *chinchaku* — calmness, composure
偉	偉	1098; 9/9. I, *era(i)* great, remarkable [WEI³ • R man & P*] 偉丈夫 — *ijōfu* — hero, great man 偉物 — *eramono/erabutsu* — great man
弾	弾	1099; 57/9. DAN, *tama* projectile; *hi(ku)* play (string instrument); *hazu(mu)* rebound, bounce [T'AN², TAN⁴ • R bow & P*] 弾丸列車 — *dangan ressha* — bullet/superexpress train 爆弾投下 — *bakudan tōka* — bomb-dropping, ⌐bombing
廃	廃 廢	1100; 53/9. HAI abandon, abolish; *suta(reru)*, *suta(ru)* die out, decline [FEI⁴ • R lean-to & P*] 廃置 — *haichi* — abolition & establishment 森林荒廃 — *shinrin kōhai* — forest devastation
蓄	蓄	1101; 140/10. CHIKU, *takuwa(eru)* store up, save [HSÜ⁴ • I: grass & store up 4–13 (cf. 1740); also R grass & P*] 蓄積する — *chikuseki suru* — accumulate 相互貯蓄銀行 — *sōgo chochiku ginkō* — mutual savings bank
普	普	1102; 12/10. FU universal [P'U³ • R sun & P*] 普及する — *fukyū suru* — (vt. & vi.) spread, diffuse 普通の — *futsū no* — usual, ordinary
簡	簡	1103; 118/12. KAN simple, concise [CHIEN³ • R bamboo & P*] 簡単な — *kantan na* — simple 簡潔な — *kanketsu na* — concise, brief
悟	悟	1104; 61/7. GO, *sato(ru/ri)* comprehend, become [WU⁴ • R heart & P*] ⌐enlightened 悟了 — *goryō* — enlightenment, perception 覚悟 — *kakugo* — resolve, readiness; perception

Figure 12. Page from O'Neill's *kanji* handbook.

has documented this amply for Mandarin; even in Japanese, the phonetics offer a moderately dependable guide to Sino-Japanese readings. For instance, as *kanji* in their own right, the phonetic (the right-hand part) of the third *kanji* from the top is read *"tan"*; the phonetic (bottom part) of the second *kanji* from the bottom is read *"kan"* (sometimes *gen*). *Kanji* may also be used to represent native Japanese words or, as here, parts of them. When so used, the remainder of the native word is supplied in *kana* (Japanese syllabic script). Of course, the phonetic components of *kanji* are unrelated to the pronunciations of the Japanese words associated with them, but the *kana* that accompany *kanji* that take native readings provide compensatory phonetic support.

But let's get back to the matter of writing *kanji*. It is easy to see, even from this small sample, that there are actually only a few basic strokes made by the brush or pen. The exact number depends on how you do the analysis. It is often said that the five strokes which make up the character 永 cover all the possibilities, but other approaches would yield a somewhat larger number.

The situation in Gregg is very similar. I have found that all the basic letter shapes in Gregg can be described in terms of five parameters: shape, length, angle, rotation, and tangency. I've improvised a cover term for the distinctive variations within each of these categories (Table 5). Using these terms, the basic letter shapes in Gregg can be described precisely, as shown in Table 6. Notice carefully the difference between the cover symbols I have chosen for Gregg letters and the English phonemes for which they stand. The cover symbols refer to the letters; the phonemes refer to sounds of English.

Just as with *kanji,* there are basic rules that govern how Gregg letters are penned. All steep strokes are written downward and right to left; all other strokes are written left to right. The right end of a right arc or left end of a left arc makes a tighter curve than the other end. These two rules are applied without exception. The basic idea is to transcribe spoken English as it sounds by combining the letters into outlines, which by analogy with *kanji* we can also call characters. But this is just the beginning.

To achieve writing speed, many adjustments in the basic principle are specified in Gregg shorthand. One technique is to let a letter stand for more than one phoneme or string of phonemes. Notice the range of values that the extra-long strokes, the circles, hooks, and loops take in Table 6.

We can call this "phoneme underspecification." Since the same phoneme may have different phonetic realizations depending on context, there can be a considerable gap between the Gregg spellings and what you actually hear. For example: the syllables /təd/, /dət/, and /dəd/ are all represented by the extra-long slant stroke; it is used to write the start of the words "today" and "detect" and the end of the word "hated." These are not only

Table 5. Basic Letter Shapes in Gregg

Parameter	Cover Term
Shape (general form)	
point	dot
line	stroke
curves	
open	
60° arc (approx.)	arc
180° arc (approx.)	hook
closed	
round	circle
oval	loop
Length (relative)	
½ unit	extra short
1 unit	short
1½ units	long
2 units	extra long
Angle (clockwise from vertical)	
15°–30°	steep
45°–60°	slant
85°–90°	flat
100°–105°	sinking
Rotation (motion of pen about center of curvature)	
clockwise	right
counterclockwise	left
Tangency (relation of two curves)	
internal	nested
external	kissing

Table 6 Gregg letter shapes

Cover Symbol	Description	Phoneme	Shape in Isolation
k	short flat right arc	k	
g	long flat right arc	g	
r	short flat left arc	r	
l	long flat left arc	l	
n	short flat stroke	n	
m	long flat stroke	m	
M	extra-long flat stroke	məm mən nəm nən	
t	short slant stroke	t	
d	long slant stroke	d	
D	extra-long slant stroke	tət təd dət dəd	
þ	extra-short slant arc	θ ð	⌐ or ⌐
p	short steep right arc	p	
b	long steep right arc	b	
f	short steep left arc	f	
v	long steep left arc	v	
c	short steep stroke	tš	
j	long steep stroke	dž	
J	extra-long steep stroke	tšətš tšədž džətš džədž	
s	extra-short steep arc	s z	(or)
ʃ	extra-short steep stroke	š	

Table 6 (*continued*)

Cover Symbol	Description	Phoneme	Shape in Isolation
h	dot	h	·
x	extra–short sinking arc	ks gz	
q	short sinking stroke	ŋ	
Q	long sinking stroke	ŋk	
TN	short slant right arc	tən dən	
TM	long slant right arc	təm dəm	
NT	short slant left arc	ənt ənd	
MT	long slant left arc	əmt əmd	
TV	= TN + f	dəf dəv tiv	
XT	= p + NT	džənt džənd pənt pənd	
a	large circle	ey æ a	
e	small circle	iy i e y	
o	small left hook	ɔ o ow	
u	small right hook	ə (stressed) u uw w	
A	large loop	ars arz ya	
E	small loop	ili# ərs ərz yi	
aw	⟨au⟩	aw	
yu	⟨eu⟩	yuw	
oy	⟨oe⟩	oy	

Table 6 (*continued*)

Cover Symbol	Description	Phoneme	Shape in Isolation
ay	large circle with nested hook	ay	⟳
L	circle with kissing small circle	li / V __	⟳
*	dot	diacritic	•
/	extra-short steep stroke	diacritic	/
–	extra-short short flat stroke	diacritic	—
\	extra-short sinking stroke	diacritic	＼
.	extra-short sinking stroke	period	＼
(	barred ⟨b⟩	left parenthesis	⨍
)	barred ⟨v⟩	right parenthesis	⨏
¶	small [⟩]	paragraph	⌐
?	small [x]	question mark	×
==	2 close parallel ⟨m⟩	dash	═══
=	2 close parallel ⟨n⟩	hyphen	══
,	comma	comma	⌐

different in ordinary orthography but are also different phonetically for many Americans: the first vowel is close to [u], the second to [i], and the third to [e]. The small left hook ⟨u⟩ (angled brackets indicate cover symbols) provides a second, important example; it can be the /ɔ/ in British "pot," /o/ as in "all," or /ow/ as in "boat." Since Gregg was born in Ireland, his speech retained the phoneme /ɔ/, which has become /a/ or /o/ in American English; nevertheless, Gregg's spellings have been retained in the system. There are diacritic marks that can be added to vowel letters, ⟨s⟩, and ⟨Þ⟩ to indicate exactly which phoneme they represent in a given word. But in the interests of speed, their use is strictly optional.

A second technique is to depart from actual pronunciation in certain situations. This might be called "string simplification." Sometimes this is done unconditionally. For example (using V for any vowel):

- Initial /kVn/, /kVm/, and /kVg/ are written ⟨k⟩. But if longhand orthography has *mm* or *nn,* or if a vowel, /r/, or /l/ follow, the combinations ⟨kn⟩ and ⟨km⟩ are written out.
- /sVs/ is written ⟨ss⟩.
- /h/ and unstressed /ə i u/ are omitted; /šən/ is further reduced to just ⟨ʃ⟩.
- Final /li/ is written ⟨e⟩; final /ili/ is written ⟨E⟩. Both these letters kiss an immediately preceding circle.
- /ks/ and /gz/ are written ⟨x⟩ if longhand orthography has *x.*

In other cases, the departures depend on context. For example: ⟨h⟩ immediately above a vowel represents /h/; but immediately after a character, it represents /iŋ/; and inside a large circle, it represents /i/ followed by ⟨a⟩. The many prefixes also belong to this class. When placed above a character, for example, ⟨A⟩ represents /agr(i)/, ⟨u⟩ represents /əndɽ/, ⟨o⟩ represents /owvɽ/; and so forth.

A third technique for improving speed involves "facultative change" in the writing of certain letters. For example: circles, which represent vowels, are generally drawn right (clockwise) except (1) before a left arc, (2) after a left arc if not followed by a right arc, and (3) before or after a stroke when /r/ follows the vowel. In these three cases, they are drawn left (counterclockwise). The loops left ⟨A⟩ and ⟨E⟩ replace the circles left ⟨a⟩ and ⟨e⟩ in the sequences /Vrs/ and /Vrz/. Arcs too are modified conditionally: ⟨s⟩ is drawn right except before and after left arcs (with or without an intervening vowel); after ⟨o⟩; after flat and slant strokes (with or without an intervening vowel); and immediately after right ⟨s⟩. In all these cases, it is drawn left. Similarly, ⟨Þ⟩ is drawn right except before and after ⟨o⟩, ⟨l⟩, and ⟨r⟩ (that is, left hooks and flat arcs). Finally, the orientation of the two hooks is conditioned: ⟨o⟩ is written like ⊂ before a flat stroke or arc unless preceded by a steep stroke or arc; otherwise, it is written like ∪. Similarly, ⟨u⟩ is written like ⊃ after a flat stroke (⟨n⟩ or ⟨m⟩) or between flat right and flat left arcs (that is, in ⟨kor⟩, ⟨gor⟩, ⟨kol⟩, or ⟨gol⟩); otherwise, it is oriented like ∩.

But beyond underspecifications, simplifications, and facultative changes, the big time-saver in Gregg shorthand is the heavy use of abbreviations or "brief forms" as they are called in the textbooks. In later versions of Gregg, the number and complexity of brief forms were reduced, but they remained a key component of the system—without them, taking dictation at a rapid clip would be nearly impossible. Table 7 presents a sampling of common brief forms from Gregg (1929) using the cover-symbol notation presented earlier. Here we see underspecification and simplification practiced on a truly massive scale. The differences that keep homonyms separate in ordinary orthography *(our ≠ hour)* are abandoned. More than one high-frequency word may be assigned to a single abbreviation (⟨c⟩ = *which* = *change*). There are numerous overlaps in the way that unrelated words are written: ⟨akr⟩ = *accord,* but ⟨akrs⟩ = *across;* ⟨kpe⟩ = *copy,* but ⟨kpt⟩ = *capital.* Note also that ⟨f⟩ = *for ≠ force, follow, fall* = ⟨fo⟩; ⟨ms⟩ = *must ≠ mistake* = ⟨mst⟩; and so on. These overlaps and arbitrary assignments create pitfalls for learners and make it hard to formulate rules that might alleviate rote memorization of entire characters.

Because brief forms are mixed together with fully spelled words in texts, you need an active inventory of several hundred of them at your fingertips to read, let alone write, Gregg fluently. Frequently they are combined into single-character phrases such as ⟨umaba⟩ = *you may be able;* from a learning perspective, these are virtually short forms themselves. There are also "intersections"—that is, characters formed by superimposing one letter on another for special classes of abbreviations, such as the names of states and cities. Students are encouraged to exploit the principles of abbreviation, phrasing, and intersection to make up their own customized set of brief forms (taking care not to override the standard set).

This heavy reliance on abbreviations makes the function of many Gregg characters highly logographic. You must learn to recall and recognize them as whole words even though every letter in a character is in theory a phonetic. Not surprisingly, handbooks of brief forms and phrases were written for aspiring students (for example, Gregg 1930). To get a feeling for the relative importance of brief forms compared with fully spelled words in context, study the version of our sample letter in

Table 7. Common Brief Forms from Gregg in Cover-Symbol Notation

a	I	bte	beauty	eve	every	k	can
A	agree	btn	between	eÞ	with, either	k‖t	quality
ab	about	c	which,	eÞt	without	ka	care
abv	above		change	f	for	kae	carry
adr	address	cel	children	fa	far, favor	kak	character
ag	ago	d	would	fay	find	katl	catalog
agn	again	D	did, date	fes	first	kay	kind
agns	against	De	duty	fge	forgive	ka∫	occasion
aj	agent	dl	deliver,	fgt	forgot	kete	committee
akr	accord		delivery	fk	effect	kf	confident,
akrs	across	do	dollar	flr	flour, floor		confidence
al	allow	dr	during, Dr.	fm	from, form	kle	clear
ans	answer	drf	draft	fml	formal	km	come
apr	appear	drk	direct	fo	follow, fall,	ko	call, quality
ar	where,	e	he		force	kol	collect
	aware	E	yes	fr	friend,	kp	compare,
ara	arrange	edu	educate,		friendly		keep
av	advantage		education	ft	future	kpe	copy
avt	advertise	eft	effort	fu	full	kpt	capital
aw	how, out	ek	week,	fÞ	further	kr	car,
ayl	while		weak	g	go, good		correct
ayr	wire	eme	immediate,	ga	gave	kre	credit
b	be, by, but		immedi-	ge	give, given	krs	course
bd	bed, bad		ately	gl	glad, girl	ks	cause,
be	believe,	en	when	gn	gone		because
	belief	enb	enable	gr	great	kt	country
bf	before	ent	went	gt	got	ku	quality
bg	big, beg	er	were	gv	govern,	kv	cover
bgan	began	erm	determine		govern-	k∫	question
bgen	begin	esl	excel,		ment	l	will, well
bk	become,		excellent,	h	a, an	la	like
	book		excellence	-*	-thing	lay	light
bl	bill, built	esp	expect,	hndl	handle	le	letter, let
bn	been,		especial	huND	hundred	let	little
	bound	espl	explain	hus	house,	lq	long
bo	body	espr	express		whose	ls	else, list
br	bring	est	yesterday	J	charge	lu	look
bs	business	ev	ever	jen	general	lv	love

Table 7. (*continued*)

m	am, more	nol	knowledge	pau	power	ret	return
ma	my	noÞ	another	pb	public,	rf	refer,
mar	mail	ns	instant,		publish		reference
mat	matter		instance	pep	people	rk	work
mayr	mile	nsp	newspaper,	pl	please	rkay	require
mc	much		inspect	pleʃ	pleasure	rkd	record
Me	money,	nstd	instead	pon	upon	rl	railway,
	many	ntu	into	pos	possible		rule
MeM	minimum	nuf	enough	poʃ	position	rm	remark,
M*	morning	num	number	pr	present,		room
mo	most	nv	never		presence	rp	represent
mpl	employ	nvs	invoice	prb	probable	rpr	report
mq	among	nʃ	insure,	prbl	problem	rs	recent
ms	must		insurance	prc	purchase	rse	receive
mst	mistake	o	of	prep	prepare	rsp	response,
mt	importance,	ob	object	prevs	previous		responsible
	important	obl	oblige	prf	perfect,	s	is, his
mu	move	od	order		proof	sat	satisfy,
n	in, not	og	organize,	prg	progress		satisfac-
na	name		organiza-	prp	purpose		tory
natr	nature		tion	prs	person	say	side
nay	night	ola	always	pt	part	sc	such
Nayr	entire	oM	woman	r	are, our,	sen	send
nb	unable	oms	almost		hour	sep	except
nd	and, end	on	one, won	ray	right, write	sers	serious
NDs	industry	ont	want	raÞ	rather	sev	several
NDv	individual	opn	opinion	re	real,	sj	subject
neon	anyone	opr	opportunity		regard	sk	ask
ness	necessary	ore	already	reg	regret,	skl	skill, school
nex	next	os	was		regular	sm	some
nf	influence	oso	also	rem	remit,	smo	small
nfm	inform	otu	altogether		remittance	sn	soon
n*	nothing	oy	point,	reM	remember	sopo	suppose
nk	enclose		appoint	rep	reply	sp	special,
nkay	inquire	oÞ	other	res	respect,		speak,
nkm	income	p	put		respectfully		speech
nkres	increase	part	particular	rese	receipt	spe	experience

Table 7. (*continued*)

spr	spirit	ʃ	ship, shall	TVn	definite	Þrut	throughout
ss	system, says	ʃd	should	Þ	the, there,	Þs	those
st	state	ʃu	sure		their	ud	word
stc	situation	t	it, at	Þa	that	ueÞ	whether
stj	strange	te	tell, till	Þaw	thousand	uq	young
sTN	stand	TMo	tomorrow	Þe	they	us	office
sto	stock	TNʃ	attention	Þe	thorough,	uu	world
stp	stop	trs	trust		thoroughly,	uun	wonder
str	strength,	tu	to, two,		three	uʃ	usual, wish
	strong		too	Þe	this	uʃl	official
suf	sufficient	tug	together	Þ*	think,	v	have
suj	suggest,	TV	different,		thing,	ve	very
	suggestion		difference		thank	vl	value
suk	success	TVk	difficult,	Þm	them	yu	use
			difficulty	Þn	then, than		

Figure 13. In this version I have marked the characters with cover symbols: not many come close to an actual transcription of pronunciation.

"WE'RE NOT IN KANSAS ANYMORE!"

Although Gregg's fundamental idea was to create a phonographic writing system, the system he perfected was heavily logographic. Even structurally, *kanji* and Gregg outlines have much in common. To facilitate a comparison, I've already introduced the idea of calling outlines characters. Now I want to introduce some additional concepts to clarify the many remarkable similarities between *kanji* and Gregg.

Let a *jot* be the visually smallest identifiable element of a writing system. Let a *letter* be a set of jots within which visible variations are not deemed distinctive. We'll call a group of jots flanked by spaces or punctuation marks (and thus identifiable as a unit of a text) a *graph*. (A single jot can be a graph, but many graphs will consist of two or more jots in a specific geometric relationship.) A set of graphs within which variations are nondistinctive will be a *character*. According to this definition, jots are *tokens* (of letters) and letters are *types* (of jots). Jots are found in

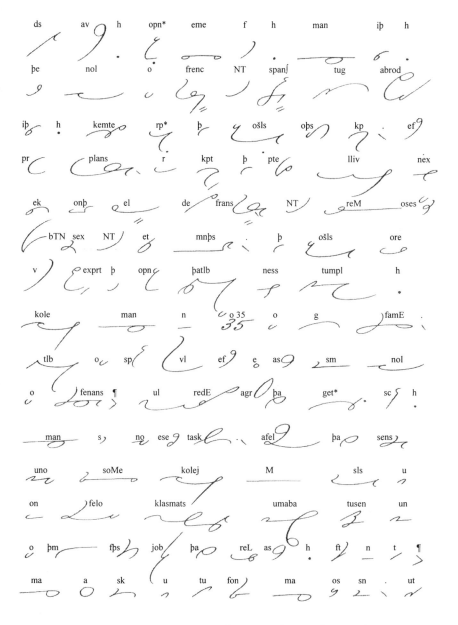

Figure 13. Gregg letter transliterated.

actual specimens of writing, whereas letters are ideal categories. Thus the letter *a* includes such variations as **A** *A* A *a* a and so on, each one a jot, in accord with the layman's sense of letter. (Thus jot and letter stand in the same relation to one another as phone and phoneme in classical linguistic analysis.) The term "letter" is not customarily applied to *kanji*, but under the definition given here, the components of a *kanji* that are identified by name in the study of calligraphy are letters. For example: there is no *kanji* consisting of a single vertical downstroke, but such a stroke is a letter in the system of *kanji*.

Given these definitions, we can now state, for both *kanji* and Gregg, the following generalizations:

- Each character consists of one or more letters.
- Simple letters can be combined to form more complex letters.
- The shapes of jots depend on what other elements are present in the letter and character.
- Letters are written in a fixed left-to-right or top-to-bottom order to form characters.
- The direction, angle, and length of pen strokes are fixed by rule.
- There is no exhaustive list of characters; new characters can be created on the model of preexisting characters.

The only one of these statements that might give pause is the last, which is perhaps more true of Chinese than of Japanese writing in modern times.

Turning from the graphic to the functional properties of characters in both systems, we can add the following facts that are equally true of Gregg outlines and *kanji:*

- Many characters in actual texts correspond to whole words.[2]
- Many characters can be read in more than one way depending on context.
- The phonetic letters in characters do not always provide sufficient information to determine their reading in context uniquely.[3]
- There is no standard collating sequence for characters.
- Characters do not have standard names apart from what they stand for in actual language.

The first three of these points are all related and easily verified by comparing the sample page from the *kanji* instruction book (Figure 12) with the list of Gregg short forms (Table 7). The last two points are worth adding because they have an impact on how people can handle *kanji* in computer environments; if there were a demand for retrieving Gregg outlines in electronic media, the same kind of problem would arise.

The cultures of learning that have grown up around Gregg and *kanji* also show profound similarities. From the standpoint of the learner of either system:

- The inventory of characters is unbounded.
- There are general rules for proper stroke shape, order, and direction, but there is no simple way to specify all possible characters by rule.
- The learner must memorize several hundred high-frequency characters in order to do any practical work.
- Daily copy practice is needed to retain active use of letters.
- The study of well-written texts is a recommended part of the learning process.

It should be added that being a native speaker of English confers an enormous advantage on a learner of Gregg. Likewise, non-Japanese students of Japanese are seldom able to pick up a pen and produce grammatically correct extemporaneous compositions in the traditional script even if their oral/aural skills and reading ability are fairly advanced. Finally, it is worth noting that the development of individual style is encouraged within limits in the writing of both Gregg and *kanji*. In both systems, there are definite aesthetic criteria for ranking samples of writing.

Of course, there are differences between the two systems that must not be ignored:

- Learners of Gregg are already proficient in standard English orthography before beginning. Learners of *kanji* have only *kana* to fall back on—and know that the use of *kana* as an expedient is not acceptable in most social situations.
- In Gregg, every letter in a character is a phonetic; every character

contains at least one phonetic. Some *kanji* lack phonetics, and none has more than one; the phonetic of a *kanji* can be mnemonic in one context but nonmnemonic in another.

· In Gregg, no letter carries extraneous phonemic information, but not all phonemes are represented in every character. In *kanji,* phonetics correspond to Sino-Japanese readings (syllables in Chinese); if a phonetic does not exactly match the syllable represented by a character, some extraneous phonemic information is therefore present.

· Gregg characters sometimes represent phrases of two or more words, whereas two or more *kanji* are needed to write many single words.

· A Gregg stenographer is the person most likely to read his or her own Gregg writing. Users of *kanji,* by contrast, generally produce a greater proportion of writing for other readers.

These differences are not trivial but do more to highlight the similarities between Gregg and *kanji* than to obscure them. Indeed, if we compare pedagogical and descriptive materials, the resemblance between Gregg and *kanji* is positively uncanny. One trick of the trade for professional court reporters in the 1920s and 1930s was to use violet ink to enhance legibility. Perhaps this choice does not rank aesthetically with the cult of inkstones and brushes in Japan, but it does show that a good deal of experimentation and effort went into details that seem to the novice quite minor—and that a guildlike consciousness informed the profession of stenography.

The following text shows how even the rhetoric used to describe the mastery of Gregg and *kanji* coincides. On the left is a verbatim reproduction of an introduction to a standard shorthand textbook; on the right are passages that convey the same message, mutatis mutandis, from a well-known book on Chinese calligraphy. An agreement or two between these texts might be ascribed to chance. But in fact, virtually every admonition and word of encouragement from John Robert Gregg himself finds a counterpart in the lore of calligraphy.

A Talk with the Beginner

Success in any study depends largely upon the *interest* taken in that particular subject by the student. This being the case, we earnestly hope that you will realize at the very outset that shorthand can be made an intensely fascinating study.

This book is not written for the benefit of those already knowledgeable on the subject, nor is it meant for any Chinese public. I shall be satisfied if it leads some people to appreciate one more form of our art, and helps them to understand more deeply the painting and other forms of our art which they already love. [p. 2]

Cultivate a love for it.

Once you can analyse the structure, and at the same time appreciate the beauty of the lines, you will have come to a real love of Chinese calligraphy for its own sake. [p. 16]

Think of it as the highest form of writing, which is itself the greatest invention of man. Be proud that you can record the language in graceful lines and curves. Aim constantly to acquire artistic skill in executing those lines and curves.

Written words can be formed to liberate visual beauties; and this is possible with Chinese characters in a greater degree, it is safe to say, than with the script of any other language, because *art,* not science or religion, was the prime end of those responsible for their development. [p. 14]

You *can,* if you *will,* make the study of shorthand a perfect joy instead of a task.

The more you study the appearance of Chinese characters, the more you will enjoy writing them. [p. 16]

Skill in the use of shorthand is a possession that has been coveted by the wisest of men and women, for it is not only a practical instrument in commercial

In former times the ability to write well was the passport to a successful official career, a good handwriting being one of the highest desiderata in the Civil work, but a much-prized and valuable accomplishment and a means of mental culture.

Be thorough. Skill in anything is attained by repetition with interest; therefore, do not shirk the careful, painstaking practice on the elementary forms given in the Manual. Write each outline many times, and aim always at the attainment of fluency and exactness in execution.

Your future success depends to a very large extent on the way you do your work now. In order that your progress may be sure and rapid, master each lesson before you proceed with the next.

In your practice, write as rapidly as you can while keeping the hand under complete control;

aim at accuracy rather than speed, but do not *draw* the char-

Service examinations. . . . Even at the present time a good hand is a social asset. . . . [W]e tend to judge a person's character from his handwriting. [pp. 12–13]

The tutor gives his pupils specimens of good calligraphy — usually written by himself — and tells them to cover them with thin paper through which the positions and constructions of the character are partly visible. . . . [They] trace the specimen characters over and over again. [p. 190]

In practising writing, we always start with K'ai-Shu, not merely because its characters are more "orthodox" than those of Hsing-Shu and Ts'ao-Shu, nor wholly because it provides such fine training in the making of beautiful patterns, but primarily because it opens the door, as it were, to those later styles. [p. 191]

When a pupil has practised for some time, the tutor places on his elbow-joint a flat weight . . . to be balanced while the writing is executed. This exercise has the effect of strengthening the muscles of the arm and intensifying the writer's control over the brush. [p. 191]

We demand that even a beginner should *write*, not fill in the

acters. You must understand at the outset that shorthand must be *written;* but you must also impress upon your mind that whatever you write you must read, hence the necessity for good penmanship.

As skill in executing the movements is obtained, the speed may be increased until the forms can be written accurately at a high rate of speed.

Some attention should be given to acquiring a capacity for writing *individual* outlines rapidly without hesitation, and with a free movement of the hand.

Aim to acquire a smooth style of writing, execute each character with an easy, *continuous* motion of the pen, and pass directly to the next without unnecessary movements. A halting, jerky movement is fatal to speed, and may be almost always traced to indecision, caused by unfamiliarity with the forms. At first carefully analyze them in detail, but after you have determined the correct outline, practice it and think of it as a *whole.*

coloured outlines as if he were *drawing.* [p. 190]

[T]he freer and more rapid movements employed for the more widely used *Hsing-Shu* and *Ts'ao-Shu* result in formlessness unless the writer constantly practises the structural shapes of *K'ai-Shu.* [p. 192]

The need for increased speed of execution brought about the establishment of *Hsing-Shu* and *Ts'ao-Shu,* both of which grew round the basic structural shapes of *K'ai-Shu.* [p. 192]

Choose some printed character and try to write it as pleasingly as you can: then compare it with the same character as written by some acknowledged master of calligraphy. [pp. 187–188]

[T]he tutor contents himself with explaining the position of the various strokes in the characters and making the pupils execute them in the right order. He does, however, insist that each stroke be made in a single movement, with the brush travelling the length of it in the right direction. It is utterly contrary to the nature of Chinese calligraphy—as it is of Chinese painting—to correct or retouch a single dot. [pp. 189–190]

Facility in the practical use of shorthand depends largely upon the stock of outlines you have at your ready command. Note the use of the word "ready." This means that you should master all the forms given in the Manual by writing them many times. This will not only impress the forms on your mind, so that you will not have any hesitation in recalling them, but will give you facility in writing them.

In shorthand, it is not sufficient to *know* how to write a word—you must not only know the form but be able to write it quickly. Hence the necessity for much *repetition practice* in writing the forms.

Most of this repetition practice should be on the forms as they occur naturally in connected matter. The repetition of isolated forms for more than five times consecutively is not in accord with modern pedagogy. Scientifically graded connected matter has supplanted the isolated form.

If, in addition to the words given in the Manual, you can add to your stock of outlines other words written under the same principles, you will have gained a great deal—will have

Never try to write until you have calmed yourself completely. Any sort of rush before writing is fatal. You would not expect to be able to play the piano well immediately after running half a mile in the park! First concentrate on the characters to be written and work out patterns for them. This will indicate a state of tranquility in your mind and enable you to execute them as you wish. [p. 201]

To achieve a perfect copy would require a lifetime's practice. In time, of course, writers are able to evolve and establish new styles of their own, but their power to do so always depends upon good early training and unremitting practice. [p. 193]

We distinguish three stages in the development of an apprentice calligrapher. At the first stage the writer finds that he can, perhaps after several attempts, make a copy of a character which seems to him to be nearly as good as the original. . . . Further practice brings him to the second stage, when he realizes the relative poorness of his work. . . . Suddenly the writer achieves a result which is really as good as the example. The wearisomeness of the endless practice falls away and he laid a broader foundation for advanced work, which will lessen the time required to attain efficiency.

Devote Much Time to Reading Well-Written Shorthand. By reading a great deal of well-written shorthand you will become not only a fluent reader, but you will enlarge your writing vocabulary.

Unconsciously you will imitate in your own work the easy execution of the forms shown in the printed plates. All expert writers have devoted much time to reading shorthand.

In addition to the work outlined in this Manual, we strongly recommend the use of the supplementary dictation material given in "Gregg Speed Studies."

[Gregg 1929, pp. xii–xiv]

realizes that his success is due to this, having at last understood the original so acutely as to be able to reproduce it. That is the third stage. [p. 196]

Writers who have passed the third stage of development seek to examine as many existing masterpieces of calligraphy as possible. [pp. 197–198]

The well-known calligrapher K'ang Yu-wei . . . once remarked, "To learn calligraphy one must start by imitating the old writers. Those who cannot acquire the good qualities of old writings cannot put their talent into their own." [pp. 199–200]

As this book is intended for those who know little or nothing of Chinese calligraphy, I do not feel there is any object in my going into the finer points of training and technique. The subject is inexhaustible. [p. 202]

[Yee 1973]

In short, generations of American stenographers have found themselves in the same kind of psychological situation as Japanese and Chinese schoolchildren. It's all very well to point out the differences between *kanji* and Gregg. But to argue that there is something culturally or linguistically unique about the use of *kanji* is clearly excessive.

Handwritten Gregg is fast disappearing. Academic interest in Gregg, measured in dissertations and theses about it, almost vanished after the advent of the affordable personal computer. Yet the basic ideas under-lying Gregg—phonographic transcription, heavy use of abbreviations, and the like—are alive and well; they have simply moved to machine-based stenography systems. In the meantime, more and more Japanese are forsaking pen and paper and doing their writing on Japanese word-processors, mostly using romanized input. The same phenomenon is tak-ing place in China. Surely the time has come to give up culturally exclu-sivist views of *kanji* (or *hanzi*) and their alleged effects on the minds of Japanese and Chinese.

After all, Kansas might as well be Kansai or Kansu for stenographers.

7 Where do hunches come from?

We must remember that the probability of an event is not a quality of the event itself, but a mere name for the degree of ground which we, or someone else, have for expecting it.
—John Stuart Mill,
Logic III.18

What is important for the speaker about a linguistic form is not that it is a stable and always self-equivalent signal, but that it is an always changeable and adaptable sign.
—V. N. Vološinov
(1973, pp. 67–68)

As explained in earlier chapters, the Ideographic Myth as it concerns Chinese characters can be traced back to Enlightenment philosophers like Descartes and Leibniz. Its deepest roots, however, go back to ancient Greece. It was Plato's belief that abstract universal entities exist outside time and space. In fact, he concluded that the only things which really or fully exist are the ideas or forms that populate the timeless universe of essences. Plato reached this view because he was preoccupied with certainty and impressed by the seeming certainty of mathematical as opposed to other kinds of knowledge. If you believe that reality consists solely of abstract essences, you have only to take a short step to imagine an encyclopedic collection of discrete ideograms that label each and every essence in that universe.

A major weakness (by no means the only one) with this Platonic view is that we come to know and talk about the alleged world of essences only through our use of language—and language is sui generis. There is nothing else like it in a person's experience or in our repertoire of behavior; nor is there any evidence of such highly evolved symbolic behavior elsewhere in the animal kingdom. We can barely bring meaning to conscious awareness in ourselves—let alone communicate it to others—until we talk about it. Any sense of certainty we have about abstract ideas is therefore just an illusion: in the end, whether mathematics or gossip, everything we know is filtered through language. Without it, we are prisoners in solitary confinement.

BEYOND THE PRIMACY OF SPEECH

But perhaps there are some kinds of writing that are meaningful at least some of the time yet do not refer to speech behavior. Surely, goes this compromise argument for Platonism, if while driving down a multilane highway I approach an intersection with a traffic light and a sign over my lane with an arrow pointing vertically upward, I don't have to give it an English translation (at least not consciously) to know that I'd better not try to turn right or left. And I'd probably understand the sign, in a purely pragmatic sense, even if I didn't know English. Likewise, to use Plato's favored example of mathematics, surely numbers actually exist in the universe apart from how we talk about them. Every arabic numeral (say, 7) has a meaning that transcends the words used to express the number in various languages. And if there is a class of written objects, including road signs, arabic numerals, and the like, that convey meaning without reference to the words of any particular language, then, in principle, there is no reason why other written objects might not, at least on some occasions, work the same way.

This watered-down Platonic argument still runs into problems when we consider the crucial role that speech and writing play in making us aware of the thoughts of ourselves and others. True, linguistic behavior is subsumed in a larger category of *semiotic* behavior: we constantly make use of learned signs and behaviors (broken branches along a forest trail, finger pointing, and such) to signal one another openly or surreptitiously—many of these, though culturally bounded, are clearly not part of language in the way that words or grammatical structures are. But they do not form a coherent system like language with its "infinitely adjustable" forms that we tailor to every new situation. Road signs and such may be nonlinguistic writing (provided we can come up with a good definition of writing dependent entirely on the physical properties of instances of writing). But they certainly aren't viable alternatives to either speech or writing as they are normally used. No collection of nonlinguistic signs is large enough to cover the range of what language covers, yet small enough to be internalized and used the way we use language.

As for numerals, the evidence is more equivocal than the compromise Platonic argument lets on. Consider, for example, the normal spoken expression for a number like 83,121 in several languages with different morphologies for number words (Table 8). It's all very well to point out that such expressions correspond to the same arithmetic value. But if words reveal anything about what goes on in the mind, the concept corresponding to 83,121 in each language is quite distinct. Furthermore, in the logic of French, *cent* (100) is countable (*deux cents*, "200"), but *mille* (1,000) is not (*deux mille*, "2,000"). In English, you need "one" between "thousand" and "hundred" when saying 83,121 (so too in German), but not in French, Hungarian, or Japanese. Whereas an American mathematician would say "two over three," her Chinese counterpart would use an expression paraphrasable as "three parts' two." In Japanese, *nijū* means "20" but "20 days" or "the twentieth of the month" is always *hatsuka*, never **nijū-nichi*, the regular form that almost all foreign students mistakenly produce the first few times around. In Hungarian, the idiomatic way to tell time involves figuring minutes before and after quarter hours, and expressions like *fél nyolckor*, morphologically "half eight time," is 7:30 (half an hour into the eighth hour), not 8:30 (half past eight). In Russian, case agreement between nouns and numerals is so complicated that describing it in detail here would be excessive.

Nevertheless, there's no point in quibbling. Some things that look like

Table 8. Spoken Expressions of the Number 83,121

English:	eighty-three thousand one-hundred [and] twenty-one $\{[(8 \times 10) + 3] \times 1{,}000\} + (1 \times 100) + [(2 \times 10) + 1]$
French:	quatre-vingt trois mille cent vingt-et-un $\{[(4 \times 20) + 3] \times 1{,}000\} + 100 + (20 + 1)$
German:	dreiundachtzigtausendeinhunderteinundzwanzig $\{[3 + (8 \times 10)] \times 1{,}000\} + (1 \times 100) + [1 + (2 \times 10)]$
Hungarian:	nyolcvanháromezerszázhuszonegy $[(80 + 3) \times 1{,}000] + 100 + (20 + 1)$
Japanese:	hachiman-sanzen-hyaku-nijū-ichi $(8 \times 10{,}000) + (3 \times 1{,}000) + 100 + (2 \times 10) + 1$

writing, albeit not ordinary writing, do seem to function outside the realm of language proper. But how exactly does this happen? Does the answer to this question require us to postulate a Platonic universe full of fixed atoms of timeless, unchanging meaning? If there were such a world, then of course it would be easy enough to imagine *Homo sapiens* ambling along at some point in natural history and affixing spoken names or written labels to each meaning. But is this the only view under which extreme, nonlinguistic kinds of writing can be explained? Suppose that, contrary to the classical ideographic view, no sign—spoken, written, or otherwise—ever exists until it is created, processed, or interpreted by someone in a communicative context. In this case all signs, including Chinese characters, and their alleged meanings are essentially private. We communicate by means of signs—but not because there is a universe of semantic invariants to which they refer. We simply engage in communicative behavior under the sort of conditions that contextualize *all* human activity. These conditions—our physiological similarities, the cultures and languages we share, and the circumstances of time and place in which our semiotic behavior occurs—constrain our behavior sufficiently to create the illusion that we are passing signs among ourselves that embody autonomous meanings. In the end, all we know is that our use of signs does or does not result in the outcomes we want. The signs themselves are just by-products of a complex game involving our senses, dexterity, collective memory, individual thoughts, and interactions with others. We can copy, remember, play with, or talk about the signs. But without human beings around to engage them (as depicted in some existentialist movies), they are just husks empty of meaning.

This is the opposite of thinking of meanings as countable, discrete, public entities that are distinct from the signs that represent them. In this view, meanings are like the values stamped on coins. Ideograms are supposed to have specific, inherent meanings unrelated to how you might express them in a particular language or on a particular occasion. Therefore, let us start by asking: what exactly is a meaning a property of? Is it a property of a class of things, to each of which we give the same name or description? A property of a single member of some such class? Or a property of the mind of the person who does the naming or describing? Each of these three alternatives finds a counterpart in applied mathematics, where the nature of probability is a central issue analogous to our problem of meaning. If we understand how to answer the question for probabilities, perhaps we can answer the question about meanings.

THREE NOTIONS OF PROBABILITY

The classical (or *frequentist*) view is that probabilities are properties of classes. University of Chicago professor Gerd Gigerenzer (1994) illustrates this view with an example from the famous mathematician Richard von Mises (1957). Take the reference class "all men insured before reaching the age of forty after a complete medical examination." Suppose that

> the number of deaths at age 40 was 940 out of 85,020, which corresponds to a relative frequency of about 0.011. *This probability is attached to a class,* but not to a particular person or a single event. Every particular person is always a member of many different classes, whose relative frequencies of death may have different values. Therefore, von Mises concluded, "It is utter nonsense to say, for instance, that Mr. X, now aged forty, has the probability 0.011 of dying in the course of the next year." [Gigerenzer 1994, p. 132; emphasis added]

In other words: you may associate a ratio of integers, like 940 over 85,020, with some arbitrary class of individuals, but this rational number does not quantify the fate of one of those individuals. This is logically impeccable yet somehow unsatisfying. After all, suppose we agree to gamble by cutting once into a shuffled pack of fifty-two cards: if I bet you even money that the card I cut to will be a spade, you'll gladly take me up since you know that, three times out of four, it won't be a spade. Yet we do not intend to play this game more than once.

This intuition, that every single event has a probability p between 0 and 1, lies at the heart of the late-twentieth-century *cognitivist* notion of probability. Bayes' Rule (Figure 14) tells you how to revise your estimate

$$p(E|N) = p(E) \frac{p(N|E)}{p(E)\,p(N|E) + p(-E)\,p(N|-E)}$$

Figure 14. Bayes' Rule.

of p as you learn new information about its associated event. This formula looks formidable but it's easy to program on computers. (It will be explained in greater detail presently.) If you believe, as many cognitivists do, that it is simply a matter of time before computers outperform human brains, then you naturally assume that this is the formula that ought to be instantiated in human brains. Hence when human judgments deviate from this formula, the problem is a defect in brain structure. As Gigerenzer explains, cognitivists have not succeeded in proving this, but it is instructive to see why they think they have.

See if you can fill in the blank in the following problem:

> If a test to detect a disease whose prevalence is 1/1,000 has a false positive rate of 5 percent, what is the chance that a person found to have a positive result actually has the disease, assuming you know nothing about the person's symptoms or signs?

$$0 < \underline{\hspace{2cm}} < 1$$

Disease X is rare, but the test for it is 95 percent accurate. Gigerenzer reports that nearly half the staff and students at the Harvard Medical School filled in the blank with a large probability. But look again at the same problem expressed in different words:

> One out of 1,000 Americans has disease X. A test has been developed to detect when a person has disease X. Every time the test is given to a person who has the disease, the test comes out positive. But sometimes the test also comes out positive when it is given to a person who is completely healthy. In fact, out of every 1,000 people, 50 of them who are perfectly healthy test positive for the disease. How many people who test positive for the disease will actually have the disease?

$$\underline{\hspace{2cm}} \text{ out of } \underline{\hspace{2cm}}$$

How would you fill in the blanks this time? Here's a hint: imagine 1,000 pennies laid out on a table in a neat rectangular array. There are 100 rows, each containing 10 pennies — your 1,000 Americans. Sweep aside 5 rows of pennies — you just put the 50 people who tested positive but are healthy in a heap by themselves. Now pick up a penny at random from any of the remaining 95 rows — the person with disease X — and put it next to the pile of 50. How many people who test positive for disease X actually have it? Easy: 1 out of 51, or about 2 percent. But according to Gigerenzer, only eleven participants in the Harvard experiment came up with that answer (Gigerenzer 1994, pp. 147–149). The reason is clear. The second statement of the problem mentions only *whole numbers* and asks for a frequency *(x out of y);* the first version talks about rates of occurrence and asks for the probability of a single event.

Of course, if you are very careful, you can still get the right answer even if you stick with the cognitivist single-event interpretation of probability. Bayes' Rule says that to obtain the probability of event E given new information N (that is, $p(E|N)$ in Figure 14), you multiply what you thought the probability of E was before knowing N, namely $p(E)$, by the *likelihood* of N, which is defined as the fraction on the right. Classic statisticians accept this formula provided that $p(E)$—called the prior probability or just "prior" for short—can be specified as a frequency, as it can in this problem. But in general $p(E)$ need not be a frequency; it might just express the degree of uncertainty you have about the outcome of event E. For instance, recall the card-cutting example: you know that my chance of cutting to a spade is ¼ because you know that an ordinary deck consists of equal numbers of spades, hearts, diamonds, and clubs. You don't have to divide 52 by 4 because the number of cards in each suit is irrelevant; all that matters is that all four numbers are the same. We will return to this point presently.

On the cognitivist account, if you got the right answer to the disease X problem, then, consciously or unconsciously, your brain performed the computation shown in Figure 15. Conversely, if like most of the subjects in the Harvard experiment you did not get the right answer, this is proof there's something fundamentally wrong with human brains. This strange cognitivist Scylla is even more repugnant than the frequentist Charybdis who says you really shouldn't think there is a definite chance of the card I cut to being a spade on any particular occasion. Fortunately, we can steer a course between this rock and a hard place. The key is to find what the two positions have in common.

The frequentist is surely right that our awareness of probability begins with frequencies—that is, in the counting and comparison of different kinds of events. The counting and comparison of events, however, presupposes categorization—that is, the recognition of certain events and outcomes as "the same" for the purpose of counting despite their discernible differences (Ellis 1993). Categories are not God-given or Platonic ideals fixed in the cosmos for all time. Each of us determines what does and does not belong to a category and, moreover, which categories are relevant to a given situation. Of course, we don't do this with complete freedom. We are constrained by the physics and chemistry of our bodies, by the world around us, and by the languages and social structures that enable us to think symbolically. Nevertheless, we do have some freedom of action. (Our lives are not completely predictable from initial conditions.) So the subjective experience of uncertainty is not a mere epiphenomenon, as the orthodox frequentist would claim.

But the constraints within which we categorize are not exclusively innate. The cognitivist conclusion—that the hardwiring between our ears is faulty—is not logically necessary. A simpler interpretation of the Harvard experiment, and the many others like it,[1] is that human beings are exquisitely sensitive to variations in linguistic form. Form matters. It can thwart our inclination to count and compare, which is the method of dealing with our feelings of uncertainty for which evolution has equipped us. It can mask the role of society and culture in establishing the categories we come to take for granted. Ironically, the problem isn't Bayes'

$$p(E|N) = 0.001 \times \frac{1.00}{(0.001)(1.00) + (0.999)(0.05)}$$

$p(E)$ = prior (unrevised) probability that patient has the disease (1 in 1,000) ($p(-E)$ is 999 in 1,000)

$p(N|E)$ = probability that test result will be positive when patient has the disease (100%)

$p(N|-E)$ = probability that test result will be positive when patient does not have the disease (5%)

$p(E|N)$ = (revised) probability that patient has the disease given that test result was positive ($\approx$0.196 or 2%)

Figure 15. Bayes' Rule with substitutions.

Rule. In fact, frequentists abhor Bayes' Rule precisely because it allows the prior to be a measure of uncertainty rather than a frequency.

To put it briefly, the frequentist criticizes the average person for ignorance or laziness while the cognitivist maintains that God never got around to debugging Adam's software. They disagree as to whether single events have probabilities, but they are unanimous that probabilities are objective properties of the universe. Scholars like Gigerenzer steer a course between these two extremes by rejecting precisely this common objectivist assumption. This, by the way, is not some newfangled idea. When John Stuart Mill wrote his *Logic,* he assumed that probabilities were purely objective—but from the second edition on, he changed his mind (Bulmer 1979, pp. 5–6), as the quotation at the head of this chapter indicates.

THE ANALOGY WITH SEMANTICS

Moving from notions of probability to notions of meaning, we may paraphrase Mill by saying that the meaning of a sign is not a quality of the sign itself—it is simply a name for the ground each of us has for making use or sense of it in a particular way. This is the underlying message in the parallel quotation from V. N. Vološinov at the head of this chapter. A statement by the linguist Roy Harris carries the same message: "A linguistic sign is not a fixed form with a fixed meaning, both of which remain regularly invariant across all the communicational episodes in which the sign is used. On the contrary, what constitutes a sign is not independent of the situation in which it occurs or of its material manifestation in that situation" (Harris and Wolf 1998, p. 24). What counts—what really does the work—is that the speaker recognizes the sign as a sign and categorizes it in relation to his or her experiences. What the sign means is partly a function of the speaker's experience of what it meant in prior "episodes," but the present episode brings its own unique conditions from which the sign's immediate meaning can never be completely separated. One might call this a Heraclitean view of language after the early Greek philosopher Heraclitus, who famously observed that you can never step into the same river twice.

Today, many descriptive linguists and postmodern theorists talk about meaning as a purely social construct—much as frequentists speak of probability as a property of categories. We must ask, however, how each individual learns to categorize things in the first place, that is, to internalize the collective know-how of his or her speech community. Cognitivist linguists, by contrast, deeply concerned with the question of language acquisition, stress the role of innate faculties in all language processing. In extreme cases, they come close to denying that genuine learning occurs at all. But this can only leave us wondering why actual language use is so lacking in computerlike regularity. If grammar is just a complex computer program, why are our conversations so full of ambiguity, vagueness, jokes, innovations, misunderstanding, and cultural idiosyncrasies? The way out of this dilemma is to adopt a view of meaning analogous to Gigerenzer's understanding of probability.

To see the relationship, think of money. Both descriptive and cognitive linguists treat meaning as if it were the value of words of the same kind—just as twenty-dollar bills are worth $20 because they have a picture of Jackson on the front and the White House on the back. Given changes in design and counterfeits, perhaps we are entitled to speak of the value "20 dollars" as if it were more real than the bills themselves. But with language, there is no excuse. Signs are not banknotes passed from one mind to another.

A better (though not perfect) metaphor, as Roy Harris (1996) has suggested, is barter. If I agree to swap my sack of rice for your bag of salt, it is precisely because we *disagree* about the value of these items at this time and in this place. You think the rice is more valuable; I think the salt is. The context of the situation—not only its physical circumstances but also whatever ideas you and I bring to them and make of them—creates a situation in which the transaction succeeds or fails for each of us. There is no guarantee we will be willing to make the same swap at some other time. And there is certainly no need to say that we unconsciously equate the value of the rice and the salt.

In other words: the pragmatic success of linguistic (indeed any) communication by means of signs does not depend on the identity of "sent" and "received" meanings. We are not biological fax machines of the sort pictured in Ferdinand de Saussure's famous *Course in General Linguistics* (Figure 16).[2] Language is not just a machine—like the Enigma of World War II fame—that we run forward or in reverse to encode or decode messages in terms of predefined, constant meanings. On the contrary, as

Harris forcefully argues, signs and meanings are created, processed, and interpreted, both mentally and physically, "on the fly." To use Saussure's terms, *la langue* is just a useful fiction; ontologically speaking, only *la parole* exists in the real world. Each of us is constantly engaging in semiotic behavior for the purpose of integrating our past experience with our consciousness of the present moment and our conjectures about the future. Categorization and metaphor, as shown by Lakoff and Johnson (1980), lie at the heart of this behavior. Interpersonal communication is just a special case. Communication works—not because all the signs and their meanings have been prearranged in some Panglossian manner in anticipation of everything the real world will ever offer—but rather because the context of each communicative act constrains the creation, processing, and interpreting of signs by each participant.

How different language looks when viewed from this perspective! The consistency of semiotic behavior is not the result of our having internalized or been born with a structure called *la langue*. Rather, the opportunity to form the abstraction we call *la langue* is afforded by this consistency. The

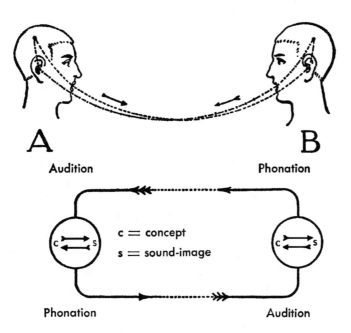

Figure 16. Saussure's talking heads.

coherence of our behavior reflects the coherence of the ever-present external pressures, both physical and cultural, that constrain but never completely determine how we use signs from moment to moment. Extreme behaviorists, who think that people must assimilate all their language and culture from the community around them, struggle to understand why individuals are not mere parrots. From our new perspective, this is no mystery. For we can see that much of language and culture is part of the *context*. Extreme cognitivists, who think of grammar as innate, machine-like, and culture-free, struggle to understand why language errors and change occur so constantly yet unpredictably. But from our new perspective, we see that linguistic behavior is inherently error-prone. It is the interplay of common physiological abilities with the context that creates the coherence of linguistic behavior we call communicating.

The key point is this: if meanings are subjective in the way that probabilities are subjective—if language is ontologically just *parole*—then there is no abstract universe of semantic invariants for ideograms or "written morphemes" (Hannas 1997) to map. Such language-independent symbols cannot exist because even the forms of language itself do not represent or refer to objects in some realm of predefined public meanings. If this theory seems too radical, consider the alternative: given either of the two conventional (objectivist) views of meaning, no sign expresses a meaning independently of language simply because that which cannot be communicated in language is not a meaning—or at least not a meaning that can be verifiably known to more than one person.

If meanings are objective, then the best we can do is to distinguish, as does John DeFrancis, partial from full writing according to whether or not it belongs to a *system* that is coextensive with some natural language. If meanings are subjective, however, then there is room for semiotic behavior outside the confines of purely linguistic behavior. This means there is a place for writing unrelated to language, including what DeFrancis would call partial writing. Musical notations, road signs, the fancy typography we see in advertising—all have a legitimate place in a theory of communication like Harris' because the success of communication in such a theory does not depend on the identity of meanings (Harris 1995). So while DeFrancis excludes pictograms, icons, mathematical notation, and other functionally limited forms of writing from consideration, Harris includes them all so long as they meet certain minimum physical require-ments.[3] Harris cheerfully agrees with DeFrancis that nontranscriptional kinds of writing are not writing in the ordinary sense. But he points out that all kinds of writing, marginal or ordinary, can in appropriate con-texts be created, processed, or interpreted without regard to language. He can say this precisely because he refuses to take meaning as an inherent feature of *la langue*—regarding it instead as an emergent property of par-ticular integrative acts of semiotic behavior, which may not even qualify as *la parole*.

This comes very close to agreeing with those who claim that Chinese characters are ideograms. They would like to say that Chinese characters represent meaning independently of any language. This isn't true if mean-ings are thought of as fixed entities transmitted by means of language. But if meanings are essentially private and the successful use of language does not depend on the exchange of identical meanings, then any sign can, for all we know, be meaningful for some person on some occasion independ-ently of speech. Notice the formal resemblance between this argument and DeFrancis' argument (1984) against the belief that Chinese charac-ters allow for rough-and-ready communication among people who don't know the same language. The fallacy in that case is thinking that only Chinese characters make this possible; in reality, any shared writing sys-tem can support this kind of translinguistic communication. Likewise, the fallacy in thinking that only Chinese characters can function nonlin-guistically is that, in reality, any kind of sign at all can have this property—in appropriate contexts.

Does this mean that the primacy of speech is a mistaken notion? Not at all. So far as we can tell, speech has always been the primary modality of language. We simply don't need to make use of this particular fact of natural history to dispel the myth of the ideogram. Neither Vološinov nor Harris nor any of the many diverse scholars who have, in one way or another, embraced a subjective conception of meaning (we will meet more in later chapters) deny the primacy of speech. Indeed, as we have seen, the key to understanding how writing can afford opportunities for communication that speech cannot is to give up the idea that meanings are separable from the forms of speech with which each of us thinks and speaks.

MORE ABOUT PROBABILITY PARADOXES

If you were amused by the Harvard experiment reported by Gigerenzer, here are two more examples of how merely rephrasing a problem can greatly alter the way we think through it. If recreational math is not your cup of tea, feel free to skip them. I've read numerous discussions of the second problem in print and on the Internet, but the analysis presented here is my own.

The Linda Problem

In a second well-known experiment discussed in detail by Gigerenzer (1994, pp. 131–133, 142–144), subjects were asked to choose *(a)* or *(b)* in the following problem:

> Linda is 31 years old, single, outspoken, and very bright. She majored in philosophy. As a student, she was deeply concerned with issues of discrimination and social justice, and also participated in antinuclear demonstrations. Which of these two alternatives is more probable?
>
> *(a)* Linda is a bank teller.
> *(b)* Linda is a bank teller and active in the feminist movement.

Depending on the exact experimental setup, 56 to 91 percent of the subjects chose *(b)*—in most cases, at least four out of five. Mathematically, however, the correct answer is *(a)*. In fact, if you were paying attention in school, you ought to know that the correct answer is *(a)* even if you didn't read the opening paragraph! After all, if "Linda is a bank teller" has probability p ($0 < p < 1$) and "Linda is active in the feminist movement" has probability q ($0 < q < 1$), then the product pq, which is the probability of their conjunction, *(b)*, must be less than p, the probability of *(a)*, or, for that matter, of q.

Now suppose we change the format of the problem slightly:

> Linda is 31 years old, single, outspoken, and very bright. She majored in philosophy. As a student, she was deeply concerned with issues of discrimination and social justice, and also participated in antinuclear demonstrations. There are 100 people who fit the description above. How many of them are:

(a) Bank tellers
(b) Bank tellers and active in the feminist movement

In this case, only 13 to 22 percent of subjects assigned a higher number to *(b)* than to *(a)*, typically fewer than one out of five. (Again the result depends on the details of the experimental setup.) Answer *(a)* is still the correct one. The only difference between the first and second versions of the Linda Problem is this: in the first version, you are forced to deal with single-event probabilities; in the second, you are allowed to think of collections of countable items, but this is enough to make it transparently obvious that the set defined by *(b)* must be a subset of the set defined by *(a)*.[4] That is: the "cognitive illusion" (called the conjunction fallacy) that some researchers claim to find in their Linda Problem data turns out to be an illusion itself.

The Monty Hall Problem

The Monty Hall Problem is named for the host of the old television program *Let's Make a Deal*, on which he regularly created a dilemma for contestants that reduces to the following game. I show you three closed boxes. Two are empty; one contains money. I know where the money is; you don't. I give you a chance to win the money by putting a mark on any box you please. We'll call it *A*. I now open a different box and show you that it is empty. I can do this regardless of which box you marked because I know where the money is and there are three boxes altogether. Call the empty box I open *B* and the remaining box *C*. I now say to you, "I'll let you take *C* instead of *A* if you want to change your mind." Are you better off choosing *A* or *C*?

Most people, including many mathematicians,[5] react to this proposition by saying that there is no basis for preferring *A* or *C*. After all, at this stage in the proceedings, there are two closed boxes, about which you know nothing, and one open box. What difference does the previous business make? Your choice at this point is not constrained by what happened before. And it seems you have as much of a chance of being right as wrong whichever box you select. Most people think this way, although they do not all act alike as a result. Some of them stick with box *A* because they believe in their own luck. Some stick with box *A* out of spite, thinking they're being tricked in some way. Yet others switch to box *C* because they think they are supposed to feel tricked and believe they should use reverse psychology. The variations go on and on. There are also people who think that picking box *A* is better than picking *C* (or vice versa) but fail to give compelling reasons for their preference. The truth is that it is always better to switch to box *C* than to stick with *A*— a fact that can be verified empirically. Nevertheless, most people doubt this statement when they first hear it. Let me try to persuade you that it is indeed better to switch.

Three explanations.   Here is an analysis that takes just two sentences to state: the odds that the money is in box *B* or *C* are 2 out of 3. The sole effect of learning that box *B* is empty is that you must assign these odds exclusively to box *C*. End of story. Most people find this explanation hard to understand, let alone accept with satisfaction, but it is logically correct. There is an implication that you were foolish to focus exclusively on the odds of guessing correctly, which are 1 out of 3 at the start of the game; you should have focused instead on the odds of failure. This seems like a trick. But I believe the chief reason this explanation seems obtuse is that it fails to provide a narrative explanation for why the odds of being wrong when you mark box *A* end up becoming the odds of finding the money in box *C*. Such a narrative explanation (see Bruner 1990) would let you escape the idea of probability as a property of a single event.

Here's a slightly longer analysis. Suppose you cheated somehow and got to peek into box *A* after marking it. If you glimpsed money in box *A*, you would not be fooled by my opening *B*. If, on the other hand, you saw nothing in *A*, you would know, as soon as I opened *B*, that the money had to be in *C*. Now if we repeat the game often, the first case will happen one-third of the time and the second case two-thirds of the time. So in any one game, you're twice as likely to find the money in box *C*. This explanation feels better than the previous one even though it just states the same facts in different words. This is because, I believe, it has more narrative development in it: first, it asks you to imagine two mutually exclusive counterfactual situations from both of which uncertainty has been eliminated; then it instructs you to change your viewpoint and judge which situation will occur more frequently. You are still using fractions "of the time" in your thinking, however, and therefore feel some pressure to think in terms of single-event probabilities.

Here is a third analysis that makes use of an analogy. Suppose we play the game with 100 boxes instead of 3. Just as in the original version, you mark any box you please as *A*. But since there are so many boxes, the futility of your guess is hard to miss. Without anyone telling you, you start off with a strong intuition that the money is almost certainly *not* in *A* but in one of the other 99 boxes. So as I open up one box after another, you wait with growing anticipation to see if I blunder and prematurely open the box with money. But I keep opening boxes until just two are left: box *A* and one other. At this point, the foolishness of thinking that this last unmarked box does not contain the money has become painfully obvious. Come to think of it, if we had started with only 75 or 50 or 25 boxes, you'd feel much the same way. But why is that? Aha! So long as there are two or more unmarked boxes to start with, the money is more likely to be in the one still unopened at the end. The more unmarked boxes, the more likely that the last one holds the money — but even as few as two unmarked boxes are enough to justify switching.[6] At last we have an argument that feels persuasive. The trick that makes the game hard to fathom is revealed: three boxes is the smallest number of boxes I can start with that makes switching always right. You don't usually think of 3 as a large number, but in this case it's large enough! As Jakob Bernoulli wrote to Leibniz in 1703, the law of large numbers is something that "even the stupidest man knows by some instinct of nature *per se* and by no previous instruction" (quoted in Gigerenzer 1994, p. 139).

This third explanation is by no means "perfect" — in fact, experience shows that even this argument will not persuade everyone. But as we go through all three explanations, they become intuitively more appealing. If this observation is correct, it confirms the subjectivist view of probability by showing that the Monty Hall "illusion" can be made to disappear. As in the cases discussed by Gigerenzer, the situation becomes clear — or at least clearer — when it is described in a way that encourages thinking in terms of frequencies. In this instance, the problem itself is not reformatted, and neither the conjunction fallacy nor Bayes' Rule is involved, yet the cognitivist interpretation is refuted.

What do our intuitions show? Cognitivist commentators on the Monty Hall Problem have looked for the source of its peculiar ability to confuse in the hardwiring of the brain. Massimo Piattelli-Palmarini (1994) argues vehemently that it reveals fundamentally illogical and therefore undesirable features of human rationality. Keith Devlin (1997) agrees that the Monty Hall Problem shows that logic and rationality are not the same, but he refrains from slapping a value judgment on rationality. Indeed, since intelligence is a product of evolution, we should expect it to include more than just logic. An animal that responds quickly though perhaps illogically to an immediate threat instead of taking the time to find the "correct" response may escape becoming some other animal's dinner. Both Piattelli-Palmarini and Devlin evidently subscribe to the metaphor of mind as computer, however, and both seek a biological explanation for the discrepancy between logic and rationality. One condemns rationality for having a bug; the other holds it blameless on account of evolution. Neither questions the appropriateness of thinking about the problem in terms of single-event probabilities.

Turning to the frequentist position, it is perhaps enough to note that adherence to the classic definition of probability by no means prevents us from falsely interpreting the Monty Hall Problem. The following line of reasoning, for example, is fallacious:

> First, I must choose one of three boxes, then one of two. So there are six combinations in all. Of these, three are "winners" and three are "losers." Each combination has probability ⅙, so it makes no difference whether I stick or switch.

This is wrong because there are really eight possible outcomes, not six. The eight possible outcomes are presented in the "decision tree" shown in Table 9. It's an improvement on the foregoing simpleminded approach, but it's still subject to misinterpretation. The root of the tree represents all possible cases; the three levels of nodes represent the three steps in the game: you mark a box; I open an empty box; you make the final choice. Here box *A* is the box with the money, not the box you mark, which may be *A, B,* or *C.* The number associated with each node is the fraction "of the time" you (naively) believe the game will proceed to the state of affairs represented by that node "in the long run."

An example of reading the tree goes like this: you will pick box *B* one-third of the time; I cannot open *A,* so I must open *C;* then you have a free choice of *A* (switch) or *B* (stick). Using this tree, you might reason as follows:

The part of the time I reach each end node is the product of the numbers associated with all the nodes on the path to it from the root. There are four cases in which I ultimately pick A (success). Summing the products in each case, the result is $\frac{1}{12} + \frac{1}{12} + \frac{1}{6} + \frac{1}{6} =$ $\frac{1}{2}$, so it doesn't matter which path I take: half "the time" I'll get A and half "the time" I won't.

The fallacy here is that even though you cannot know whether I have a free choice of opening B or C (because you picked A) or must open B or C (because you picked the other), you can be certain that, in "the long run," my hand will be forced two out of three times. If you ignore this advance information and proceed blindly, you will end up choosing A "half the time" at the third step, but you need not do so. Those $\frac{1}{2}$'s attached to the third-level nodes are not preordained: you're in control! You can decide to switch your original choice in every case. The frequencies of the third-level nodes then become 0 or 1 as shown in Table 10. It's now easy to see that you definitely lose $\frac{1}{6} + \frac{1}{6} = \frac{1}{3}$ of the time and definitely win $\frac{2}{3}$ of the time. Furthermore, this is the best you can do since, at the third level, only A is common to each of the four final binary choices.

Clearly knowledge of frequencies does not immunize us to confusion. Whether we conceive of probabilities as properties of single events or properties of classes of events, we can arrive at false conclusions if we forget that identifying events or classes of events depends on categorizations, the identity of which is not epistemologically guaranteed. The laws

Table 9. Naive Decision Tree for the Monty Hall Problem

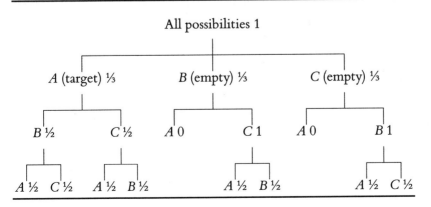

Table 10. Correct Decision Tree for the Monty Hall Problem

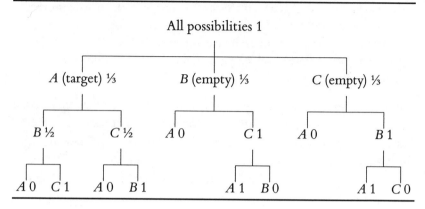

of probability are therefore somewhat analogous to Boyle's and Charles'
Laws. Although high-school students of chemistry are routinely taught
that these are purely objective laws of nature,

> in actual fact, these laws only approximate the real behavior of gases.
> For instance, for pressures greater than ten atmospheres or for cer-
> tain gases such as water vapor and carbon dioxide near liquefaction,
> Boyle's law is not very accurate. . . . These relationships are derived
> from the general kinetic properties of individual gas molecules act-
> ing in an aggregate. A gas may appear to be following Boyle's and
> Charles' laws, yet in actuality these laws have no existence except
> in the minds of scientists. Such laws are meta-descriptive devices
> that scientists use to talk about the properties of gases. In no literal
> sense can it be said that individual gas molecules follow these laws.
> [Skousen 1989, pp. 139–140]

8 In the basement under the Chinese Room

Any twenty-first-century book about Chinese characters needs to include a chapter on computers. But a book that zeroes in on the notion that Chinese characters are ideograms needs such a chapter more than most. Not only are computers and the Internet changing the way that uncommon scripts are being used throughout the world, they are also the interface between the burgeoning realm of computer science and the general public. They constitute a house of many rooms, each of which deserves a visit—starting, naturally enough, with the room created in a seminal article by Berkeley professor of philosophy John Searle.

JOHN SEARLE'S CHINESE ROOM

Searle's 1980 article initiated a long, often heated, but in many ways productive debate between proponents and critics of artificial-intelligence (AI) research and related R&D projects. It appeared in the journal *Behavioral and Brain Sciences,* which not only published the article but also invited prepublication rejoinders from a wide assortment of academic peers and an omnibus surrejoinder from the author himself. All the essays appeared together in a single issue of the journal and still make for exciting reading. Although the original article has been widely reproduced, summarized, and discussed in print and electronic formats, it has also been misunderstood or misrepresented on various occasions. For this reason, I want to be cautious in describing what I believe are the essential points of Searle's core idea.

Searle's aim was to show, through a cleverly designed thought experiment, that a computer program which can scan a newspaper article and answer questions about it is not necessarily intelligent. A computer program that could perform such a task with moderate success was devised in the late 1970s and ballyhooed, together with several other programs, as evidence that it is possible to reduce intelligent behavior to a series of computational processes. Although there were computer programs to do other tasks that seem to require what we usually call intelligence, such as playing chess, Searle latched on to the newspaper analyzer because the task seemed typical of the sort of thing people actually do in daily life.

Searle suggests that we compare a computer running the newspaper analysis program with an imaginary setup that simulates all its parts on a larger scale. This setup involves a man in a room who knows only the English language and can communicate with us (outside the room) only by passing sheets of paper under the door. The idea is to simulate what the computer does by providing input to the man in the room, having him carry out with pencil and paper what the computer does with electrons, and getting him to produce output like that of a computer given similar instructions.

Since our man is perfectly ordinary, he unquestionably embodies human intelligence. We have no idea whether the computer embodies intelligence or not, but we know exactly what it does when it runs a program. To ensure that the man is never given an opportunity to apply his intelligence to do more than the computer, we conduct our experiment using a newspaper article and a question about it written in Mandarin Chinese in customary orthography. Assuming that the man does what he's told, he has precisely the same chance of producing a correct answer to the question, in written Chinese, as the computer. That is: we use the man's total ignorance of Mandarin or any language other than English to ensure that our imaginary model truly simulates what the computer does.

The program instructions we pass to the man under the door may include Chinese characters, but they only refer to them as visually distinguishable blobs of ink. Although this point is absolutely crucial, many commentators on the Chinese Room have overlooked it. We are not permitted to give the man English translations of any kind. So far as he is concerned, individual Chinese characters are just graphic objects to be compared or copied as such. He has no idea why they have the shapes they do, how they correspond to Chinese or English words or phrases, or why they are in a certain order in the newspaper article, the question, or parts of our instructions. We simply feed him orders like the following:

Step 1517.   Check if the next two characters are any of the pairs listed on pages 203–864 of your instructions. If so, then go to Step 6320; else go to Step 1518.

Step 3823.   If the next character in the text matches any of the following 112 characters, copy it in the next vacant position on page 964 of the instructions.

Step 10,755.   Write the third character in the text after the one you are currently pointing at on page 3492 in the next available space.

Step 1,210,572. Push page 10324 under the door.

The poor devil carries out essentially the same instructions the computer would execute, only much, much slower. He can tell when two characters are alike and when they are not; he can draw each one on paper as required. But beyond this, the characters are for him just arbitrary meaningless chicken scratches. Throughout his Herculean labors—perhaps we should say Sisyphean—he doesn't have a clue what the newspaper article is about or even that he is composing the answer to a question about it. (Fortunately for our consciences, he's just imaginary.)

Because the man in the room carries out exactly the same instructions, he enjoys the same chance for success as a computer running the equivalent program. If we ignore irrelevant variables such as time and neatness of handwriting, the answers to the question generated by man and computer are indistinguishable. Whether we are impressed by them or laugh at them makes no difference; what matters is that the same answer was generated by a computer and by our imaginary man. Therefore, if we cannot say that the man in the room behaved intelligently, we have no business saying that the computer did either. This is the key. For although the man in the room is doing many chores that require intelligence (reading documents in English, keeping track of vast amounts of paper, visually comparing one Chinese character with another, deciding whether they are the same or not, copying them as best he can, sharpening pencils), the overall plan of his behavior is as obtuse, plodding, and absurd as anything Kafka or Sartre ever dreamed up. Our man simply isn't behaving intelligently on the level of any ordinary activity such as reading. To see this, just put yourself (assuming you can read Chinese) in his place. The article and question are not just meaningless character strings to you. It may take a while before the purpose of the fiendishly long set of instructions you keep getting under the door dawns on you, but if the process is more hell for you than the imaginary man, it is because you know Chinese! The computer never wonders "Why am I doing all this?" while it carries out one command after another, but you surely would.

This is a devastating argument against the underlying assumptions of AI because it uses introspection in a novel way. It asks you to compare your common everyday experience of thinking with what the poor man in the Chinese Room is doing—and for most people, it is obviously not at all the same thing. Since this is such a good argument, it has roused a wide range of objections, none of them convincing. One approach is to assert that our conscious experience of language use, including meaning (semantics), is just an illusion: there is only syntax—you just *think* that there's more going on. This is rather like saying that pain is unreal because what's really going on is just a bunch of neurons firing off in a certain way in your skull. It is certainly true that there are different scales at which we can observe and describe pain and other physical processes, but what privileges the smallest scale? Nothing other than our history of talking about atoms, so-called elementary particles, and most recently quarks.

A weaker response is to say that the man in the room actually understands Chinese; he just doesn't know that he does. This is like saying that maybe there is more to language than just syntax; but even if there is, we're unaware of it. (A variation on this theme is to claim that the entire experimental apparatus is a system that knows Chinese; the man is just a cog in a wheel, so to speak.) This concession does not entirely remove the scaling problem that flawed the previous objection. And, moreover, it runs into another problem: since humans actually do better at the task than computers (and therefore better than the man in the Chinese Room), they must be doing something different from what's specified in the program. So long as the experiment is a large-scale analogue of a program plodding along, one instruction at a time, in a von Neumann machine, it doesn't matter how you tinker with it. Of course, if you could exactly simulate every cell of a living, breathing, educated reader of Chinese by electromechanical means and wire them all together in exactly the right way, your robot would presumably do what a living, breathing, educated reader of Chinese does. Unfortunately, the claim made by most AI researchers is precisely that such physiological simulation is unnecessary.

Given the defects of the foregoing objections, the Chinese Room poses a formidable argument against what Searle called "strong AI" or what his Berkeley colleague Hubert Dreyfus later termed GOFAI, "good old-fashioned artificial intelligence." Strong AI needs to be distinguished from the use of computers as tools in the investigation of human cognition. Using a computer to simulate what would happen in a portion of an ideal brain under various conditions is an example of weak AI—and to the extent that such simulations are used only to motivate hypotheses about what happens physiologically in real brains, no one finds fault with them. The contentious point is precisely the claim that a computer program, by its very nature, is to a greater or lesser extent intelligent. For the dwindling few who still cling to this claim, all meaning can be reduced to information in the narrow sense of mathematical information theory. Meaning, in this view, is just a matter of organization or structure in patterns; any physical system that contains nested patterns (larger ones composed of smaller ones) and the means for changing one pattern into another allegedly possesses the necessary and sufficient conditions for being intelligent. This radical view, popular in certain engineering circles from the late 1960s to early 1990s, is usually stated with numerous qualifications these days, but it still lies at the core of much AI research.

Whether or not you agree that Searle's famous Chinese Room argument demolishes the case for strong AI, there are two important points to notice. First, the strong-AI position that Searle is attacking is very similar to the theory of meaning implied in the Ideographic Myth of Chinese characters. After all, there are only a finite number of Chinese characters whereas the realm of meanings seems unbounded. If someone comes along with a huge book that claims to list every possible meaning, it's easy to dream up a meaning not in the book by sticking a relative clause into an item listed in the book or by combining listings ("an X that is purple," "something neither A nor B," and the like). So even if every character carried a well-defined meaning, syntactic arrangements of characters must also carry meanings. But strong-AI theory claims that syntactic arrangements of symbols *instantiate* meaning. (For computational purposes, single characters are just trivial cases of strings—strings of one character. Definitions of the meanings of single ideograms are just more strings of symbols.)

Second, to make his thought experiment vivid, Searle chooses Chinese. But why not a Vietnamese room or a Bulgarian room? After all, the key point is that the man in the room knows only English. Clearly Searle wanted to make it crystal clear that his hypothetical man could not possibly be thinking on his own and thus using his intelligence to do more than execute the instructions passed to him under the door. The force of the thought experiment, after all, arises from the fact that the man in the room is as free to exercise his intelligence as an ordinary reader—yet artificially is prevented from doing so. To make sure this point wasn't missed, Searle chose the stereotype of inscrutability par excellence. How ironic that, in constructing a powerful argument against a theory of meaning historically inspired by Chinese characters, Searle resorted to our culture's crudest preconceptions about Chinese characters to drive his point home.

In short, the Chinese Room is a story that can be interpreted on at least two levels. As a philosophical argument, it punches a hole in claims for strong AI. As a rhetorical move, however, it pays homage to the very myth it is designed to refute. One might justifiably complain that while Searle does a good job showing that meaning must be more than just nested arrangements of physical objects, the Chinese Room isn't very helpful in making clear what meaning is.

THE DUPLEX HOUSE

Not surprisingly, the constellation of issues raised by Searle's Chinese Room thought experiment has led to a certain polarization among those who study the cognitive sciences. The mainstream group, who generally assume the possibility of artificial intelligence and all the philosophical assumptions about human intelligence underlying it, have pretty much appropriated the adjective "cognitive" for their line of thinking. The rest, who think AI reductionism is incapable of comprehending the full range of human cognitive abilities, are treated like total outsiders to the scientific discourse. Compare, for example, Steven Pinker's *Language Instinct* (1994) and Michael Agar's *Language Shock* (1994), two excellent introductions to linguistics published in the same year by the same company. Two books so diametrically opposed would be difficult to find in any field.

Agar, an anthropologist then working at the University of Maryland, focused on how language is used in different cultures and how cultures only become perceptible to us when two or more of them come into contact. At one point, Agar remarks that Benjamin Lee Whorf (1897–1941) is one of the few people in the past he wishes he could go back to meet. Whorf was the maverick scholar who floated the hypothesis that the structure of your language impinges on the structure of your thoughts. Pinker, however, a linguist working at MIT, singles out Whorf for special ridicule, calling him at one point a "charlatan." For Pinker, the interesting stuff in language is almost all unrelated to culture, in which it swims somewhat like the yolk floating in an egg white. Pinker is concerned about figuring out how babies acquire language. He thinks it all depends on innate neural structures for handling language up to and including syntax, which he sees as the sine qua non of true linguistic behavior.

According to this view, the brain is a wet computer. Every brain comes equipped with an abstract substrate like an operating system, sometimes called Mentalese, which enables the process of language acquisition. Language works the way it does because of the abstract structure of Mentalese and the actual languages that work under it like application software. Just as a piece of software can be "reverse engineered" by observing its output without seeing its source code, so too we can deduce the rules of a language by comparing how its speakers interpret utterances in it. It doesn't matter that we have only a very sketchy idea of how these rules are physiologically embodied in the brain; they must exist because without them it seems impossible to explain the properties ("universals") found in all languages, the robustness and economy of the language acquisition process, and the ability of linguistically competent people to create and interpret novel utterances.

It was proof of the dominating appeal of this view of language that it was Pinker, not Agar, who became a star in 1994. And it is easy to see why it was so appealing. We are heirs to a long tradition of science fiction (Isaac Asimov's robot novels, Arthur Clarke's HAL, made real for millions by Stanley Kubrick) based on the notion that there is no difference in principle between what happens in a computer and inside our skulls. Vast amounts of money have been plowed into R&D projects that rely on the same premise. As Searle (1992) has pointed out, the approach to language that Pinker pursued, when taken to its logical extreme, purports that syntactic rules themselves and their interrelationships instantiate meaning. All that other stuff—our feelings, beliefs, and culturally bounded interpretations—is just epiphenomenal. So if we properly replicate the syntactic rules of, say, English in a computer program, the program will not merely simulate but will actually possess the linguistic competence of a native speaker of English. Small wonder that MIT has led the way in efforts to produce machine translation and so-called artificial intelligence.

Philosophers like Hubert Dreyfus (1993), stressing the importance of the body in cognitive activity highlighted by Merleau-Ponty, have forcefully criticized this brain/computer metaphor. In this he is supported by recent advances in neurophysiology and empirical results obtained with connectionist computational models. The former have been summarized by Philip Lieberman, whose comments show that objections to the concept of innate syntactic competence are by no means purely philosophical:

> Chomsky's model of the brain still seems to be based on the digital computers that were being developed at MIT when he first developed his linguistic theories in the mid-1950s. The technologies that now allow clinicians to image the brains of patients suffering brain damage that destroys their capacity to understand and produce language did not exist at that time. The state of knowledge concerning the human brain had hardly changed since the nineteenth century, and so it was reasonable for Chomsky to propose that the human brain contained an additional "organ," a language "module" that wasn't present in the brains of closely related animals such as chimpanzees. Chomsky's model, moreover, was a reasonable interpretation of the traditional textbook treatment of the human brain, which attributes language to two parts of the brain—Broca's and Wernicke's areas, named after the nineteenth-century scientists who were among the first clinicians to study the effects of brain damage on language. However, though these parts of the brain are involved in language, the data of hundreds of independent research projects using new techniques show that there is much more to the story. [Lieberman 1998, pp. 99–100]

Connectionist models show how a network of elementary computational units, in which no component corresponds to a formal rule, can nevertheless behave as if rule-governed. Such "neural nets" are to patterns of complex behavior what holograms are to three-dimensional scenes: they have no local parts that correspond one-to-one with parts of what they "represent."[1] It has only been within the past twenty years or so that computers capable of supporting connectionist models have been available at reasonable cost. So Lieberman's point applies here too.[2]

Connectionist results, which have greatly affected the course of AI research over the past decade, offer what Searle would call a weak-AI approach to language: using computers as tools for discovering what can be accomplished pragmatically with various computational procedures. Perhaps the most thorough effort along these lines is found in the work of Ronald Langacker (1987; 1991). He presents a wide range of linguistic data that are difficult to explain in terms of the "basic, deeply entrenched folk model" of language as a conduit:

> According to this model, linguistic expressions are vehicles for transporting ideas along a conduit leading from the speaker's mind into the hearer's. These vehicles are strings of words each of which contains a finite amount of a substance called "meaning." The speaker assembles and loads the vehicle, and then sends it along the conduit; the hearer unloads it to determine what idea the speaker *has in mind* and wants to *get across* by *putting it into words*. [Langacker 1991, p. 508]

Implicit in this model are two related ideas: "a word's meaning is strictly limited and distinct from general knowledge" and "the meaning of a complex expression is constructed just by stacking together the meanings of its parts in accordance with general combinatory rules" (p. 508). These may be handy metaphors for talking about language. But if we enshrine them as theoretical axioms, they prevent us from seeing that "only sound waves actually travel from the speaker to the hearer," that the hearer must therefore actively participate if the linguistic act is to succeed pragmatically, and that complex linguistic structures often display "emergent or contextually induced properties that no individual component is capable of evoking" (p. 508).

This, of course, puts Langacker on a collision course with generative theories of the sort favored by Pinker and Chomsky. These theories zero in on syntax and postulate that it "constitutes a separate irreducible level of linguistic structure" autonomous of meaning (Langacker 1991, p. 515). For Langacker, by contrast, all grammar (including but not limited to syntax) "is inherently symbolic; only units with semantic and phonological import are required for its proper characterization" (p. 516). Nevertheless, he does not see his own theory, which he calls "cognitive grammar," as completely opposed to the generativist approach. Rather he contrasts it not only with generativism, which tries to discover rules of syntax as if they were statements in a computer program, but also with connectionism, a cover term for computational models in which large networks of simple processors interact. Although each processor is programmed in the traditional sense to perform certain operations depending on the inputs it receives from the processors adjacent to it in the network, the network as a whole follows no preconceived rules. Its global behavior depends only on the initial conditions of its many interconnected processors—including the ways in which they are "wired" together—and data received from outside the network. The number of possible states that such a network can theoretically take is beyond reckoning. But experimental work shows that, given properly chosen initial conditions, the global state of the network shifts over time in such a way that it produces (almost) only outputs that are appropriate responses to the inputs. For example: a suitably configured "neural net" primed with English texts can "learn" to synthesize a speech stream (almost) identical to what someone reading the texts out loud would produce—even though no single component in the network contains any rules about changing letters into phonemes. For this reason, some generativists think of connectionism as a "mind-as-mush" view of language. Some connectionists return the favor by describing generative syntax as "empty-symbol-pushing" (Langacker 1991, p. 530).

Langacker sees his own theory—cognitive grammar—as a middle-of-the-road position that avoids the excesses of both generativist and connectionist approaches while acknowledging their respective insights. For him the central problem is to develop a theory that explains where the regularities in language come from (1991, pp. 533–536) without resort to rules autonomous of meaning or a blanket denial that rules exist. For our purposes, however, the important feature of Langacker's work is his stance on meaning:

> In discussing the relationship between meaning and grammar, theorists tend to presuppose that the former—reducing to conditions on objective truth—is known or at least straightforwardly determinable; hence, they conceive the issue as being whether aspects of grammar can be characterized or predicted on that basis. . . .
> [C]ognitive grammar conceives . . . the situation as being quite

different. Meaning is a conceptual phenomenon, and by virtue of construal a given objective situation can be coded by any number of expressions all of which are semantically distinct. Furthermore, construal is generally as invisible to us as a pair of glasses or contact lenses — despite its formative influence on how we view a scene, our awareness is focused on the scene itself. *There is consequently no sense in which an expression's semantic characterization is known prior to linguistic analysis* or available as an independent basis for prediction. [Langacker 1991, p. 517; emphasis added]

Royal Skousen is another linguist who has adopted a weak-AI approach. Skousen has developed a theory, "analogical modeling of language," that is even more radical than the sort of connectionist work to which Langacker refers. AML, as its practitioners call it,

> eliminates the need for Chomsky's distinction between competence and performance. . . . This distinction arises in rule-based approaches since rules are used to account for "normalized" behavior and performance factors are left with the task of accounting for "violations" of these rules. On the other hand, in an analogical approach . . . [t]here is no independent description of the data; there is only predicted behavior for given contexts. *Usage is the description, and performance is competence.* [Skousen 1989, p. 76; emphasis added]

This is the kind of conclusion that Agar might come up with, yet it arises from work on a highly sophisticated mathematical model of language use.

There are critics even more radical than Dreyfus, Searle, Langacker, and Skousen. Varela, Thompson, and Rosch (1991) find fault even with connectionist models. They advocate a view of cognition allied with Buddhist philosophy in which subject, object, and the action that relates them are distinct but ontologically interdependent. But even short of this position, it is clear that the metaphor of the von Neumann machine is not the only one available for serious thinking about language and cognition.

HOME PRODUCTS

The ordinary person for whom the computer is now an everyday practical tool may feel that all this philosophical give-and-take is just so much hairsplitting. Surely computers confer upon Chinese, Japanese, Koreans, and anyone else who wants to use Chinese characters in a computer-based environment the freedom to do so. People buy these contraptions, so presumably engineers must have found methods that make it not merely possible but actually efficient and satisfying to use Chinese characters electronically. Forget about the philosophical debates. Just look at how consumers use *kanji*. This will show what sort of symbols they really are! This sharp attack certainly seems to cut through the Gordian knot of the ideogram problem. (Note the resemblance to the Successfulness Myth discussed in Chapter 1.) But it leads to some unexpected answers to the problems it purports to solve.

Many Japanese believe that Japanese word-processing (JWP) technology has eliminated all the difficulties associated with the thousands of multifunctional *kanji* that crowd Japanese texts. Nanette Gottlieb (2000) is the latest to attempt to explain why. In her study of JWP, she covers the historical background, surveys mainstream Japanese opinion on JWP proliferation, and even reports on what Japanese say they feel when reading and writing with JWP equipment. Most are moderately satisfied customers, but it is far from clear why. Gottlieb's discussion doesn't shed much light on the reasons because she does not distinguish functions shared by all word-processing systems (such as cut-and-paste editing) from those needed expressly to accommodate the Japanese writing system.

Twenty years ago, Japanese documents were literally handcrafted. JWP has changed this—boosting production and reducing the time needed for revisions and formatting. But the personal computer (PC) did at least as much, and faster, where alphabets are commonly used. According to the latest Economic Planning Agency white paper (*Asahi Shimbun*, 22 June 2000), fewer than 15 percent of Japanese had Internet access in 1998 compared with almost 25 percent of Singaporeans (in whose tiny nation English is the main language of government and education) and the rate of increase in Internet users between 1995 and 1998 was slightly lower in Japan than in Malaysia. Gottlieb herself observes (2000, p. 6): "In 1997, only around 20 percent of Japanese had PCs, compared to over 40 percent in the United States and about 35 percent in Australia." If this fact reflects difficulty in handling Japanese script on computer, the problem must lie specifically in the man/machine interface through which users input *kanji* and *kana* since computers can certainly display and store files containing Japanese script.

Figures compiled by the Economic Planning Agency suggest that the input bottleneck is indeed an important factor. The percentage of Japanese households reporting that they owned a PC rose from 10.6 percent in 1990 to 15.6 percent in 1995, 38.6 percent in 2000, and 50.1 percent in 2001 — which would seem to indicate that Japanese families are happy PC users. During the same period, however, the percentage of households reporting that they owned a special-purpose JWP machine increased from 24.1 percent in 1990 to 39.4 percent in 1995 and then held fairly steady (39.0 percent in 2000, 37.6 percent in 2001). The key fact about PCs and JWPs is that, with the right program loaded, any PC marketed in Japan can do what a JWP does — but a JWP cannot in general be programmed to do everything that a PC can. With this in mind, let us treat the foregoing percentages as probabilities — in 1990, for example, the odds were that 10 or 11 of every 100 households owned a PC — and calculate how many households had two, one, or no machines for handling Japanese script. This will lead us to a more telling analysis. (See Table 11.)

Consider first the changes from 1990 to 1995. During this period, the ratio of JWP-only households to PC-only households went up from 21.5/8.0 = 2.7 to 33.3/9.5 = 3.5. The proportion of households owning both a PC and a JWP went up too, but some increase was inevitable since even compulsively trend-conscious Japanese consumers are reluctant to throw away costly purchases the instant they become redundant. In fact, since it is likely that few of the 16.7 percent of no-machine households that bought a JWP or a PC between 1990 and 1995 bought both, most or all of the new two-machine households probably came from the JWP-only group, where they were replaced by new entrants from the no-machine group. So apart from the 1.4 percent of new PC-only households, all the rest — 15.3 percent, or more than ten times as many — started off with a JWP.[3]

Now remember: there's nothing you can do with a JWP that you can't do on a PC with the right software, but plenty you can do on a PC that you can't do with a JWP. From the foregoing figures we can therefore deduce that, up to 1995, Japanese consumers were fascinated by the possibility of producing documents on a machine, rather than by hand, but were put off by PCs. Working with spreadsheets, using databases, programming as a hobby, and browsing the net were not worth the investment in time and effort needed to handle the PCs of the period, which were rather slow, more expensive than JWPs, and used operating systems that required some confidence in English.

Manufacturers purposely priced JWPs low to attract first-time buyers in a fiercely competitive market (Unger 1987, pp. 166–169). But for affluent consumers, the price difference was probably only a minor disincentive. Likewise, though slow by today's standards, faster machines at the same price level simply were not available at the time. The real problem from the consumer's perspective was that the machines didn't "run in Japanese." More precisely, inputting Japanese script was too demanding to be used for anything other than word processing, so why bother to get an expensive PC when a cheaper JWP would do?

Table 11. Percentage of Japanese Households Owning Japanese Word-Processors and Personal Computers

1990		PC	No PC		
		10.6	89.4		
JWP	**24.1**	2.6	21.5		
No JWP	75.9	8.0	67.9		
1995		PC	No PC	Change	1990–1995
		15.6	84.4		
JWP	**39.4**	6.1	33.3	3.6	11.7
No JWP	60.6	9.5	51.1	1.4	−16.7
2000		PC	No PC	Change	1995–2000
		38.6	61.4		
JWP	**39.0**	15.1	23.9	8.9	−9.3
No JWP	61.0	23.5	37.5	14.1	−13.7
2001		PC	No PC	Change	2000–2001
		50.1	49.9		
JWP	**37.6**	18.8	18.8	3.8	−5.2
No JWP	62.4	31.3	31.1	7.7	−6.3

Note: Figures in bold are taken from Economic Planning Agency reports; others are calculated.

By 1995, most PCs sold in Japan offered similar versions of character-conversion *(kanji henkan)* input routines—transcriptive input programs—which get the job done but are intrinsically slow and stressful compared with true touch-typing. When doing transcriptive input, users must constantly check for wrong *kanji* and make style choices. They must refrain from accepting whatever the program offers first, especially when writing extemporaneously, because most programs simply suggest whatever *kanji* was most recently used for a particular pronunciation. Things are not made easier by manufacturers who vie to cram ever more *kanji* and archaic forms into their look-up dictionaries; this practice just increases the need for users to be cautious and make choices. Experiments have proved that when mistakes are made using transcriptive input programs, the homophonic errors generated are more difficult to catch later during proofreading than all other kinds of *kanji* errors (see Chapter 3).

Returning to the foregoing statistics, we can see that things changed in the period 1995–2001. Households with PCs jumped from 15.6 to 38.6 percent in the first five years and then to 50.1 percent the next year. Why did this happen? The introduction of the Microsoft Windows 95 operating system and succeeding versions did much to boost PC sales and spark interest in the rapidly expanding Internet. (It should not be forgotten that it was the way Microsoft bundled its web browser with Windows 95 that eventually led to the still unresolved antitrust lawsuits brought against it.) Japanese consumers began to want to do more than print New Year's greeting cards: they wanted to surf the web and exchange e-mail. Meantime, the steady long-term decline in all hardware prices made the lower cost of JWPs less important and their limitations more noticeable. As JWPs broke down, they were replaced with PCs rather than with newer JWP models. This is shown by the drop in the ratio of JWP-only to PC-only households—to 3.5 in 1995 to 1.0 by 2000 and then to 0.6 by 2001—and by the greater increase in two-machine households relative to PC-only (first-time buyer) households.

One thing that did not happen between 1995 and 2000 was a radical improvement in Japanese script input technology. Although PCs began to gain ground over JWPs during this period, we can see that it was not because of greater satisfaction with transcriptive input. We can do this by applying the same kind of analysis we just performed on PCs and JWPs to PCs and facsimile machines (Table 12). For the purpose of sending electronic messages, faxes and PCs overlap in function: you can write some-thing on a sheet of paper and transmit it "as is" (retaining the original) or type in your message and send it as e-mail. Fax technology languished in the West but was aggressively developed by Japanese companies pre-cisely because it accommodates handwritten material (Negroponte 1995, pp. 187–189). Prior to 1995, the expense of fax machines and the need to attach them to existing phone lines made them unattractive to nonbusi-ness consumers. But after 1995, as large numbers of households consid-ered buying PCs, many weighed that option against buying a fax because their main goal was communications, not computing.

Unlike JWPs—which functionally are just stripped-down special-purpose PCs—the trade-offs between fax machines and PCs are more complex: fax machines obviously can't do spreadsheets, databases, and

Table 12. Percentage of Japanese Households Owning Fax Machines and Personal Computers

1990		PC	No PC		
		10.6	89.4		
Fax	**2.0**	0.2	1.8		
No Fax	98.0	10.4	87.6		
1995		PC	No PC	Change	1990–1995
		15.6	84.4		
Fax	**10.0**	1.6	8.4	1.3	6.7
No Fax	90.0	14.0	76.0	3.7	−11.7
2000		PC	No PC	Change	1995–2000
		38.6	61.4		
Fax	**32.9**	12.7	20.2	11.1	11.8
No Fax	67.1	25.9	41.2	11.9	−34.8
2001		PC	No PC	Change	2000–2001
		50.1	49.9		
Fax	**35.5**	17.8	17.7	5.1	−2.5
No Fax	64.5	32.3	32.2	6.4	−9.0

Note: Figures in bold are taken from Economic Planning Agency reports; others are calculated.

other computational tasks; but they can accept messages at no extra charge (as long as the line isn't busy) whereas a PC must be connected to a network server in order to send or receive e-mail. Most important, fax machines don't require transcriptive input; until very recently, putting handwritten graphics into PC files and sending them via e-mail was a difficult and slow process, and even now it requires more than the standard package of software and peripheral hardware devices. From this perspective, the fact that in 2000 and 2001 the percentage of Japanese households with a fax, whether or not they owned a PC, exceeded the percentage with only a PC is telling. It shows that consumers are still not comfortable enough with the technology currently available for inputting Japanese script to exploit their PCs in the way their American, European, and Australasian counterparts do.

NETWORKING EAST ASIA

But beyond the input problem, Japanese also must deal with a sociolinguistic fact of life: not many non-Japanese take the time and trouble to learn to read and write Japanese well enough to use any kind of JWP technology, understand Japanese Internet postings, or make productive use of them. One must wonder whether Japanese can ever become a language of international electronic communication unless romanization becomes an alternative to customary script, at least in cyberspace. "There are now 14.2 million [Internet] users each of Spanish and Japanese," notes Nanette Gottlieb (2000, p. 185). But whereas there are many nations in which Spanish is the principal language, there is only one Japan—and for the very reasons that Japanese native speakers find JWP helpful, the written form of their language remains a daunting challenge for most foreigners. According to a 1998 survey of American universities, where Japanese has risen to fifth place among foreign languages, Italian had more students—and Spanish, which is now virtually the second domestic language of the United States, was an order of magnitude more popular than Italian. In short: aside from themselves, Japanese can't expect to have many Internet users to communicate with so long as they insist on using Chinese characters for every kind of writing they do. (Table 13 shows the distribution of Internet servers in Asia.)

The same conclusion is suggested by a survey conducted by the Carnegie Foundation for the Advancement of Teaching. From 1991 to 1993, the foundation asked 20,000 faculty members in fourteen nations, where the university systems were judged "relatively comparable," to rank the quality of support they receive at their home institutions. Table 14 shows the percentage in each country who rated the item shown in each heading as "good" or "excellent" at their own institution.

If you look at the rightmost column in Table 14, you can see that professors in Japan and South Korea were not as pleased with their institution's library holdings as professors in Hong Kong. This finding reflects the well-known fact that in countries where Chinese characters are traditionally used, libraries are relatively underdeveloped; Hong Kong is an exception because it is highly bilingual. Note that when faculty were asked to rate computer facilities (leftmost column), Japan and South Korea were again near the bottom of the list while Hong Kong was near the top; the same pattern shows up in the ratings of teaching technology and research equipment, where computer software often plays a role. Why should the ratings be low in Japan and South Korea yet high in Hong Kong? Again the most likely explanation is dissatisfaction with software for handling Chinese characters. In this case, the conclusion is strength-

Table 13. Distribution of Internet Servers in Asia

Location	Number of Servers	
	Total	Per 10,000 Population
Singapore	8,208	29
Hong Kong	15,392	26
Japan	159,776	13
Taiwan	16,166	8
South Korea	23,791	5
Malaysia	1,087	0.6
Thailand	2,481	0.4
Indonesia	848	0.04
China	1,023	0.009

Source: Asahi Shinbun, 1 November 1995.

ened by the fact that in terms of culture and academic life, Hong Kong has much in common with Japan and South Korea except for the much greater extent to which English is used.

In short, the realities of computer and Internet use let us look at the myth of the ideogram from a fresh perspective. Anyone who wants to claim that Chinese characters, and only Chinese characters, make it possible for educated people throughout East Asia to communicate with each either despite ignorance of their respective languages must eventually come to grips with a simple fact: so far only English, with all its awful spellings, idioms, and dialects, has approached the status of a genuinely universal cyberspace language. Of course, this fact has much to do with the history of the second half of the twentieth century, Hollywood, television, rock-and-roll, airport culture, Microsoft, coca-colonization, and

Table 14. Percentage of Faculty Members Rating Support as Good or Excellent

Computer Facilities		Teaching Technology		Research Equipment		Library Holdings	
Netherlands	69	Hong Kong	61	Netherlands	57	Netherlands	66
Hong Kong	69	Netherlands	59	Sweden	50	Sweden	62
Sweden	68	United States	48	Germany*	46	Germany*	53
United States	61	Sweden	47	Hong Kong	44	United States	50
Germany*	60	Germany*	44	United States	42	Hong Kong	49
Israel	56	Australia	36	England	31	Australia	40
Australia	53	Mexico	33	Australia	28	Russia	39
England	48	England	30	Mexico	22	Mexico	39
Mexico	43	Israel	29	Israel	22	Israel	38
Chile	33	Chile	22	Brazil	15	England	37
Japan	25	Russia	18	Chile	15	Brazil	34
Brazil	25	Japan	14	Japan	14	Japan	31
Russia	15	South Korea	9	South Korea	9	Chile	22
South Korea	13	Brazil†		Russia	7	South Korea	7

* Includes only institutions in the former West Germany.
† Data not available.
Note: Data have been sorted to make it easy to see relative ranks of countries where Chinese characters are used.
Source: Chronicle of Higher Education Almanac, 1 September 1995, p. 33.

all the other distinctive features of this waiting-for-Star-Trek world we inhabit. Still, the humble QWERTY keyboard plays a role. For all its well-known design faults, including a blatant bias in favor of English, it's a virtual standard and makes touch-typing possible—and that is enough. After all, we still reckon that circles have 360 degrees of arc for no better reason than that's the way the Babylonians did it thousands of years ago.[4]

9 Converging strands: can "ideogram" be salvaged?

McLuhan was overstating the case when he claimed that "until writing was invented, man lived in acoustic space." What he should have said was that until writing was invented, *language* lived in acoustic space. In a preliterate culture, the world of language is the world of sound. Writing changes all that. With writing, language *invades the world of visual communication*. It enters into competition—and partnership—with pictorial images of all kinds. The integration of writing with speech is what ushers in the misguided concept of language as something that is medium-transferable: sounds . . . can be spoken, "transferred" into a different form where they are visible but no longer audible, and then "transferred" back again into speech. [Harris 2000, pp. 235–236]

THE EMERGING PARADIGM

If in the preceding chapters I have been severe in criticizing those who think that Chinese writing is ideographic or that Chinese characters always function logographically, it is partly because there are much better approaches to understanding the aspects of Chinese characters that sustain the Ideographic Myth. In Chapter 7, I introduced such an approach by drawing an analogy between the notions of subjective probability and private meaning. To put the idea in a nutshell, it's all right to say that a red, octagonal stop sign is an ideogram—provided that you don't claim there is an abstract Platonic universal STOP that the sign embodies or represents. In other words: you get to say that a stop sign functions ideographically if and only if members of a culture, which has rules about how to behave when you see a stop sign, follow these rules appropriately in a given context.

Context is important because each instance of encountering a stop sign is unique. Although many encounters are similar to one another, exceptions that prove the rule sometimes occur. A schizophrenic may claim the stop sign is a burning bush from which God speaks to him. If a hurricane hurls an uprooted stop sign into a jungle, where it is chanced upon by someone with no experience of automobiles, roads, English, manufacturing, or paint, there's no telling what she'll make of it, literally or figuratively. That archaeologists in the distant future might very well misunderstand the function of an unearthed stop sign is amply demonstrated by the way twentieth-century archaeologists misunderstood Mayan civilization until the breakthrough decipherment of Mayan writing. On any particular occasion, the sign "means" what it does because of the biological, social, and circumstantial constraints entailed by the context of the occasion. Though I may use linguistic shorthand like "You know it means 'stop!'" it is impossible for me to crawl into your head and get a certain idea of what you're thinking when you see a stop sign. I can only make educated guesses—on the basis of your behavior on specific occasions—that what I take as a sign, you do too, and that it does (or does not) work for us, as a sign, in the same way.

This is a far cry from the concept of meaning that dominates much scientific and humanistic research today—the idea of meaning as the product of algorithms or collections of logical propositions that satisfy certain truth conditions—but it is not without its own intellectual tradition. Its roots can be traced back at least as far as anthropologists like Bronislaw Malinowski and linguists like John Firth. A wide range of scholars from several different disciplines have all, in their different ways, developed alternatives to the dominant view—alternatives that seem to be converging on a single coherent position. I hinted at this trend in Chapters 7 and 8 when I cited the ideas of Roy Harris, V. N. Vološinov, and Ronald Langacker. Since there are crucial differences among the theories of the many writers I have in mind, a full discussion of this alternative approach would take up a book by itself—indeed, Michael Toolan (1996) has already written one that does the job well. But to understand how these ideas relate to the problem of the Ideographic Myth, it is enough to give a sense of the essential issues by discussing just a few of these notions: dialogism, integrational semiology, and language/brain coevolution.

DIALOGISM

Writing after Stalin's rise to absolute power, Vološinov was obliged to lace his prose with gratuitous Marxist rhetoric and make obsequious references to Stalin's favorite linguist Nikolai Marr, whose ideas were as pseudoscientific as those of the notorious Trofim Lysenko, who set back Soviet biology for at least a generation. If we strip away this self-protective veneer, we are left with a theory of meaning that might be called dialogism. In this view, language is constantly in a state of becoming through conversational use. The myriad verbal exchanges among members of a speech community contribute to the unfolding of its language over time. Because language always involves dialogue, either real or virtual, monologic speech is the least representative kind of language and a poor basis upon which to build a theory of language.

Since Vološinov is, at the most superficial level, concerned with establishing a linguistics compatible with Marxism, he casts his theory as a dialectical synthesis of two earlier trends in linguistics. The "thesis," with which he is largely in sympathy, is represented by the views of the nineteenth-century German philologists Alexander von Humboldt and Karl Vossler—a "romantic" philosophy that Vološinov calls "individualistic subjectivism." It is characterized by the following four propositions:

1. Language is activity, an unceasing process of creation *(energeia)* realized in individual speech acts.
2. The laws of language creativity are the laws of individual psychology.
3. Creativity of language is meaningful creativity analogous to creative art.
4. Language as ready-made product *(ergon)*, as a stable system (lexicon, grammar, phonetics), is, so to speak, the inert crust, the hardened lava of language creativity, of which linguistics makes an abstract construct in the interests of the practical teaching of language as a ready-made instrument. [Vološinov 1973, p. 48][1]

These axioms stand in antithetical opposition to the "neoclassical" theory of Saussure, which Vološinov calls "abstract objectivism" and summarizes with four contrasting propositions:

1. Language is a stable, immutable system of normatively identical linguistic forms which the individual consciousness finds ready-made and which is incontestable for that consciousness.
2. The laws of language are the specifically linguistic laws of connection between linguistic signs within a given, closed linguistic system. These laws are objective with respect to any subjective consciousness.
3. Specifically linguistic connections have nothing in common with ideological values (artistic, cognitive, or other). Language phenomena are not grounded in ideological motives. No connection of a kind natural and comprehensible to the consciousness or of an artistic kind obtains between the word and its meanings.
4. Individual acts of speaking are, from the viewpoint of language, merely fortuitous refractions and variations or plain and simple distortions of normatively identical forms; but precisely these acts of individual discourse explain the historical changeability of linguistic forms, a changeability that in itself, from the standpoint of the language system, is irrational and senseless. There is no connection, no sharing of motives, between the system of language and its history. They are alien to one another. [Vološinov 1973, p. 57]

As one can guess from his pejorative use of "philologism" as an alternative name for this approach, Vološinov dwells longer on the inadequacies of abstract objectivism than on those of individualistic subjectivism. In the end, however, he conjoins the negations of both approaches to form the following synthesis:

1. Language as a stable system of normatively identical forms is merely a scientific abstraction, productive only in connection with certain particular practical and theoretical goals. This abstraction is not adequate to the concrete reality of language.
2. Language is a continuous generative process implemented in the social-verbal interaction of speakers.
3. The laws of the generative process of language are not at all the laws of individual psychology, but neither can they be divorced

from the activity of speakers. The laws of language generation are sociological laws.

4. Linguistic creativity does not coincide with artistic creativity nor with any other type of specialized ideological creativity. But, at the same time, linguistic creativity cannot be understood apart from the ideological meanings and values that fill it. The generative process of language, as is true of any historical generative process, can be perceived as blind mechanical necessity, but it can also become "free necessity" once it has reached the position of a conscious and desired necessity.

5. The structure of the utterance is a purely sociological structure. The utterance, as such, obtains between speakers. The individual speech act (in the strict sense of the word "individual") is *contradictio in adjecto*. [Vološinov 1973, p. 98][2]

Vološinov elaborates his understanding of meaning in this synthesis by distinguishing theme, meaning, and evaluation. Theme is, so to speak, the "upper limit" of semiotic content; meaning is its "lower limit." Theme is tied to the historical context of each act of communication, while "meaning is the technical apparatus for the implementation of the theme" (p. 100). The question "What time is it?" thus has a different theme each time it is asked, but its meaning remains the same on all occasions. These semiotic values do not, however, exhaust the significance of an utterance: the value judgment that each participant places on the utterance in context is an inseparable part of its significance for that participant. Two things flow from this requirement: first, verbal communication can never be divorced from the concrete situation in which it occurs; second, no synchronic description of a language corresponds to the reality of the language as experienced by any of its users. Together these conclusions deny the validity of Saussure's distinction of *langue* from *parole*—or, rather, imply that the notion of a purely synchronic *langue* is merely a useful fiction.

INTEGRATIONAL SEMIOLOGY

Whereas Vološinov wants, on the surface at any rate, to fashion a proper Marxist philosophy of language, Harris is concerned by the failure of linguists to pursue Saussure's call to embed linguistics within a more general theory of semiotics, or "semiology" as he prefers to call it. Consequently, Harris talks generally about communication, of which speech is just a special case. In fact, he relishes the opportunity, when it arises, to stress the creative potentials inherent in writing that are not found in speech. Nevertheless, his conclusions are strikingly similar to Vološinov's.

According to Harris, for example, three kinds of conditions—biomechanical, macrosocial, and circumstantial—are attendant upon each concrete communicative situation and constrain the way participants form, process, and interpret signs in that situation. The three activities of sign formation, processing, and interpretation correspond to Vološinov's theme, meaning, and evaluation, though Harris is more concerned about the activities themselves whereas Vološinov conceptualizes their outcomes.

Of particular interest are the macrosocial conditions, for they include social conventions such as language. Harris, like Vološinov, rejects the reality of a synchronic *langue.* Linguistic structures do not come with preassigned, invariant meanings—what Harris calls "fixed codes" and Vološinov calls "signals." Traffic lights are fixed codes: the metonymies "green is go" and "red is stop" are arbitrary and invariant. By analyzing the many different ways in which such fixed-code systems can fail to function, Harris shows that they "are invariably superimposed upon a natural *laissez-faire* situation, to which communication immediately reverts when the code breaks down" (1996, p. 250). Language is part of this "natural *laissez-faire* situation." To use fixed codes as a model for language, therefore, is to make the mistake of, in Vološinov's terms, building a theory starting from monologic speech.

In Harris' "integrational semiology," each participant in a communicative situation finds or rather creates signs in a context much as, in gestalt psychology experiments, the observer discovers what constitutes figure and what ground. The gestalt depends not only on the physical situation but also on the mental state and past experiences of the observer. The context as well as the signs (including their "meanings") do not exist outside the communicative situation, and there is no guarantee of their identity for different participants or even for the same participant on different occasions: "The sign does not exist outside the context which gives rise to it: there is no abstract invariant which remains 'the same' from one context to the next. Nor, *a fortiori,* is there any overarching Saussurean system to guarantee that invariance" (Harris 1996, p. 22).[3]

And lest there be any doubt, "there are no contextless signs" (Harris 2000, p. 81). Harris illustrates by contrasting a photograph of "an old-fashioned fingerpost" with a photo of a heap of "discarded signposts, complete with their lettering" and construction-site cones (pp. 90–92). In the first case (Figure 17), "the traveller's understanding of what a signpost is contributes to the semiological value of the written forms. The metal upright and the horizontal arm provide the installation for the text, thus turning what would otherwise be just sequences of letters into a message. This is not a simple conjunction of elements but a functional complementarity." In the second case (just a pile of junk), the signposts "survive as material objects long after having ceased to play a role in any system of communication. . . . [T]hey do not carry their semiological status around with them."

According to Harris, Aristotle got it right when he chose the word *"sumbolon"* for "sign." This Greek source of English "symbol" was "one half of an *astragalos* [knucklebone] or similar object that two *xenoi* or parties to a contract broke in two, each keeping half as proof of the contractual relationship" (Harris 2000, p. 23). The two halves had "no value at all individually." Only their relationship to each other mattered; one symbol does not represent or stand for the other:

> They are not identical, nor equivalent. Substituting one for the other is a meaningless operation. (It would leave things exactly as they were.) Nor is there any question of one half being a copy of the other. (On the contrary, it is important that they should differ.) The whole point is that they are both *different* and *unique*. Both their dif-

Figure 17. Harris' road sign.

ference and their uniqueness are united in their complementarity. [2000, p. 24]

Aristotle thus distinguished representation from symbolism. And so, says Harris, should we:

> Signs . . . are not pairings of form and meaning already set up in some pre-established code. They arise from actual events and circumstances in which the participants are involved. Thus, in a particular situation, *any* object, action, etc. can acquire a semiological value. [Notice the similarity with DeFrancis and Unger's rebuttal to Sampson in Chapter 2.] Furthermore, it is not essential that all the participants should agree on what that value is, or even agree on which particular features of a given communication situation have such a value. On the contrary, everyday life is full of situations which are of such semiological complexity as to defy any definitive interpretation, whether by the participants or by an observer-analyst. [2000, pp. 81–82]

Harris classifies signs as emblems, tokens, and duplex signs (signs that are both emblems and tokens simultaneously).[4] He uses the example of Robinson Crusoe's "calendar" to illustrate the token/emblem distinction. If Crusoe had made a notch in a stick each day, the notches would have been mere tokens of the days. Their exact shape and placement on the stick do not matter; the crucial thing is that Crusoe makes one notch every day without fail. But if he makes the notches in a linear order along the length of the stick and makes the notch for each Sunday consistently longer than the rest (as Defoe says he does), then the notches become emblems as well as tokens; long notches are emblematic of sabbaths, short notches of ordinary days, in addition to being tokens of days in general. Emblems that aren't tokens also exist. But it is the fact that signs can function as tokens and emblems *simultaneously* that makes communication by means of signs possible. This ability of signs to be iconic and, at the same time, to objectify and integrate past experience with the present moment is what gives their use in communication the appearance of what Harris derisively calls "telementation." In reality, says Harris, as if echoing Vološinov's denial of Saussurean postulates, telementation is at most a useful fiction: no ideas or thoughts are actually carried by signs from one mind to another. Communication is just a name for the way each of us integrates his or her activities by means of signs.

From this standpoint, as noted in Chapter 7, certain kinds of writing can legitimately be said to be autonomous of speech—for example, pure emblems such as signatures (Harris 1995; 2000).[5] The category "writing" should, in Harris' view, be broad enough to include both glottic (transcriptional) and nonglottic varieties:

> Alphabetic writing is one form of language-based, or "glottic" writing. Reading this sentence aloud would be a trivially easy task for millions of people; but impossible for anyone—even if literate— who knew no English. Similarly, anyone who knows no Thai will be hard put to it to read a Thai newspaper (either aloud or silently), even though Thai writing is also alphabetic. These disparities are diagnostic indicators of glottic writing. However, the alphabet as such is not a glottic system. Furthermore, glottic writing is not the only kind of writing human ingenuity has devised. Musical and mathematical notation do not require any knowledge of English (or Thai), but they do require an understanding of the principles on which the notation is based. These principles, however, are quite different from those of glottic writing. Which is why you do not read a musical score or a mathematical table in the same way as you read this page (or any other page of glottic writing). [2000, pp. viii–ix]

This is very much in the spirit of McCloud's picture-plane theory (Chapter 2) and explains why Harris criticizes DeFrancis' (1989) distinction between partial and full writing (Harris 2000, p. 153) . For DeFrancis, nonglottic writing is just a contradiction in terms; for Harris, it makes no difference that musical notation fails to map the same realm as, say, the Chinese writing system because the purposes of musical notation and Chinese writing are different. He continues: "If anyone wants to insist that glottic writing has to do with speech, they are merely . . . harping on a tautology" (p. 201).

In keeping with this outlook, Harris takes pains to define what counts as writing in terms of specific physical properties.[6] He does not think that every human artifact or action constitutes a text, as Jacques Derrida and other postmodernists would claim. Nor does he believe that, say, written English is a complete and autonomous language distinct from spoken English, as such scholars as Josef Vachek have argued. It is simply that "all signs have a biomechanical basis, provided by the human body and its sensory equipment" (Harris 2000, p. 85). Therefore, "utilitarian" theories of literacy (Harris uses this term pejoratively) linking writing exclusively to the transcription of language are to be rejected.[7]

Harris' position therefore puts him at odds with linguists like DeFrancis, Hockett, and Bloomfield who see the primacy of speech in language as sufficient reason for focusing attention exclusively on glottic writing. Yet he also criticizes so-called autonomists such as Llorach, Lyons, Hjemslev, Uldall, and Vachek who (not all for the same reasons) claim that writing can function autonomously of speech:[8]

> There are no autonomous signs and no autonomous sign systems. Nor could there be. For signs exist only as contextualized products of particular communication situations. This applies as much to the written sign as to any other kind of sign. In the case of glottic writing the debate about "autonomy" is particularly futile, since the whole function of glottic writing is to act as an interface between biomechanically different modes of communication. [2000, pp. 201–202]

The essence of Harris' criticism is that both speech-primacy and autonomist theories rely on the idea of representation. According to Harris, the notion of representation is neither necessary nor salutary for a theory of semiology. After all, communication does not necessarily require intent:

> Intentional theories of communication in effect rule out of court whole areas of semiological experience—perhaps even the greater part of social interaction—in order to focus on cases where it seems plausible to assess the success or failure of the enterprise by reference to the purposes of its initiator (insofar as these can be ascertained). An integrational theory of communication, by contrast, views this as an unwarranted adoption of one participant's point of view. [1996, p. 65]

For the same reason that Harris rejects both the "utilitarian" and autonomist approaches to language, he also rejects the two best-known hypotheses about how writing and speech interrelate in literate societies:

> According to one, writing serves to record linguistic units and structures already recognized by speakers of the language in question. According to the other, writing itself serves as the model for the recognition of such units and structures.

What neither hypothesis offers is a direct answer to the question of *how* the written sign comes to play the role hypothetically assigned to it. [2000, p. 211]

It is only by abandoning the notion of representation that we find the correct answer: "Any graphic configuration acquires a certain linguistic value insofar as it serves to articulate the integration of one form of verbal activity with another, or verbal activities and non-verbal activities" (ibid.). Writing and speech thus fit together like the two *sumbola:* one does not represent or parallel the other.

For all his discussion of emblems and tokens, Harris for the most part explains how one goes about doing integrational semiology only indirectly—by showing how "segregational" theories that view signs as ready-made representations fail to account for all the facts in pragmatically rich situations. Bradd Shore (1996), an anthropologist, engages current methodologies more directly. His goal is to develop a theory that reunites psychology with anthropology by bridging the gap between culture and the mind of the individual. Like Vološinov, Shore finds the two dominant views of language (in his case, Frege's "realism" and Saussure's "nominalism") at an impasse and strives for a synthesis. Like Harris, Shore sees meaning as something constructed by individuals, not as a kind of mental currency passed from mind to mind:

> Culture theory has been beset by a false choice between nominalist and realist theories of meaning. Extreme forms of realism reduce cultural systems to their real-world adaptive functions and stress the ultimate referential character (and thus the empirical motivation) of cultural symbolism. Extreme nominalism, by contrast, emphasizes the relative freedom of cultural forms from real-world constraints and the conventional and contextual motivation of cultural symbols. Neither approach deals in any significant way with *psychogenic motivation,* with culture as a property of a particular mind. [Shore 1996, p. 332; emphasis added]

This lacuna can be filled, according to Shore, by adopting an approach to meaning construction that combines Lakoff's theory of metaphor (Lakoff and Johnson 1980) and categorization (Lakoff 1987) with insights gained from connectionist work in computer science. Notably, however, Shore qualifies his enthusiasm for the Lakoff-Johnson approach in ways that echo Harris' concerns: "what happened to the individual?" (p. 334). Are metaphors and categories the same for all members of a speech community? And why is speech accorded a privileged position?

Similarities with Vološinov and Harris are seen in other of Shore's remarks:

> For native speakers, the *experience of linguistic signs* is transformed from one of historical arbitrariness to one of virtual psychological identity. Whatever linguists tell us about the arbitrariness of our words, any native speaker knows better. In our experience, our words do not *represent* concepts: they *present* them in a wholly transparent way. . . . [N]ative speakers do not normally speak *in* their language, but *through* it. [p. 357]

This notion of speaking "through language" is close to Harris' "natural *laissez-faire*" state of communication. Indeed, Shore's search for a unified theory of meaning construction by the individual and the culture in their environmental setting is paralleled by Harris' identification of biomechanical, macrosocial, and circumstantial constraints on the use of signs.

LANGUAGE/BRAIN COEVOLUTION

The approach of Terrence Deacon (1997), a neuroscientist, differs greatly from those of Harris and Shore, yet his conclusions about how signs work are remarkably similar. Deacon thinks the arguments advanced by Pinker (1994), Bickerton (1990), and others for an innate "language acquisition device" (LAD) and "universal grammar" are based on a naive view of how evolution works. Patterns of behavior like language, he points out, evolve in a quasi-organismic way — and at rates many orders of magnitude faster than actual organisms do. Furthermore, syntax is what makes it possible for us to mold language instantly to any unforeseen situation. Yet adaptations arise only when nature presents countless generations with the same challenges, which reproductively successful members of a species meet in the same way.

These facts make it difficult to explain how an innate LAD and universal grammar could have come into existence — and postulating an innate LAD and universal grammar is by no means the only way to account for the ease of language acquisition by children or the existence of linguistic universals. On the contrary, it makes more sense, Deacon argues, to see the rapidity of early language acquisition and the existence of universals across languages as products of *language* evolution rather than human evolution. Just as the biological species alive today are only a small fraction of all those that have ever lived, the languages we can observe today, for all their glorious variety, most likely represent the descendants of only the most successful attempts at linguistic behavior. (Remember that writing and historical linguistics permit us to see back into the past only a few thousand years and not always with complete clarity.) It is reasonable to assume that the facility with which children pick up the language of their surroundings, whatever it may be, and the common features that all languages seem to share are due to the fact that languages that did not afford ease of acquisition or the right features fell into disuse tens of thousands of years ago.

Deacon thinks that the proper evolutionary time frame for language and its precursors is on the order of 2 million years, during which time countless innovations were tried and discarded.[9] Since those features of language to which the universal grammar is claimed to give rise are precisely the ones that endow language with its mercurial flexibility, they cannot, Deacon argues, be the product of the evolution of bodies and brains. If there is anything innate in the brain other than our ability to handle the acoustical and articulatory aspects of language, it is not syntax but a more fundamental capacity for symbolic thinking. Deacon shows how all of the many physical and cognitive adaptations necessary for language follow from the coevolution of language and brain in hominids who started to use simple symbol systems.[10]

Symbol for Deacon is the third of Charles Peirce's well-known triad of icon, index, and symbol—that is, signs motivated by similarity, by spatial or temporal correlation, or by convention. Deacon is more liberal than Harris on the question of what things or behaviors can be used as signs. But on the crucial point—that signhood is in no way intrinsic to the signs themselves—they are in agreement. Many animals make use (whether consciously or not) of quite complex iconic and indexical signs. In biological terms, the perception of similarity is nothing but the failure to perceive certain differences. The body of a praying mantis, for example, which looks like a twig, functions successfully as an icon if a potential predator fails to distinguish it from other twigs.[11] Indices involve three icons: the category of referents, the category of indices that co-occur spatially or temporally with the members of the referent category, and the category of relevant correlations. In the case of smoke as an index for fire, for example, the organism must have categorical memories of smoke, fire, and smoke/fire co-occurrences; it is the association of the first two categories by way of the third that constitutes the index, and many organisms are capable of such associationistic learning.

Just as indices are built from icons, symbols are constructed from combinations of indices. This is a two-step process. First-order indices are grouped into second-order indices by virtue of certain pragmatic correlations. Vervet monkeys have different warning calls for eagles and for leopards, for example, corresponding to the fact that these predators typically attack from different directions (up from the ground, down from the sky). Each call is a first-order index. The broader category "warning call" (which vervet monkeys may or may not have) is a second-order index. As the number of first-order indices grows, the number of uncorrelated combinations among them (combinations with no pragmatic value) inevitably grows faster than the number of correlated combinations (combinations that do have some pragmatic value). That is, most of the possible combinations will never be needed because their correlates do not co-occur in the environment. Members of the group may therefore come to supplement keeping track of the constantly changing parameters of the environment (including their own behavior) with recall of just the combinations of first-order indices they experience. Associating these "proven" combinations with new indexical signs of their own (second-order indices) permits the continued expansion of the group's sign system in a more efficient way, saves mental effort, and allows each group member to benefit (at least potentially) from the alertness of other members of the group. Eventually a switch from mostly first-order to mostly second-order indexical sign use becomes advantageous. Deacon, using Frege's terms, describes this as a switch from reference to sense. ("The morning star" and "the evening star" have different senses but the same reference: the planet Venus.) It is when this switch takes place that the second-order indices become symbols and syntax (the semantically distinctive ordering of symbols) can emerge.

Only humans, among all animals, are adapted to the fundamentally different kind of learning involved in the use of symbols as opposed to icons and indices. This is clear from the fact that iconic or indexical relations can be changed or destroyed by altering or eliminating the motivating stimuli from an animal's environment—whereas symbolic connections, once learned, remain even when the motivating stimuli are absent or contrary stimuli are present. Deacon exemplifies this situation with the legend of the Boy Who Cried Wolf: the symbolic (linguistic) meaning of the boy's utterances is never in doubt, but their indexical value soon is. Higher primates, such as chimpanzees and bonobos, can be taught symbolic systems if exposed to lengthy multistage training regimens at a sufficiently early age, but such conditions are absent in their natural environments. Indeed, it is far from easy to imagine what sort of environmental conditions could have led to the rise of symbolic learning in our immediate human ancestors, though we know such conditions must have existed. (We need not go into Deacon's conjectures about them.)

It should be clear that this theory of signs is very similar to Harris'. Deacon's symbols, indices, and icons are more or less Harris' duplex signs, emblems, and tokens. (Frege's sense/reference distinction thus parallels Deacon's index/icon and Harris' emblem/token distinctions.) The role Deacon accords to the individual interpretation of signs in context fits Harris' notion of integration closely, and nowhere does Deacon slip in semantic invariants. The differences between Deacon and Harris seem to result from the former's concern with evolution—which predisposes him to think of signs in nature prior to the advent of distinctively human cognition—and the latter's preoccupation with the relationship between speech and writing, which predisposes him to ignore evolutionary questions. These differences are, I believe, superficial. We should not let them obscure the much larger differences between both Deacon and Harris, on the one hand, and those on the other who espouse the orthodox context-independent concept of meaning, most recently seen in cognitivist approaches to language.[12]

DEATH OF THE IDEOGRAM

It is remarkable that scholars coming from backgrounds as diverse as those of Vološinov, Harris, Shore, and Deacon (I could have introduced more) have, in their various ways, come up with a theory of communication in which there is neither a need for nor a possibility of knowing, with certainty, what precisely constitutes meaning in the minds of others. Each in a different way highlights how we mislead ourselves by speaking of signs as representational. And this, of course, is why this excursion into their theories is so valuable: no representation of thoughts implies no ideograms. By suggesting a way to liberate semiotic theory from reliance on the notion of representation, however, these theories throw open the door to an appreciation of what Harris calls nonglottic writing, which some might like to characterize as ideographic writing under a different name. But Harris' nonglottic writing is unencumbered by the dead hand of the Ideographic Myth.

By introducing the distinction between subjective meanings (what Vološinov would call theme) and the lexical conventions of language ("literal meanings"), and by refusing to subordinate the former to the latter in a general theory of human communication, this alternative approach explains in an intuitively appealing way why languages and cultures are ever-changing and robust behavioral systems. It provides a natural reason for the historical continuity of languages and cultures despite the innumerable differences among the people who sustain them. It eliminates the mystery of why the allegedly perfect computational machinery of language production and comprehension running in individual brains should get bogged down in misunderstanding and ambiguity with such regularity. It makes clear why one culture does not instantly fall to pieces upon contact with another.

Thus, at the deepest level, the lesson we should learn from the mythology that has grown up around Chinese characters is one that transcends the particulars of East Asian history and comparative studies of cultures. As Harris says: "How people think about writing is bound up in many subtle ways with how they think about their fellow human beings. There is more to rethinking writing than just looking for a more satisfactory intellectual analysis of particular communicational practices" (2000, p. viii). Once we see that the infrastructure of Platonic meanings to which ideograms allegedly refer is a fiction, we can see that the search for disembodied intelligence that has become so important in our postindustrial world is fundamentally misguided. If we someday perfect computers smart enough to fool us into believing that they actually think, it will only be because they never produce strings of symbols that tip us off to their artificiality. Magicians may be entertained, smitten with admiration, even baffled when they see their colleagues perform, but they know they are watching a trick. With computers, the challenge is remembering that the apparatus would not exist without us. There may come a time when nothing will prevent us from interpreting what computers have to tell us any differently from what our in-laws or coworkers, our friends or our enemies, tell us. At that point, we will have only ourselves to blame if we are foolish enough to ascribe humanity to our artifacts. For they will no more be capable of exercising free will than a Chinese character is capable of meaning something in an empty universe.

Notes

Introduction

1. For those eager to read Chinese dinner menus, there is no handbook more sophisticated in matters linguistic or culinary than the late James D. McCawley's *The Eater's Guide to Chinese Characters* (1984).

Chapter 1 Agony and bliss

1. Or to quote the jolting warning my colleague Galal Walker gives students: "If you study Chinese with the goal of making Chinese listen to the same stuff you say in English to Americans, you're just learning how to piss off a billion people the hard way."

2. The claim is actually more invidious than this because it implies that speakers of any other so-called monosyllabic language (such as Vietnamese) who do not write their language with Chinese characters necessarily inhabit a world of dysfunctional literacy. This is probably why some writers go beyond mere indispensability to argue that the Chinese writing system is actually superior in some way to all others.

3. As Baron explains: if one uses a cutoff of 65 percent (the standard now used with American schoolchildren), only 13 percent of the 1992 sample of adults end up in the lowest level. To eliminate the chance that subjects assigned to the lowest level could perform the test tasks in nontest situations, the cutoff needs to be lowered to 20 percent, at which point the lowest level comprises only 5 percent of the sample.

4. It is said that when Descartes explained to the brilliant Queen Christina of Sweden that people were really nothing more than elaborate watchworks, she remarked that she had never seen a watch give birth to baby watches. A bright student!

5. In India, by contrast, where the Vedic scriptures were traditionally passed down by oral memorization, the theory of Sanskrit phonology and morphology was highly developed by the middle of the first millennium BCE. Korean and Japanese scholars, who had to learn literary Chinese much as educated Europeans once had to learn Latin and were sometimes concerned with the proper sound of words related to Buddhism, showed somewhat greater curiosity about the workings of language than the Chinese.

Chapter 2 **Cryptograms vs. pictograms**

1. For more details see Michael D. Coe's succinct "Spillover to the Americas: The Ideographic Myth as a Barrier to Deciphering Maya Writing" (Erbaugh 2002, pp. 225–227).

2. To use a greatly simplified example, the ancestor of the Hebrew letter מ, Greek M and μ, Roman M and m, was originally a picture of water, a word that coincidentally began in ancient Semitic languages with an [m] sound (a bilabial nasal): the breakthrough idea was seeing that one could use the letter to represent not just water but the sound [m] wherever it occurred in words. All letters in the world's "old" alphabetic or syllabic systems of writing (that is, excluding historically recent inventions) arose from pictograms in this way.

3. Elkins adds: "Examples of notations are heraldry, graphs, charts, and other maps, tables, and mathematical notation" (p. 257).

4. Note that speech is generally necessary to make such prearrangements. Thus even if semasiographic writing systems existed, one wonders how their alleged autonomy from speech could ever be established with certainty.

5. We need to speak of first languages, not just a first language, because bilingualism is widespread. Acquisition differs from learning not only because it happens during one's first encounter with a certain kind of knowledge and skill set but also because it happens while one is passing through a unique stage of physical development and social relationships that do not occur again later in life.

6. I cannot resist interjecting that Robert A. Heinlein (1907–1988), a giant among science fiction writers, fully understood and made good use of this fact in his classic novel *The Moon Is a Harsh Mistress,* a story of how exiled convicts and their descendants on the Moon successfully win their independence in 2076. In chapter 12, the one-armed computer technician Manuel O'Kelly Davis explains (in lunar dialect) why a fellow conspirator needed to smuggle a codebook Earthside:

> A cipher can be incredibly subtle, especially with help of a computer. But ciphers all have weakness that they are patterns. If one computer can think them up, another computer can break them.
>
> Codes do not have same weakness. Let's say that codebook has letter group GLOPS. Does this mean "Aunt Minnie will be home Thursday" or does it mean "3.14157 . . ."?
>
> Meaning is whatever you assign and no computer can analyze it simply from letter group. Give a computer enough groups and a rational theory, involving meanings or subjects for meanings, and it will eventually worry it out because meanings themselves will show patterns. But is a problem of different kind on more difficult level. [Heinlein 1997, p. 173]

7. These facts were summarized by Ho-min Sohn in "Language Purification Movements in the Two Koreas," a lecture presented at the Association for Asian Studies annual meeting, Washington, D.C., 4–7 April 2002. Much of the vacillation

in South Korean policy seems to have been prompted by the desire to distance the South from the North; whatever the reason for reintroducing characters in the North, which is unclear, the cumulative effect of educational policies on both sides of the 38th parallel has been to make it quite unlikely that *hanja* will play a significant role in the everyday lives of Koreans if and when the country is reunified.

8. Note the importance of clear terminology in this analysis. Examples of confused definitions can be found in Elkins: "*Semasiographic* and *glottographic* are *near synonyms* for a number of other pairs, the commonest of which is *logographic* and *phonetic*" (1999, p. 126; emphasis added). A code is "a system of conventional signs (such as letters) given unusual denotations or a system of invented signs. Codes can depend on more *intricate* rules than ciphers" (1999, p. 254; emphasis added). Unless Elkins means arbitrary or unpredictable by "intricate," which is not clear, this is simply false. A cipher is "a code in which the unusual *denotations* are explained or generated by a *key* (that is, a single formula or table of correspondences)" (ibid.; emphasis added). But in a cipher, words are not replaced by other words ("denoted"), and it is common to write out ciphertext using five- or six-letter groups to disguise true word boundaries; moreover, not all ciphers use a "key," which in cryptography refers specifically to an auxiliary word or phrase employed in conjunction with the rules of the cipher.

9. In the widely used terminology of Charles S. Peirce, an icon is a sign that resembles what it represents—a sense completely inappropriate for McCloud's purpose, which is to overcome the dichotomy between picture and language.

10. It is particularly fitting to contrast McCloud's theory with Elkins'. The closer an image is to McCloud's Language Border, the more it is what Elkins would call a notation. The closer to the apex of the triangle, the less latitude exists for distinctively picture-like or writing-like formatting. But McCloud does not let his notion of iconicity get in the way of seeing that line *CO* is a *border*. He is thus ready to accept DeFrancis' definition of writing, whereas Elkins, struggling to explain a deep semiotic continuity between pictures and writing (that is, prove the border doesn't really exist), falls into the same trap as Sampson, though each chooses different examples of "semasiography."

Chapter 3   The Great Wall of China and other exotic fables

1. Lest one think that this instance of left-brain/right-brain pseudoscience is an isolated case, one may recall Tsunoda Tadanobu, who in the 1980s claimed to have proved through stimulus/response key-tapping experiments that people who speak Japanese or languages with few consonants, such as Maori and Tongan, between the ages of six and eight end up processing sounds in their brains differently from people who speak other languages during these critical ages. Tsunoda has since faded from view because no one could replicate his experiments, a difficulty he came to attribute to phases of the moon and other celestial phenomena. Those seeking a Chinese example should read Moser (2001).

2. The key is to use the anatomical fact that many of the nerve pathways ending in the left hemisphere of the brain originate on the right side of the body and vice

versa. By presenting conflicting stimuli to the left/right ears or left/right visual fields and seeing which tend to dominate over many trials, one builds up a statistical case for right/left hemisphere dominance in the mental processing needed to produce the correct responses to the stimuli.

Chapter 5   How would a magician memorize Chinese characters?

1. Lorayne doesn't use phonetic notation and is a little vague on the details. Judging from examples in the book, it appears that the digraph ⟨th⟩ is treated as if it were /t/ + /h/; likewise, ⟨ng⟩ is taken as /n/ + /g/, at least when pronounced as in "finger" (compare "singer").

2. There are of course rare individuals, like the Indian prodigy Srinivasa Ramanujan (1887–1920), for whom numbers seem to have had individual personalities. The British mathematician J. E. Littlewood famously recalled "once going to see him when he was lying ill at Putney. I had ridden in taxicab number 1729, and remarked that the number seemed to me rather a dull one, and that I hoped it was not an unfavorable omen. 'No,' he replied, 'it is a very interesting number; it is the smallest number expressible as the sum of two cubes in two different ways' " (Hardy, 1967, p. 37). If you have memorized the first dozen cubes, you might notice that $1,729 = 1,728 + 1 = 12^3 + 1^3 = 1,000 + 729 = 10^3 + 9^3$. But unless Ramanujan was simply recalling a result he had found at leisure earlier, it is remarkable he could assert *immediately* that no smaller integer can be likewise partitioned.

3. Hunt (1982, p. 114) describes another, simpler "peg" system, which uses rhymes: one ~ *bun;* two ~ *shoe;* three ~ *tree;* four ~ *door;* and so forth. Notice that it too relies on phonetic similarities.

4. In reality, the so-called meanings of *kanji* are just a by-product of how they are used in Japanese orthography. It is the morphemes of Japanese that convey meaning; the *kanji,* which sometimes represent a string longer or shorter than a whole morpheme, merely pick it up by association.

5. It is not so clear what the tag would be for the word *"baka"* 馬鹿 (dunce, fool). If 馬 is "horse," then 鹿 must be "deer"—but that, as the expression goes, doesn't add up. Words like this illustrate the dangers of thinking that every *kanji* has a fixed core meaning.

6. 莫, read *"mò"* in Chinese and *"bo"* or *"baku"* in Japanese, stands for what Chinese grammarians aptly call an "empty word" in contrast to semantically pregnant nouns, verbs, and adjectives, which are "full words." It marks rhetorical negative questions or phrases; hence the adjectival phrase 莫大 (Ch. *mòdà,* J. *bakudai,* "enormous"; that is, "surely none greater").

7. Indeed, in modern Chinese 書 serves to write *"shū"* (book), a noun, and in Japanese only the invariant *"ka"* part of *"kaku,"* which has dozens of other grammatical forms *(kakō, kaita, okaki ni narimasu, kakaserarenakattara).*

8. Interestingly, for *on* or Sino-Japanese readings of *kanji,* Heisig relies heavily on the fundamental fact that most *kanji* contain phonetic elements that provide a cue to

the syllables in the reading. He does this in full knowledge that this signific-phonetic analysis is often at odds with the mnemonic linking stories he develops in vol. 1.

9. In fact a whole act can be developed around this one technique, as described in Hugard and Crimmins (1961, pp. 426–445). Although the phonetic code and peg words are different from Lorayne's, the mnemonic techniques are identical. To the uninitiated, the order of the cards looks totally random—and therefore impossible to memorize—but it can be memorized and is, moreover, carefully designed to enable a number of effects beyond those that depend on knowing the location of every card. Using false shuffles that leave the order of the cards undisturbed, the magician can, for example, miraculously deal himself unbeatable hands in hearts, bridge, or poker.

10. On the fallacy of thinking that memorizing a *kanji* dictionary is sufficient for reading Japanese see Eleanor H. Jorden, "Teaching Johnny to Read Japanese: Some Thoughts on Chinese Characters" (Erbaugh 2002, pp. 92–104). Jorden distinguishes reading from mere "decoding" and "*kanji* hopping." As for winning at poker see Wallace (1977).

Chapter 6 Lord Chesterfield and the Mandarins

1. The proliferation of the desktop PC also led to the demise of keypunch operators; typing, however, remained a vital skill.

2. The percentage of "whole-word" *kanji* in Japanese texts is commonly exaggerated. *Kanji* that do not correspond to whole words usually represent only part of a word; in Gregg, by contrast, non–"whole-word" characters generally represent a multiword phrase.

3. Again, in Chinese, the number of such characters is greatly exaggerated. In the case of Japanese, the use of *kanji* to stand for (parts of) native morphemes increases the number of cases in ordinary texts in which this insufficiency occurs, but this is compensated for by the context provided by *kana*, which disambiguates *kanji* readings in most cases.

Chapter 7 Where do hunches come from?

1. See the end of this chapter for another example and further discussion.

2. Roy Harris (1981) coined the handy term "telementation" to describe this view of how language works.

3. Braille is writing but sign language and electromechanical recordings of speech are not because writing is never an event or "kinetic." Musical scores and dance notations are writing but barcodes are not because only the former exploit relative as well as absolute locations in graphic space (involve "script," not just "chart"). Typographers' "greeking" (Rviqw xle ucw, . . .) is writing but drawings are not because written text must have certain "contrasts of proximity, alignment, size, inclination, and colour" (Harris 1995, p. 127) even when purposely contrived to lack linguistic significance.

4. By comparison, neither the algebraic fact that, for all $p > 0$ and all $q < 1$, $pq < p$, nor the relevance of this algebraic fact to the problem at hand is particularly obvious.

5. Even the legendary mathematician Paul Erdős was taken in by it (Schechter 1998, pp. 107–109).

6. In fact, if you're mathematically inclined you might generalize this conclusion and note that even if you got to mark, say, three boxes out of thirty at the start, you'd still be better off switching at the end. If I open all but one unmarked box, the odds of its having the money is 0.9 since the odds that *any* of the marked boxes contains the money is 0.1. If you must choose when there are three unmarked boxes remaining (the same number you marked at the start), you are three times more likely to get the money by blindly choosing one of them instead of one of your original three choices.

Chapter 8   In the basement under the Chinese Room

1. Indeed, I hedge on the word "represent" because when we say that a graph or chart "represents," for instance, the costs versus the revenues of a business, we tacitly assume that the constituent parts of the graph or chart correspond one-to-one with real, separable features of what is being represented. But this one-to-one relationship is precisely what is absent in the case of a hologram.

2. When precursors of connectionist models were proposed around the time that Chomsky's *Syntactic Structures* was becoming influential, they were attacked by Seymour Papert and Marvin Minsky, also at MIT, who claimed they could prove mathematically that such models could never emulate human intelligence. For critical comments on this episode see Crick (1994, pp. 181–182) and Johnson (1992, p. 143).

3. This amounts to saying that the four conditions (owning or not owning a JWP or a PC) were not entirely independent of one another. However, the inferred tabulated percentages are still probably valid as a rough first approximation to actual rates of ownership.

4. The Babylonians used a base-sixty counting system. A circle with a diameter 60 units long has a circumference 360 units long if you use the crude estimate $\pi \approx 3$; hence 360 degrees. The Greeks never bothered to change that even though it's impossible to construct an angle of less than 3 degrees with just an unmarked straightedge and compasses, their classical tools. Only lately have engineers started dividing the circle into 400 "grads" instead of 360 degrees.

Chapter 9   Converging strands

1. In this and the following passages quoted from Vološinov, he and his translators make excessive use of emphatic italics, which I have removed.

2. For Vološinov, "ideological" is virtually a synonym for "cognitive" in its modern sense. Point 4 seems to have been included to assure the reader that the synthesis is suitably Marxist. Points 1, 2, 3, and 5 are clearly the counterparts of points 1 through 4 in the previous summary statements.

3. This idea should not be confused with other recent theories of meaning. Barrett observes: "For the deconstructionist, the referential aspects of language—the claim that language refers to definite things, objects, people—are not the central fact

about language. More important in the case of any symbol are the multiple links it establishes with all other symbols within the whole symbolic matrix" (1986, p. 129). As Harris points out, this idea is as committed to the notion that signs are "surrogational"—that is, stand for or represent things—as the Saussurean idea of "difference" that it caricatures.

4. Token versus emblem, Harris' distinction, is very different from the token versus type distinction of the American logician Charles Sanders Peirce. To grasp token in Peirce's sense, think about counting words in a text. When you want to make sure that a document you're writing does not exceed 1,000 words, you need to count every token of a word in the text; if you want to know the size of Shakespeare's dramatic vocabulary, you need to count all the different words (types of words) in the plays.

5. What defines a signature is that it is produced by a particular individual and no other. It need not be a transcription of speech, nor absolutely uniform from instance to instance, yet a forgery is not an authentic signature. Thus provided that a signature is an authentic instance of writing, it "works" as a symbol by virtue of properties that are unrelated to the chunk of language with which someone might associate it.

6. See note 3 in Chapter 7.

7. In fact, Harris begins *Rethinking Writing* by saying: "An alternative title for this book might have been: *The Tyranny of the Alphabet and How to Escape from It*" (2000, p. vi). This has the unfortunate consequence of suggesting to some readers that "what Harris is mainly trying to do is completely separate writing from the oral language it supposedly stands for, and give it autonomous existence as a separate system of signs" (Ionita 2001, p. 192), which is not the case.

8. On this account, Hannas too would be an autonomist.

9. In the same way, the animals that live today represent the progeny of only a few of the many kinds of animals that flourished in the first great explosion of multicellular organisms millions of years ago, most of which can be regarded as failed evolutionary experiments (Gould 1989). Although we have no fossils of languages as we have of animals, we may imagine a similar pattern of evolution in which the modern diversity of forms—though astonishing in itself—is but the extension of a tiny slice of an earlier, totally different diversity left to us by a combination of evolutionary change and historical contingency.

10. One is reminded of Julian Jaynes' extraordinarily bold hypothesis (1976) that consciousness follows rather than precedes the origin of language. It is interesting that Jaynes, like Lakoff and Johnson, stresses the essential role of metaphor in language. (Of course, as Deacon explains, Jaynes' extremely late date for the rise of consciousness and his account of hemispheric lateralization are both contradicted by current understanding of brain function. And, as Lieberman remarks, hemispheric lateralizataion is not confined to humans.)

11. Harris (1997) criticizes the example of patterns on a moth's wings that protect the moth by resembling the eyes of a large animal, and it is certainly true that the moth is no more a willful former of signs than its would-be devourer is a conscious

interpreter of signs. Nevertheless, if such natural situations are not precursors to the *processing* of signs, then how can the human capacity to process signs, let alone form and interpret them, be explained in evolutionary terms?

12. Harris (1997) criticizes Deacon for using "reference" as a "catch-all term for any kind of recognised association. Thus, for anyone who knows what skunks smell like, the smell 'refers to' the skunk." But Deacon's use of Peirce's taxonomy of signs does not, as far as I can detect, commit him to saying that semiotic associations must be the same for all observers or that the category to which a sign "refers" is given a priori—and these are the points to which Harris (1996) objects in his critique of Peirce. Surely we don't want to say that when an animal smells a skunk and backs off, it necessarily goes through a mental process in which the odor serves as an indexical sign that conjures up a virtual skunk, the thought of which causes the backing off, but one cannot deny that the animal alters its behavior in response to a specific condition. If such frequently observed behavior in lower animals is not the precursor of the semiotic behavior of humans, one can only wonder what could be.

References

Books and Articles

Although the following list is far too idiosyncratic to qualify as a formal bibliography, I've included brief comments on those books that are most likely to help readers interested in the terrain explored in the text.

Agar, Michael. 1994. *Language Shock.* New York: Morrow. Agar asks the reader to draw a circle around what we think of as language proper: phonology, syntax—all that boring stuff you had to learn to pass high school French. But all the interesting things about language, says Agar, lie outside this circle. (Pinker says in effect that anyone who works outside the circle isn't doing linguistics.)

Ahmad, Aijaz. 1992. *In Theory: Classes, Nations, Literatures.* London: Verso. Ahmad's Marxist stance and rhetorical richness can be offputting, but his critique of postmodernist theory is right on target.

Baron, Dennis. 2000. "Will Anyone Accept the Good News on Literacy?" *Chronicle of Higher Education,* 1 February.

Baron, Naomi S. 1981. *Speech, Writing, and Sign.* Bloomington: Indiana University Press. History has shown that Baron was wrong about the role of phonographic elements in Mayan script, but she brings together many interesting examples of marginal kinds of writing and makes an honest if flawed attempt to craft an integrated, functional approach to semiotic behavior.

Barrett, William. 1986. *Death of the Soul: From Descartes to the Computer.* New York: Doubleday. Among Barrett's many insightful remarks, my favorite is: "In France any intellectual cause that attains sufficient notoriety is likely to end as a literary movement." Insofar as deconstructionism seems to be the last (or at least the latest) refuge of writers incapable of producing anything except literary criticism, I take this observation to mean that deconstructionism has outlived whatever usefulness it may have had.

Barry, Dave. 1992. *Dave Barry Does Japan.* New York: Random House.

Bickerton, Derek. 1990. *Language and Species.* Chicago: University of Chicago Press. Bickerton's book (like Pinker 1994) zeroes in on syntax, in Chomsky's sense, as the sine qua non of language. Unlike Pinker, who jeers at Benjamin Whorf, or Chomsky, who simply rules culture out of bounds for serious linguists, Bickerton has studied pidgins and creoles and tries to buttress the innatist position by showing that they reveal a primitive level of linguistic development in which the universal grammar is better exposed than in most "ordinary" languages. This approach has been challenged by other pidgin/creole researchers, who dispute some of Bickerton's factual claims, and by historical linguists, who point out that we are hardly in a position to identify "ordinary" versus creolized languages with the degree of confidence that Bickerton's theory seems to require.

Bruner, Jerome. 1990. *Acts of Meaning.* Cambridge, Mass.: Harvard University Press.

Bulmer, M. G. 1979. *Principles of Statistics.* New York: Dover.

Chen, Xiaomei. 1995. *Occidentalism: A Theory of Counter-Discourse in Post-Mao China.* New York: Oxford University Press.

Clarke, J. J. 1997. *Oriental Enlightenment: The Encounter Between Asian and Western Thought.* London: Routledge. Clarke traces the often incoherent development of Western thought about the East, particularly from India eastward, and shows that on balance Western romanticization of the East has been a "counter-movement . . . which in various ways has often tended to subvert rather than confirm the discursive structures of imperialist power" (p. 9). Clarke's broader perspective and his more nuanced historical approach make his study superior to Edward Said's celebrated *Orientalism.*

Coyaud, Maurice. 1985. *L'ambiguïté en japonais écrit* [Ambiguity in written Japanese]. Paris: Association Pour l'Analyse du Folklore. Though hard to find and in French, this book is a classic in a perverse way, proving that scholarly misunderstandings die hard. [Reviewed in *Journal of the Association of Teachers of Japanese* 30(2) (1998): 55–63.]

Crick, Francis. 1994. *The Astonishing Hypothesis: The Scientific Search for the Soul.* New York: Scribner's. This Nobel laureate, codiscoverer of DNA, is a consummate curmudgeon.

Deacon, Terrence W. 1997. *The Symbolic Species: The Co-evolution of Language and the Brain.* New York: Norton. [Reviewed in *Modern Language Journal* 82(3) (1998): 437–439.] Deacon deftly turns the innatist arguments of Chomsky and Pinker on their heads.

DeFrancis, John. 1984. *The Chinese Language: Fact and Fantasy.* Honolulu: University of Hawai'i Press. Without a doubt, the best one-volume introduction to Chinese linguistics for those readers of English who know no Chinese. DeFrancis tells the story of Gaspar da Cruz. DeFrancis used the term "digraphia" in an article of the same title in the journal *Word* 35(1) (1984):59–66. [Reviewed in *Journal of the Association of Teachers of Japanese* 20(2) (1986):232–240.]

———. 1989. *Visible Speech: The Diverse Oneness of Writing Systems.* Honolulu: University of Hawai'i Press. Besides unmasking the Yukaghir "love letter," this book is also notable for DeFrancis' critical review of writing system classifications, especially those of Archibald Hill and Geoffrey Sampson. In hindsight, trying to classify entire writing systems is probably not the best way to think of them, since within any writing system, different signs can function differently depending on context. (See Mark Hansell, "Functional Answers to Structural Problems in

Thinking About Writing," in Erbaugh 2002, pp. 124–176.) If one is unwilling to embrace Harris' (1996) semiotic approach to writing systems, there is no choice but to take DeFrancis'.

DeFrancis, John, and J. Marshall Unger. 1994. "Rejoinder to Geoffrey Sampson, 'Chinese Script and the Diversity of Writing Systems.'" *Linguistics* 32(3):549–554.

Devlin, Keith. 1997. *Goodbye, Descartes.* New York: Wiley. An enjoyable excursion into mathematics and logic taking a stance opposite to that of Piattelli-Palmarini (1994) yet sharing an implicit faith in the objectivity of mathematical concepts.

Donald, Merlin. 1991. *Origins of the Modern Mind: Three Stages in the Evolution of Culture and Cognition.* Cambridge, Mass.: Harvard University Press. Donald's speculations on the origins of culture are thoughtful and fascinating, but they are flawed toward the end by his needless digressions into the notion of ideogram. An interesting exercise is to consider how Donald's theory might be rewritten to eliminate this digression.

Dreyfus, Hubert L. 1993. *What Computers Still Can't Do: A Critique of Artificial Reason.* Cambridge, Mass.: MIT Press. The most recent edition of *What Computers Can't Do* (1973), this book deals more directly with the claims of AI researchers and reaches conclusions as devastating as Searle's.

Eco, Umberto. 1995. *The Search for the Perfect Language.* Translated by James Fentress. Oxford: Blackwell. Eco explains the context in which the Western fascination with Chinese characters took hold.

———. 1998. *Serendipities: Language and Lunacy.* Translated by William Weaver. New York: Columbia University Press. Chapter 3 of Eco's book (pp. 53–76) explains the Egyptian background that predisposed da Cruz, Kircher, Leibniz, and other key "proto-sinologues" to think of Chinese characters as hieroglyphic. Curiously, Eco fails to mention Müller or the fact that Chinese characters and Mayan writing were, like hieroglyphics, principally phonographic.

Eisenstein, Sergei. 1949. *Film Form: Essays in Film Theory.* Edited and translated by Jay Leyda. London: Dennis Dobson.

Elkins, James. 1999. *The Domain of Images.* Ithaca: Cornell University Press. As his discussion of the Yukaghir "love letter" suggests, Elkins is not always fit to judge the quality of the wide range of scholarship he surveys. Although the many examples of images he reproduces from the gray zone between writing and picture are thought-provoking, the dutiful references to philosophers from Derrida to Wittgenstein seldom add clarity to the discussion. Elkins uses the term "full writing" but doesn't cite DeFrancis, and he evades the question of whether or not the rebus principle is decisive in distinguishing writing from other kinds of drawing.

Ellis, John. 1993. *Language, Thought, and Logic.* Evanston, Ill.: Northwestern University Press. [Reviewed in *Times Higher Education Supplement* (London), 12 August 1994.]

Erbaugh, Mary E., ed. 2002. *Difficult Characters: Interdisciplinary Studies of Chinese and Japanese Writing.* Pathways to Advanced Skills Series, vol. 6. Columbus, Ohio: National East Asian Languages Resource Center. This anthology of papers might be thought of as a companion volume to this book. Besides Erbaugh's superb essay on the pretensions of French deconstructionism and Mark Hansell's chapter on a functional approach to writing systems, the chapter by Sachiko Matsunaga on Japanese psycholinguistics explaining eye-tracking experiments that corroborate Horodeck's findings (see my Chapter 3), and Ovid Tzeng and Daisy Hung's survey of other literature on the psycholinguistics of Chinese characters, are especially worthwhile.

Fenollosa, Ernest. [1936] 1968. *The Chinese Written Character as a Medium for Poetry.* Edited by Ezra Pound. San Francisco: City Lights. There was a time when aspiring writers could be excused for using this starry-eyed view of Chinese as an introduction to the mysteries of the East, faute de mieux, but no longer. Incidentally, Fenollosa taught the Japanese philosopher Inoue Tetsujirō, who in 1894 appears to have been the first Japanese to use the term *"hyōi moji"* (ideogram) to refer to Chinese characters.

French, Howard W. 2000. "The Rising Sun Sets on Japanese Publishing." *New York Times,* 10 December.

Gardner, Martin. 1982. *Logic Machines and Diagrams.* 2nd ed. Chicago: University of Chicago Press. The first twenty-seven pages discuss the ideas of the late medieval logician Ramón Lull, whose concepts influenced the "proto-sinologist" Athanasius Kircher (Mungello 1989, pp. 174–188; see my Chapter 1). Indirectly Gardner affirms the intellectual lineage leading from Lull through Kircher to modern AI theory. Actually Matteo Ricci's "memory palaces" (Spence 1984) bear a greater similarity to Lorayne's "links." Gardner, longtime mathematics columnist for *Scientific American* and exposer of pseudoscience, is incidentally a proficient amateur magician; Hugard, Lorayne, and Randi are pros.

Gigerenzer, Gerd. 1994. "Why the Distinction Between Single-Event Probabilities and Frequencies Is Important for Psychology (and Vice Versa)." In *Subjective Probability,* ed. George Wright and Peter Ayton. West Sussex: Wiley. The best short history of probability theory I have encountered so far.

Gottlieb, Nanette. 2000. *Word-Processing Technology in Japan: Kanji and the Keyboard.* London: Curzon. Gottlieb's work is always strong on reporting the gamut of Japanese opinion, but she hesitates to examine those opinions in terms of the objective constraints of the technology. In this book she faithfully records Yamada Hisao's (1983) reasons for supporting romanization only to dismiss them—rather like an apologist for automobiles damning Ralph Nader with faint praise. [Reviewed in *Times Higher Education Supplement* (London), 12 October 2001.]

Gould, Stephen Jay. 1989. *Wonderful Life: The Burgess Shale and the Nature of History.* New York: Norton. The last four words in the subtitle are no boastful joke. Far more than a discussion of Cambrian fossils by an enthusiastic paleontologist, this beautifully crafted book presents with arresting clarity the late Stephen Gould's ideas on the role of historical contingency in evolution.

Gregg, John Robert. 1929. *Gregg Shorthand: A Light-Line Phonography for the Million.* Anniversary ed. New York: McGraw-Hill.

————. 1930. *Gregg Shorthand Dictionary*. Anniversary ed. New York: McGraw-Hill. Countless other textbooks are available in libraries and secondhand bookstores.

Hannas, Wm. C. 1997. *Asia's Orthographic Dilemma*. Honolulu: University of Hawai'i Press. Unlike many books on Chinese characters, which dwell on China, Japan, and Korea, this one includes a discussion of Vietnamese. [Reviewed in *Journal of Japanese Studies* 24(1) (1998):197–201.]

Hardy, G. H. [1940] 1967. *A Mathematician's Apology*. Foreword by C. P. Snow. London: Cambridge University Press.

Harris, Randy Allen. 1993. *The Linguistics Wars*. New York: Oxford University Press. One of two highly accessible histories that include Chomsky and the development of generativist syntax. Randy Harris is chattier than Stephen Murray and focuses on the conflict between Chomsky and his disciples.

Harris, Roy. 1981. *The Language Myth*. London: Duckworth. Harris held the chair of General Linguistics at Oxford for many years, during which time his views alienated many of his British colleagues, no doubt because of his radical rhetoric. (Note also the essay "The Dialect Myth" in Harris and Wolf 1998, pp. 83–95.)

————. 1986. *Origins of Writing*. London: Duckworth. Largely superseded by the more carefully worded *Rethinking Writing* (Harris 2000), perhaps because this book led to confusion about Harris' stand with respect to postmodernist theory.

————. 1995. *Signs of Writing*. New York: Routledge. Harris' Diogenes-like and sometimes obscure style is particularly evident in this book. [Reviewed in *Modern Language Journal* 82(1) (1998):123.]

————. 1996. *Signs, Language, and Communication: Integrational and Segregational Approaches*. New York: Routledge. The clearest exposition of Harris' theory of semiotics. [Reviewed in *Modern Language Journal* 82(2) (1998):289–290.]

————. 1997. "Pillow Talk for Cavemen." *Times Higher Education Supplement* (London), 7 November. This review shows Harris at his curmudgeonly best. In personal correspondence, he also criticized Vološinov, though I really don't understand why.

————. 2000. *Rethinking Writing*. Bloomington: Indiana University Press.

Harris, Roy, and George Wolf, eds. 1998. *Integrational Linguistics: A First Reader*. Oxford: Pergamon. Despite friction with other linguists, Harris has attracted a small band of followers, of whom the best known in the United States is probably Talbot Taylor. This collection of essays gives a good sense of the radicalism inherent in Harris' approach to language and semiotics.

Heinlein, Robert A. [1966] 1997. *The Moon Is a Harsh Mistress*. New York: Orb.

Heisig, James W. 1977. *Remembering the Kanji I: A Complete Course on How Not to Forget the Meaning and Writing of Japanese Characters*. Tokyo: Japan Publications Trading Company.

————. 1987. *Remembering the Kanji II: A Systematic Guide to Reading Characters*. Tokyo: Japan Publications Trading Company. Notice the change in the subtitles between vols. I and II. The original title of the set was *Adventures in Kanji-Land*, an obvious allusion to the strangeness of Alice's famous adventures.

Hobbs, James B. 1986. *Homophones and Homographs: An American Dictionary.* Jefferson, N.C.: McFarland. A wonderful reference for linguists, though perhaps more likely to be found on the bookshelves of Scrabble aficionados and crossword-puzzle fiends.

Hugard, Jean, and John J. Crimmins Jr., eds. 1961. *Encyclopedia of Card Tricks.* London: Faber & Faber. Chapter 20 of this classic on conjuring describes how to memorize and use the Nikola Card System, which makes it possible to execute a mystifying group of seemingly unrelated effects. The similarity to Lorayne's memorization techniques is striking.

Hunt, Morton. 1982. *The Universe Within: A New Science Explores the Mind.* New York: Simon & Schuster. Though twenty years old, this rich introduction to cognitive science makes it clear why simplistic hypotheses about so-called artificial intelligence are not likely to be correct.

Ikegami, Yoshihiko, ed. 1991. *The Empire of Signs: Semiotic Essays on Japanese Culture.* Amsterdam: John Benjamins.

Ionita, Maria. 2001. "Quiet, Please!" Review of Harris (2000). *Literary Research* 18(5): 192–197. Ionita complains that Harris ignores Derrida: "Harris seems surprisingly incapable of grasping his philosophy. The chapter on signatures, 'On the Dotted Line,' for example, completely ignores Derrida's work on the subject in *Limited Inc,* although part of his conclusions coincide with Harris." In fact, Harris' ideas differ from Derrida's in crucial respects. Ionita's review illustrates how easy it is for the currently popular academic paradigm in literary studies to distort the reception of new ideas.

Jaynes, Julian. 1976. *The Origin of Consciousness in the Breakdown of the Bicameral Mind.* Boston: Houghton Mifflin. One of those scientific works—like Kepler's early attempts to relate the regular Platonic solids to the orbits of the six planets known to him—that are worth reading even though they propose a failed theory invalidated by later findings.

Johnson, George. 1992. *In the Palaces of Memory: How We Build the Worlds Inside Our Heads.* New York: Vintage Books. How do we maintain long-term memories in a body where cells are continually dying and being replaced?

Kanō Yoshimitsu. 1994. *Yomesō de yomenai kanji 2000* [Two thousand characters you thought you could read but can't]. Tokyo: Kōdansha. The Japanese quiz book referred to in Chapter 5. As the title indicates, it contains much more than what I have summarized.

Kennedy, George A. 1964. *Selected Works.* Edited by Tien-yi Li. New Haven: Far Eastern Publications, Yale University. Includes Kennedy's brilliant essay on the how the Chinese word for "butterfly" is written and a scathing critique of Ezra Pound's pronouncements about Chinese. Interestingly, Kennedy analyzes but does not translate Fenollosa's poem.

Kess, Joseph F., and Miyamoto Tadao. 1999. *The Japanese Mental Lexicon: Psycholinguistic Studies of Kana and Kanji Processing.* Amsterdam: John Benjamins. The most recent summary of the literature, with strong emphasis on Japanese sources. Bends over backward to be fair to researchers claiming to have found evidence that *kanji* convey meaning without reference to language. [Reviewed in *Word* 52(3) (2001): 479–483.]

Kida Jun'ichirō. 1994. *Nihongo daihakubutsukan: Akuma no moji to tatakatta hitobito* [The great Japanese language museum: The men who battled the devil's own characters]. Tokyo: Jasuto Shisutemu [Just Systems].

Koestler, Arthur. 1961. *The Lotus and the Robot.* New York: Macmillan. Perhaps the first postwar "Japan bashing" book.

Lakoff, George. 1987. *Women, Fire, and Dangerous Things: What Categories Tell Us About the Mind.* Chicago: University of Chicago Press.

Lakoff, George, and Mark Johnson. 1980. *Metaphors We Live By.* Chicago: University of Chicago Press. One of those deceptively small books in simple style that introduces radically new and important ideas—in this case the notion that metaphors, rather than logical propositions, are the building blocks with which we construct meanings.

Lakoff, George, and Rafael E. Núñez. 2000. *Where Mathematics Comes From: How the Embodied Mind Brings Mathematics into Being.* New York: Basic Books.

Langacker, Ronald W. 1987. *Foundations of Cognitive Grammar.* Vol. 1: *Theoretical Prerequisites.* Stanford: Stanford University Press.

———. 1991. *Foundations of Cognitive Grammar.* Vol. 2: *Descriptive Application.* Stanford: Stanford University Press.

Leibniz, Gottfried Wilhelm von. 1981. *New Essays on Human Understanding.* Edited and translated by Peter Remnant and Jonathan Bennett. Cambridge: Cambridge University Press.

Leroi-Gourhan, André. 1993. *Gesture and Speech.* Translated by Anna Bostock Bergerand. Cambridge, Mass.: MIT Press.

Lieberman, Philip. 1991. *Uniquely Human: The Evolution of Speech, Thought, and Selfless Behavior.* Cambridge, Mass.: Harvard University Press.

———. 1998. *Eve Spoke: Human Language and Human Evolution.* New York: Norton. Lieberman emphasizes the evidence from physical anthropology for the primacy of speech in the natural history of human evolution.

Lorayne, Harry. 1957. *How to Develop a Super-Power Memory.* New York: Frederick Fell. Other easily obtainable paperback books by magicians contain a chapter on "head magic," which often includes a discussion of mnemonic systems.

McCawley, James D. 1984. *The Eater's Guide to Chinese Characters.* Chicago: University of Chicago Press.

McCloud, Scott. 1993. *Understanding Comics.* New York: Paradox Press. A brilliant dissertation on comics as an art form but far more than a historical or theoretical appreciation of the comics genre. A practitioner-storyteller rather than a critic-theorist, McCloud comes up with an insightful, intuitive theory about pictures and writing that can be extended to include the menagerie of visual artifacts that Elkins (1999) assembles but without Elkins' ponderous nomenclature or doubtful assumptions about the relationship between language and writing.

Mises, Richard von. 1957. *Probability, Statistics, and Truth.* London: Allen & Unwin.

Moser, David. 2001. "Pseudo-Science in the Chinese Linguistics Circle: a Brief Summary of the Ongoing Academic Dispute Between Xu Dejiang (徐德江) and Wu Tieping (伍铁平)." *Waiyu jiaoxue yu yanjiu* 外语教学与研究 [Foreign language teaching and research] 33(6):450–463. In November 1995, Xu Dejiang, a self-styled scholar of language, sued the linguist Wu Tieping for having published an article accusing him (justifiably, as Moser shows) of academic fraud. More than seven hundred linguists, including twenty from outside China, petitioned the court on Wu's behalf, and it refused to hear the case in 1998. Xu is, however, still active.

Mungello, D. E. 1989. *Curious Land: Jesuit Accommodation and the Origins of Sinology.* Honolulu: University of Hawai'i Press. Mungello describes the intellectual milieu of early sinology, including Müller, Leibniz, Kircher, Ricci, and the other Westerners who contributed to the Ideographic Myth of Chinese characters, but primarily he is interested in the history of Chinese-European contacts.

Murray, Stephen O. 1994. *Theory Groups and the Study of Language in North America: A Social History.* Amsterdam: John Benjamins. Better than Randy Harris' effort in breadth of coverage of the range of schools and periods of American linguistics but definitely an academic work.

Nara, Hiroshi, and Mari Noda, eds. 2003. *Acts of Reading.* Honolulu: University of Hawai'i Press.

Negroponte, Nicholas. 1995. *Being Digital.* New York: Knopf. Negroponte is co-founder and chair of the prestigious MIT Media Laboratory.

Nitobe Inazō. 1972. *The Works of Inazō Nitobe.* Edited by Takagi Yasaka et al. Tokyo: University of Tokyo Press.

Norman, Donald A. 1993. *Things That Make Us Smart: Defending Human Attributes in the Age of the Machine.* New York: Simon & Schuster. Norman's book *The Invisible Computer: Why Good Products Can Fail, the Personal Computer Is So Complex, and Information Appliances Are the Solution* (Cambridge, Mass.: MIT Press, 1998) contains additional food for thought, but it isn't hard to think of counterexamples to his conclusions about what makes successful products successful.

O'Neill, P. G. [1973] 1998. *Essential Kanji: 2,000 Basic Japanese Characters Systematically Arranged for Learning and Reference.* New York: Weatherhill. O'Neill's guide might be called the traditional approach to learning *kanji* as opposed to Heisig's (1977; 1987) approach (described in my Chapter 5).

Packard, Jerome. 2000. *The Morphology of Chinese.* Cambridge: Cambridge University Press. Knockdown arguments from synchronic linguistics proving beyond doubt that modern Mandarin has plenty of polysyllabic words. It is instructive to contrast Packard's cogent argumentation with that of Sproat (2000).

Paradis, Michel. 1998. "The Other Side of Language: Pragmatic Competence." *Journal of Neurolinguistics* 11:1–10. Takes the wind out the sails of proponents of radical hemispheric laterality theories.

Paradis, Michel, Hiroko Hagiwara, and Nancy Hildebrandt. 1985. *Neurolinguistic As-*

pects of the Japanese Writing System. New York: Academic Press. Now superseded by Kess and Miyamoto (1999), this classic study is more forthright in criticizing claims of *kanji* ideographicity based on experimental and clinical reports. [Reviewed in *Journal of the Association of Teachers of Japanese* 20(2) (1986):232–240.]

Petroski, Henry. 1989. *The Pencil: A History of Design and Circumstance.* New York: Knopf. Though not as scintillating as James Burke's *Connections* (Boston: Little, Brown, 1978) and later excursions into the role of serendipity in invention, this impeccably thorough history of a fundamental tool of modern life is full of unexpected twists and turns.

Piattelli-Palmarini, Massimo. 1994. *Inevitable Illusions.* New York: Wiley. An entertaining but unremittingly reductionist approach to logic and therefore not as satisfactory as Devlin (1997), with which it nevertheless shares an implicit faith in the objectivity of mathematical concepts.

Pinker, Steven. 1994. *The Language Instinct.* New York: Morrow. Not his newest or most famous work, but the book that started Pinker on the road to intellectual stardom—and therefore perhaps his least self-conscious effort.

Porter, David. 2001. *Ideographia: The Chinese Cipher in Early Modern Europe.* Stanford: Stanford University Press. Porter discusses the formation of European ideas about language and symbolism inspired by contact with Chinese writing (especially pp. 49–72) in greater detail than does Mungello (1989).

Randi, James. 1987. *The Faith Healers.* Buffalo: Prometheus Books. The famous French magician Robert Houdin defined a magician as an actor playing the part of a wizard. Those who pretend to be true wizards are not entertainers: they are charlatans and frauds who use deceit to take profit from the gullible. Randi, a professional magician, has dedicated himself to unmasking these frauds and educating the public on the need to be skeptical. In this enterprise he does science and society a great service; see especially pp. 39–44. Randi's books deserve a much wider readership.

Rasula, Jed, and Steve McCaffrey, eds. 1998. *Imagining Language: An Anthology.* Cambridge, Mass.: MIT Press. A convenient source for seventeenth-century attempts to concoct logically perfect languages, but includes much more.

Said, Edward W. 1979. *Orientalism.* New York: Random House. This book must be mentioned because it made "orientalism" a shibboleth for postmodernist cultural studies. But Said's narrow focus on Western approaches to the Islamic world weaken his claim that orientalism was a monolithic ideology in the service of imperialist hegemony. Clarke (1997) does a better job explaining the relevant intellectual history; for a sharp critique of Said grounded in Asia's recent political history see Ahmad (1992). And lest one think that only Westerners exploit the foreign as a source of rhetorical authority, see Chen (1995).

Sampson, Geoffrey. 1985. *Writing Systems: A Linguistic Introduction.* London: Hutchinson.

———. 1994. "Chinese Script and the Diversity of Writing Systems." *Linguistics* 32(1): 117–132. Sampson thinks that every writing system embodies some dominant "principle" of operation, but he presents no evidence that this principle actually plays a role in reading and writing and does not consider the possibility that the same signs can function differently in different contexts. His 1994 article defends his 1985 position.

Schechter, Bruce. 1998. *My Brain Is Open: The Mathematical Journeys of Paul Erdős*. New York: Touchstone. I recommend this book to anyone even mildly interested in mathematics.

Searle, John R. 1980. "Minds, Brains, and Programs." *Behavioral and Brain Sciences* 3:417–457. The seminal article.

——. 1992. *The Rediscovery of the Mind*. Cambridge, Mass.: MIT Press. The book-length follow-up.

Senzaki Manabu. 2001. "Taikenteki waga unō-sanō ron" [My personal theory of "right-brain/left-brain"]. *Shūkan bunshun* (February):133.

Shaw, George Bernard. 1962. *Androcles and the Lion, an Old Fable Renovated. With a Parallel Text in Shaw's Alphabet to Be Read in Conjunction Showing Its Economies in Writing and Reading*. Baltimore: Penguin Books. The terms of Shaw's will specified that this play should be published in a parallel edition with his original English spellings and a new "phonetic," space-saving orthography on facing pages. Shaw himself used Pitman shorthand, and the winning alphabet turned out to be one devised by a descendant of Isaac Pitman himself.

Shlain, Leonard. 1998. *The Alphabet Versus the Goddess: The Conflict Between Word and Image*. New York: Viking. A classic blend of politically correct blather, wishful thinking, pop psych, and pseudoscience. I've quoted only the chapter on China; others can tear apart Shlain's forays into other parts of the world. The jacket identifies Shlain as a surgeon.

Shore, Bradd. 1996. *Culture in Mind: Cognition, Culture, and the Problem of Meaning*. New York: Oxford University Press. Because of the lengthy chapters on baseball and Samoan society, it takes some time to get to Shore's theoretical message, but he writes wonderfully and the excursions are well worth the effort.

Skousen, Royal. 1989. *Analogical Modeling of Language*. Dordrecht: Kluwer Academic. A mathematically elegant alternative to formalist linguistics as now practiced.

Spence, Jonathan. 1984. *The Memory Palace of Matteo Ricci*. New York: Viking. Constructing a memory palace was a mnemonic technique: to deal with a topic, you imagined a museumlike building with galleries and rooms containing memorable objects about each of its salient features so that a mental tour of it would allow you to recall its contents. For the serious student of such a technique, the idea that Chinese characters are ideographic is easy to swallow. (See my Chapter 5 for a more modern version of visualization as an aid to memory.)

——. 1992. *Chinese Roundabout: Essays in History and Culture*. New York: Norton. Spence presents the story of Müller as a delightful vignette but does not probe the linguistic aspects of the story.

Sproat, Richard. 2000. *A Computational Theory of Writing Systems*. Cambridge: Cambridge University Press. Sproat strives with limited success to construct a theoretical formalism within which one can justify calling Chinese characters logograms.

Thornton, Tamara Plakins. 1996. *Handwriting in America: A Cultural History.* New Haven: Yale University Press. Since this study is otherwise complete, it is odd that Thornton passes over stenography with hardly a comment.

Toolan, Michael. 1996. *Total Speech: An Integrational Approach to Language.* Durham, N.C.: Duke University Press. This specialist study shows how such writers on linguistics as Grice, Hacket, Halliday, Slobin, Sperber and Wilson, and Tannen lend support to (and differ on crucial points from) Harris' integrational semiology.

Toulmin, Stephen. 1990. *Cosmopolis: The Hidden Agenda of Modernity.* New York: Free Press. A beautifully written history particularly valuable for the chapters in which the author explains how revulsion with the atrocities of the Thirty Years War informed the switch from humanism to rationalism. (The argument in the latter half of the book, in which Toulmin argues that we are returning to the lost humanist tradition in our age, is, I fear, too optimistic.)

Unger, J. Marshall. 1987. *The Fifth Generation Fallacy: Why Japan Is Betting Its Future on Artificial Intelligence.* New York: Oxford University Press. Applies the ideas of Searle and Dreyfus to the problem of inputting Chinese characters.

———. 1989. "Language Engineering versus Machine Engineering: A Linguist's View of the Character Input Problem." In *Text Processing Chinese by Computer: Characters, Speech, and Language,* ed. Wesley A. Clark. Washington, D.C.: National Academy of Sciences.

———. 1990. "The Very Idea: The Notion of Ideogram in China and Japan." *Monumenta Nipponica* 45(4):392–411.

———. 1991. "Memorizing Kanji: Lessons from a Pro." *Sino-Platonic Papers* (27):49–58.

———. 1992. *Literacy and Script Reform in Occupation Japan: Reading Between the Lines.* New York: Oxford University Press.

———. 1996. "Taking Digraphia Seriously: Future Software for East Asia." *Journal of the Chinese Language Teachers Association* 31(3):45–55.

———. 2001. "Functional Digraphia in Japan as Revealed in Consumer Product Preferences." *International Journal of the Sociology of Language* (150):141–152.

Unger, J. Marshall, and John DeFrancis. 1995. "Logographic and Semasiographic Writing Systems: A Critique of Sampson's Classification." In *Scripts and Literacy,* ed. David R. Olson and Insup Taylor. Dordrecht: Kluwer. This 1995 paper was actually presented in 1988 at a conference at the McLuhan Center of the University of Toronto.

Vachek, Josef. 1973. *Written Language: General Problems and Problems of English.* The Hague: Mouton. Perhaps it is inevitable that some Czechs, Hungarians, and other speakers of landlocked languages with relatively few speakers should feel that a language without a writing system is, in some essential respect, inferior to a language that has one. After all, when one's contact with the outside world depends so heavily on the printed word and on translation, when one is under such pressure to become fluent in one or more of the "big languages" in which important books are written, the primacy of speech must be hard to swallow.

Varela, Francisco J., Evan Thompson, and Eleanor Rosch. 1991. *The Embodied Mind: Cognitive Science and Human Experience*. Cambridge, Mass.: MIT Press. This is about as "far out" as it gets in linguistics.

Vološinov, Valentin Nikolaevič. [1930] 1973. *Marxism and the Philosophy of Language* [Marksizm i Filosofija Jazyka]. Translated by Ladislav Matejka and I. R. Titunik. New York: Seminar Press. Vološinov was a colleague of Bakhtin, lately a favorite of postmodern theorists; controversy swirls around the authorship of this work and Vološinov's true position on Stalinism. As explained in my Chapter 9, the similarities between Vološinov's dialogism and Harris' integrational semiology are uncanny.

Waldron, Arthur N. 1989. *The Great Wall of China: From History to Myth*. Cambridge: Cambridge University Press. Waldron explains that the structure referred to today as the Great Wall was for the most part built quite recently, in the Ming dynasty. The story of a continuous wall from the sea to the desert built in pre-Han times was just that—a story—that the Portuguese picked up from Arabs with whom they came into contact during the age of exploration. Neither the Chinese themselves nor such occasional visitors as Marco Polo ever mention the Great Wall because there was no such thing—just an accumulation of forts and towers built here and there over many centuries of Chinese history. The same Gaspar da Cruz who started the Ideographic Myth started the myth of the Great Wall too.

Wallace, Frank R. [1968] 1977. *Winning Poker: A Guaranteed Income for Life by Using the Advanced Concepts of Poker*. Must reading for anyone who thinks that poker is just a matter of skill at cards, blind luck, or some combination of the two. At first you'll get a Schadenfreude buzz from Wallace's tips and techniques, but eventually you realize you are reading something more like a novel, a moral confession by a hardened, compulsive hustler masquerading as a how-to book. You have glimpsed what goes on in the cynical mind of the sort of charlatans that Randi (1987) seeks to expose.

Yamada Hisao. 1983. "Certain Problems Associated with the Design of Input Keyboards for Japanese Writing." In *Cognitive Aspects of Skilled Typing*, ed. W. E. Cooper. New York: Springer. Still the best discussion of the history of keyboards and their application to the problems of Japanese script input. Yamada developed a true touch-typing method for inputting Japanese script (*kana, kanji*, alphanumerics, punctuation marks, and all) at the same typing rate as achieved in English—as well as a method that makes it possible to train Japanese typists in roughly the same time needed to train English typists. Nevertheless, Yamada has been a longtime advocate of using romanized Japanese on computers (see Unger 1987).

Yee, Chiang. [1938] 1973. *Chinese Calligraphy: An Introduction to Its Aesthetic and Technique*. 3rd ed. Cambridge, Mass.: Harvard University Press. A charming treatise on Chinese characters from the era when readers of English were likely to be introduced to Chinese aesthetics by the works of Arthur Waley or Lin Yutang.

URLs

We live in an age when the venerable institution of peer review is facing what may be its greatest challenge since it became common scholarly practice. The Internet and the Worldwide Web now make it extremely easy to find documents on a vast array of topics, but for this very reason they lay traps for the intellectually unwary. There are so many documents to wade through, so many webpages that come and go and change names unpredictably: here today, gone (or lost) tomorrow. And of course, without some expert knowledge or guidance, it is difficult to distinguish self-proclaimed authorities from genuinely reliable sources. With these caveats in mind, here are webpages from which I have drawn in the book.

Chapters 1–4

On Blissymbolics:

home.istar.ca/~bci/research1.htm
www.symbols.net/blissre.htm
www.geocities.com/Athens/Troy/1642/bliss.html

On Interglossa:

www.rick.harrison.net/langlab/i0.html

On the Shavian alphabet:

www.simonbarne.com/shavian

Mark Rosenfelder has produced an excellent webpage that explodes naive ideas about the structure of Chinese characters with cogent arguments:

zompist.com/yingzi/yingzi.htm

For promotional material on Shlain's anti-masterpiece:

www.alphabetvsgoddess.com

Chapter 5

The following website is loaded with useful information on the history of the script reform movement in Japan with a focus on the problems of using traditional orthography on computers. English and Japanese texts are available. The excellent quality is what one expects from Kida Jun'ichirō.

www.honco.net/japanese/index.html

Chapter 6

Stenography is now done mostly on machines that use chord keying (the simultaneous depression of combinations of keys). This keeps the total number of keys small and enhances speed. Nevertheless, the principles of Gregg are still widely incorporated into these systems. The following websites talk about machinery, training courses, and career opportunities:

www.phoenixtheory.com/
www.cyberdawg.com/gemini/
www.depo.com/

Chapter 8

Since it is not easy to get international statistics on computer ownership and usage, this extrapolation by Douglas Huang from data collected by the Search for Extraterrestrial Intelligence (SETI) project based at the University of California, Berkeley, is quite interesting. As of 12 July 2000, more than 2 million computer users connected to the Internet were letting SETI use their computers during idle moments to process data. Huang interprets "the percentage of SETI users in a given country's population" as an indicator of the extent of computer penetration and Internet access in that country. Japan, the world's second-strongest economy, ranked 39 out of 102 countries with SETI participants; by comparison, the United States came in fifth, outranked only by Iceland, Denmark, Canada, and the Netherlands.

www.texaschapbookpress.com/computerusage.htm

Chapter 9

Ionita's (2001) review of Harris (2000) is available on the Worldwide Web at the following address:

www.uwo.ca/modlang/ailc/old35/ReviewsIonita-Harris.htm

Index

Greek alphabet, 170
Gregg shorthand, 84. *See also* shorthand
Gregg, John Robert, 95, 104–110

handwriting, 85–86, 103, 108
han'gŭl, 8
hanja, ix, 31–32. *See also* Chinese characters
hanzi, ix. *See also* Chinese characters
Harris, Roy, 119, 155–162, 175–176; and DeFrancis, 122–123
Hebrew, 30, 42–43, 45, 170
Heisig, James, 78–82
hemispheric laterality, 46, 50–53, 171–172
Heraclitus, 119
hieroglyph, 1, 17–18, 57–58
hiragana, 8
Hjemslev, Louis, 160
Hockett, Charles, 160
holograms, 138, 174
homographs, 68–70
homophones, 8–9, 43, 145
Hong Kong, 148–149
Horodeck, Richard Alan, 48–49
Humboldt, Alexander von, 153
Hungarian, 113
hyōi moji, 180. *See also* ideogram

icon, 34, 122, 163–165, 171
iconography, 34–35
ideals, 111
identity of meaning, 120, 123, 156
ideograms, 46, 111, 122, 166
Ideographic Myth, 3–5, 44, 122, 140–141, 166; alternatives to, 151–152; and Artificial Intelligence (AI), 16, 135; believers of, 19; and Blissymbolics, 13–14, 16. *See also* semasiography
imitation, 109
index, 163–165
India, 169
individualism, 153
information, 52, 135
innatism, 137–138, 163
Inoue Tetsujirō, 58, 180
input, Japanese, x, 9, 12, 49–50, 142–145
integers, 115–117

intelligence, 132–134
international language, 147, 149
Internet, 12, 131, 142, 145–148, 190
intuition, 115, 127–130
invariants (semantic), 114, 156–157

Japan, 6, 11–12, 169
Japanese, 54, 77, 81, 113, 147, 172; borrowings into, 65–67; word-processors, 110, 142–147. *See also* Classical Japanese
Japanese writing: compared with Gregg shorthand, 103–104; glosses in, 80–81; *kana* in, 32, 81–82; use of *kanji* in, 61–70
jukujikun, 64
JWPs, 110, 142–147

kana, 8, 32, 81–82
kanbun, 62, 64–65
kanji, ix. *See also* Chinese characters
kanji henkan input, 145
kan-on, 65
Karlgren, Bernhard, 8
katakana, 8
Kennedy, George, 7, 17
keyboard, 150
Kircher, Athanasius, 18, 180
kokuji, 69
Korea, 10, 12, 31–32, 169–171; North, 32; South, 148–149
Korean, 8, 67
Kristeva, Julia, 58
kun readings, 64, 80–82

Langacker, Ronald, 139–141, 152
language, 2, 111, 151, 166; acquisition of, 137, 163; international, 147, 149; manual and sign, 33
language acquisition device (LAD), 162
language learning, 77–78, 81–83, 104
language policy, 9–10, 170–171
langue, 58, 121–123, 155
Latin, 8, 169
laws, scientific, 127, 130
learnability, 19, 28
learning, xv–xvi, 120, 164; of second language, 54, 77–78, 81–83, 147;

vs. acquisition, 28; of writing, 85,
103–110
"left-brain / right-brain." *See* hemispheric
laterality
Leibniz, Gottfried von, 2, 13, 17, 18, 127
Leroi-Gourhan, André, 57, 62
letter, 92, 100
lexicon, 9
linguistic behavior, 52–53, 112
linguistic form, 118
lists, 45
literacy, 10–12, 110, 169
literal meaning, 166
Literary Chinese. *See* Classical Chinese
literati, 86, 106
Llorca, Emilio Alarcos, 160
loanwords (in Japanese), 67–68, 89
logic, 19, 72, 74–76, 78, 80, 83
logography, 28–31, 39, 48, 54
longhand, 96. *See also* handwriting
Lorayne, Harry, 71–78

machine translation, 138
magic, 72, 82, 166–167, 185
Malaysia, 142, 148
Malinowski, Bronislaw, 152
manga, 11, 33. *See also* comics
manual language, 33
Marxism, 153, 155, 174
mathematics, 3, 111, 150, 174; notation of,
122, 159
Mayan, 20–21, 170
McCloud, Scott, 32–39, 159, 171
McLuhan, Marshall, 84, 151
meaning, 114, 155–156, 165–166; of
Chinese characters, 48–49, 57, 78;
familiarity as, 76; non-verbal, 33, 47–
48; origins of, 53, 152, 158; syntax
and,135–136
memorization, 71–72, 186. *See also* mnemonics
Mentalese, 137
Merleau-Ponty, Maurice, 138
metaphor, 34–36, 121, 161
Mill, John Stuart, 111, 119
Minsky, Marvin, 174
mnemonics, 73–82

models: of communication, 120; of handwriting, 109; of language, 130–140
Mongolian, 46
monosyllablic words, 7, 169
montage, 57
morphology: Chinese, 6–8, 44–45;
Japanese, 63–64, 68, 172
Müller, Andreas, 18–19
music notation, 122, 159, 173
myths, 41, 54; emulatability, 2, 6–7;
indispensability, 3, 8–10, 43, 169;
monosyllabic, 3, 7–8, 43–44, 169; successfulness, 3, 10–12, 142; universality,
2, 5–6, 15, 17, 44, 123, 149–150. *See
also* Ideographic Myth

names, 42, 68–69, 103
Needham, Joseph, 47
"neural nets," 138–140
Nitobe Inazō, 47
nominalism, 161
notation, 24, 28; mathematical, 122, 159;
musical, 122, 159–173
numbers, 5, 74, 115–116
number words, 113
numerals, 5. *See also* arabic numerals

objectivism, 128, 153–154
operating system, computer, 137, 145
on readings, 9, 63–65, 67–68, 89, 91
orientalism, 1, 185
origins: of language, 2, 28; of writing, 21

Papert, Seymour, 174
Paradis, Michel, 51–53
parole, 121–123, 155
partial writing, 21, 26, 122, 159
patriarchy, 41–42
patronymics, 42–43
PCs, 85, 142–147
Peirce, Charles Sanders, 163, 171, 175–176
performance, linguistic, 141
personal computers, 85, 142–147
phonemes: English, 73–74, 91, 93–95;
Japanese, 68
phonetic elements, 4, 19, 66, 89–91,
103–104, 172–173

About the Author

J. Marshall Unger is professor of Japanese and chair of the Department of East Asian Languages and Literatures at the Ohio State University. He is the author of *The Fifth Generation Fallacy* (which predicted that Japan's costly search for artificial intelligence would end without any breakthrough) as well as dozens of scholarly works on the history of the Japanese language and its writing system. He has also written on Japanese language pedagogy and chaired the committee that produced the NEH–College Board supported *Framework for Introductory Japanese Language Curricula in American High Schools and College* (1993).

Production Notes for Unger/*Ideogram*
Cover design by Santos Barbasa Jr.
Text design by Josie Herr with text in Bembo and display in Tekton
Composition by Tseng Information Systems, Inc. in Buffalo TEX
Printing and binding by The Maple-Vail Book Manufacturing Group.
Printed on 60 lb. Sebago Eggshell, 420 ppi